MY GREATEST DAY IN NASCAR

Also by Bob McCullough

New York Running Guide

Washington, D.C. Running Guide

My Greatest Day in Baseball

My Greatest Day in Golf

As told to
Bob McCullough

MY GREATEST DAY IN
NASCAR

The Legends of Auto Racing
Recount Their Greatest Moments

THOMAS DUNNE BOOKS • St. Martin's Griffin ⋈ New York

THOMAS DUNNE BOOKS.
An imprint of St. Martin's Press.

www.stmartins.com

Library of Congress Cataloging-in-Publication Data

McCullough, Bob.
    My greatest day in NASCAR / Bob McCullough.
       p. cm.
    ISBN 0-312-25254-4 (hc)
    ISBN 0-312-28048-3 (pbk)
    1. Automobile racing drivers—United States—Anecdotes.   2. NASCAR (Association)—
    History.   I. Title
  GV1032.A1 M39   2000
  796.72'0973—dc21   99-055496

First St. Martin's Griffin Edition: May 2001

10 9 8 7 6 5 4 3 2 1

The interviews were originally compiled during the 1999 NASCAR season, and several were originally intended to be part of a magazine series. The intent was to capture the flavor of the NASCAR experience, primarily through the perspective of the drivers (past and present, stars and aspiring stars), but the collection also includes car owners, crew chiefs, track owners, NASCAR officials, and others who have helped give this sport its unique mystique and character. I hope the collection conveys some of the grit and glory of the sport, both for those familiar with NASCAR and stock car racing and for those fans just coming into the field. The author would like to thank those who participated for sharing their thoughts, feelings, and memories, and those who helped out for their time, effort, and diligence.

CONTENTS

MY GREATEST DAY IN NASCAR

■ *Bobby Allison had two greatest days in auto racing . . . one of which stands clear as a bell in his memory, the other of which he literally can't recall. The leader of one of racing's foremost families talked briefly of the 1988 Daytona 500 and the injury that stole his memory of the race, then gave a full account of his first 500-mile victory, when he literally had just enough car to cross the start/finish line.*

Well, my day, I have no memory of. . . . My greatest day would have had to have been the 1988 Daytona 500, which I won for the third time at age fifty, with the best young man in racing second behind me. However, a few months later, June 19, 1988, I was injured severely at Pocono . . . head injury, caused a lot of memory loss. I have zero memory of Daytona 1988 . . . even today. I know it happened, I've got a lot of written stuff and so forth, I've had a tape of the race which I haven't watched in a long time, but even the tape from way back wouldn't do anything for me in terms of helping me remember anything.

I just accept that I have no memory. . . . They tell me that I won the race, and I've got some written record of having won the race, I've got some pictures of me, and the race team, and the family, and Davey Allison, and victory lane.

You know, all head injuries are quite different, but traditionally, memory loss and the loss of being able to put things together to support what should be a memory, is fairly common, I guess, with a head injury. And so, what I did early on in my recovery, I said, Okay, I hurt, and I can't remember this, and I can't do some things that I used to do, but I'll try to focus on the positive side and go from there. And that's what I've done.

Now, talking about racing, I remember way on back some things fairly well. And, of course, my first 500-mile win certainly always comes to mind when I talk about special days in my career. It was my first ride ever for Holman and Moody, and Fred Lorenzen was the crew chief, and Ralph Moody was the team director, and of course I had a pit crew that Ralph Moody had put together.

We won that 500-miler at Rockingham, I guess it was late October, November 1967. . . . The date doesn't come to mind right at this very second, but I've got plenty of verification of it. That 500-miler, that was one of the really great days; now, there are some others, but that always comes first, so I guess I would have to say that would be the greatest day.

Okay, we'll go all the way back to the Monday of the week coming up to that race, and I was in my little garage at my other place in Hueytown, Alabama . . . backyard garage, house on Crescent Drive, which is where we lived before we moved here. . . . I was working on a brand-new car for the Rockingham race, tired and hot and sweaty, and I had a paid employee or two and maybe a volunteer helper or two assisting, and we had probably been up through the night working for a day or two, and the telephone rang.

And the voice said, "You're gonna get a phone call in two minutes, the answer's yes, good-bye." And I looked at the phone, I said, "I kinda recognize that voice, but this is a person that I know and respect, but is not really my friend—I mean, I don't really have a personal friendship with him, a relationship."

That was Ralph Moody that [had] just made that phone call, and Ralph Moody had a reputation for a lot of great things, but he also had a reputation for being a little bit of a prankster. And so I said, Why is he aggravating me—right now I've got all this work to do, and he doesn't know what I'm doing or anything like that—but why this? And I hung the phone up and I went back to welding a part on the car.

The phone rang again. It was Freddy Lorenzen, Freddy Lorenzen said, "Ford gave me a car, will you drive it at Rockingham?" So I already had the answer—"the answer's yes"—so I said, "Yes, I will." He said, "Okay, come to Charlotte, meet me at Charlotte, we'll adjust the seat, look the car over"—in those days, see, you could go to the racetrack a day or two early if you wanted to—"and we'll just go on down to Rockingham the next day."

So I hung the phone up, and I told the guys, I said, "Okay, guys, everybody can go home and get some rest, we've got a total change of plans, this project is coming to a stop. I'm going to drive for Holman and Moody at Rockingham." They all went, "Yay," "Hurray," "Hurray"—they were all thrilled for me.

I got in my little Moody airplane and flew to Charlotte, North Carolina. Went to the Holman-Moody shop, just to see—first of all picked out the car that we agreed would be the best effort for that particular race, they had the car that Mario had won the Daytona 500 with earlier in the year, it was sitting there. But they also had some of the number 17s that David Pearson was driving; they had the number 66 that Jack Bauscher was driving some—they had a pretty good stableful of cars, so there was a pretty good group to select a car from.

But the car that Mario had won Daytona with had been redone, and lightened-up with a smaller engine installed in it—I guess for somebody to run somewhere like Milwaukee, somewhere like that—but it had a 396 engine in it. And in those days in NASCAR, the weight of the car was determined by the size of the engine, so a 396 car could run lighter than a 427-powered car. So that also made me think that on this kind of racetrack, the lighter car possibly would be better on tires in the long run, and so the car might have a shot at winning this 500-mile race.

So we chose the little number 11, got the car ready, and took it over to Rockingham and did some testing, and boy, I was really surprised, 'cause, boy, this car was good. The car was fast, the car drove really well, Freddy really did a nice job of adjusting the car to get it to be the best all the way around the racetrack, adjusting the chassis settings and everything.

But he kept on all week, he kept making little adjustments and little changes, and, "Try this again, no, let's go back to the other, try this. . . ." We ran a lot of different things on the car, but we'd only run for a lap or two, and then we'd talk about it, and then he'd say, "Let's try this," or "Let's try that." I was really happily impressed with how Freddy addressed the adjustment of the car.

When it was time to qualify, we were in line to qualify—in those days you qualified whenever you wanted to. Well, a couple of cars, the Ford cards, had gone ahead and qualified, and we were gonna be on the pole, our times were the best of anybody.

Trying to address this particular part properly, especially if you're gonna document it, it needs to be as accurate as we can have it. The Holman and Moody cars, the Ford cars, had come up with the information that the tire with no inner liner was faster in qualifying than a car with an inner liner. Well, the rules said you have to have 'em, but they didn't check 'em. And so the Ford cars that were already qualified all had on inner liners.

So while I was in line to qualify, one of the already-qualified cars reported to NASCAR that I didn't have inner liners. And so NASCAR came and pulled us out of line and made us take those tires off and put on tires that had inner liners. Well, that made me qualify third instead of on the pole.

So we went on, we accepted that, and as we got ready for the race Freddy said, "Now, you've gotta listen to me, you can't kill the car." And all these—at the time they were Grand Nationals, that's what the Winston Cup was called in those days—all these Grand National cars are killable, the Fords, the Chryslers, anything of the 500-mile really is a long endurance race for the car. You've gotta take care of the car.

"Now, I don't want you to go as fast as you can go, I want you to go a good competitive speed, but we don't have to be in the front until way late in the race. And if you're going too fast, I will signal you with the key word—we'll use *'think'* as the key word. If you see *'think'* on the blackboard, that means to slow down, you're going too fast." So I said okay.

And he said . . . "We didn't get the pole, and we need to show those guys that we can beat 'em, so we need to lead a lap early in the race." I said okay.

So we come around for the start, I'm third in line, I'm second row inside. We get a green flag, the guys in the front row take off, and I pull into line pretty good, and the caution light comes on immediately, there's a spinout behind us. And, of course, in those days you race back to the flag, but in a 500-miler, knowing that there's something that happened right at the start of the race, it's not very smart to go wide open around there to see if there's a big wreck or a little wreck.

So I just kind of eased up, and we all came around, so I'm still third, and I'm under the caution. So we run a couple of caution laps, there's no big problem, somebody had spun, but they got the guy going, or whatever. And we get a green flag again in about the fourth lap. Well, now we're single-file, because in those days NASCAR had single-file restarts, if one happened at the beginning of a race today, it would be a single-file too, so there's this long line of cars.

We come around and get a restart, and, boy, I'm gonna go ahead and drive into the lead, because I am easily quicker than anybody else there. I passed the guy that was third, and the caution light comes on again. So we come around, and we're back under the yellow, and now I'm second, and four or five laps go by while they clean out this spinout or whatever it is.

In about the 10th lap we get the third restart of the race, our third green flag of the race. We go around, I lead the 11th lap, the next lap I come back around, and Freddy Lorenzen is standing out on the far outside of pit row, with a signboard that says, *"Think."* There are lots of pictures that have been printed of that over the years, it was never made really public that *"Think"* was our code word—him conveying some of his knowledge over to me, who was a real youngster, a novice.

So I backed off, and I went back to about third or fourth or fifth in line, and I stayed there pretty much all day long. About the 400th lap of the race, the 390th lap of the race, Cale Yarborough was leading the race, and he was coming to lap me. And Freddy Lorenzen walked out with a sign board that said *"Go."*

I went ahead and mashed down on the gas, and I pulled away from Cale. Cale attempted to chase me, and his engine blew up, and so Cale was out of the race. That left me leading the race with a big lead over whoever was behind me, because by then everybody else had run fast and failed. So it left me there with a big comfortable lead, and Freddy walked right back out on pit road with the sign board with *"Think"* on it, and I eased up.

With about fifty laps to go, forty-five laps to go, I began to get a strange vibration in the car, and I just kept soft-pedaling the thing, babying the car, and all I could think about was that something was gonna break, I'm gonna be out of this thing, here I can win this race and something's gonna break.

With about twenty laps to go I start seeing grease inside the car. Now something under the car is leaking grease, and I don't know if it's something in the rear end, the rear-end coolant system—in those days we didn't have a transmission cooler. But there's grease on the floorboard, but it's obviously gear grease and not engine oil; I could tell from the smell of it that it was gear oil.

So I began to be very concerned about this, and I continued to baby this car, and I finally get that white flag, and I get that checker flag, and I have won my first 500-mile race ever. I come around to go into victory lane, and the transmission falls out. It had broken around the casing, on the back part of the transmission—the back of the transmission falls off and takes the drive shaft with it, and they have to push the car up into victory lane.

But I'm there.

It was just a great celebration, it was a great win for me, it was my first 500-mile win. I had won a few of the short races up till then. But it was just a tremendous day for me.

Afterward I told Freddy thank you, and "you were really right, you do have to take care of the equipment, because the equipment all is a little bit weak for as hard as we're pressuring it."

Certainly it was a great learning experience for me. Up until that point I had raced hard for every win I had gotten, whether it be on a modified or a sportsman or a late model on the short tracks, or a Grand National, you know, my first Grand National events. There were all these races that I ran really hard, and I finally got a win, but also I had already been through several events where I had run really hard and the car broke right at the end . . . not thinking that, Golly, if I'd've taken it a little easier I still could have won, and maybe the car would have finished.

See, that just wasn't part of the general nature at the time—they dropped the green and then you go wide open. So that was a great learning experience for me, and it certainly helped me from there on.

Certainly the 1967 American 500 at Rockingham was a great day, it was a great kickoff to a superspeedway-winning career that still is at the top of the list. It's always gonna be special. The 1988 Daytona 500, I'll have to rely on the idea that the information says that I won the race. And at age fifty, to win the Super Bowl of stock car racing with the best young man in racing second behind you, and that being your own son, there's gotta be no better achievement in any profession.

■ *Like his brother Bobby, Donny Allison had two greatest days, and his first was also a Rockingham race that put him on the map in the world of NASCAR. His second was a win at Charlotte that kept him on the map during a pivotal moment in his career, and together those two events are memorable additions to the Allison legacy.*

There's a lot of 'em. . . . Probably the first one that was really a big highlight was the first race I ever won in a Winston Cup car, and that was in 1968 in Rockingham, North Carolina. The race at that time was really an endurance race as well as a speed race, and I was in a factory Ford owned by Banjo Matthews.

It was really a situation where I really wasn't even supposed to even run the race, and I ended up driving [Matthews'] car there, and at that particular time Ford was bringing in a little motor, which was a 390, but I run a 427, which was supposedly a disadvantage. The other Ford factory cars had some kind of problem, or whatever, I don't know—anyway, I ended up winning the race and Bobby ran second.

After the race I will never forget Banjo and Richie Lane, tears running down their cheeks, because they thought I'd never win another race [for them] as a car owner, and of course that would be my first race, it was a really, really special thing for me.

During the race I don't really remember a whole lot about the competition between Bobby and myself; I do know that at the end of the race they let me know that he was second. We didn't have radio communication, we did it by [chalk] board. All I could do was sit there and hope that nothing happened to my car, and that I could keep going as strong as I was going, because if I did I knew he couldn't outrun me.

I think that was probably around 450 miles [when they told me that] there was 50 miles left to go. Of course, at that particular time in the race, you're imagining that everything is going wrong, but really nothing was.

I think that they had a problem with some of the other 390 engines, and of course the 427 was a well-proven race engine at the time, and I didn't have any kind of a problem. I think I did gain an advantage from that.

I think the other one that really, really stands out most of all would be the National 500 at Charlotte Motor Speedway in 1977. It was my first one with Hoss Ellington, in either 1977 or 1976, I think it might have been 1976. I was a teammate with A. J. Foyt; he drove Hoss's primary car and I drove the supposedly secondary car. But I had the best car.

I went on to win that race, and not only did it do a lot for Hoss, but it did a lot for my career, because I had been let go as a driver from the Diehard team and supposedly couldn't drive anymore. . . . Anyway, I won that race, and I did it in quite a style. I passed, I think, sixteen cars, and I got the lead and led all day.

I had quite a race with Cale Yarborough—I got by him probably with one pit stop to go, with one 80-mile stretch to go, and he and I raced to the wall and I did get away from him. But all day long, whoever was there to race I could outrun. I came out of the pits, I might lose the lead and go back to second or third, and I'd go right back and get the lead.

It was quite a race for me.

My career when I got in the car was down pretty bad, as far as Winston Cup went, and I just opened a door and turned on a new light.

After the race, the celebration wasn't with A.J., it was with Hoss

Ellington and myself and, of course, the crew. They were ecstatic, because my crew was the secondary crew of Hoss Ellington's, not the primary one—the primary one was on A.J.'s car. And, of course, when he fell out of the race, which he did, they all came to my pit. In fact, I looked over, and when we first saw Hoss there, and A.J. was still in the race. Then Hoss was in my pit, and I said, I wonder what he's doing in my pit?

It was quite an afternoon for everybody concerned.

We had a Monte Carlo, and A.J. had a Chevrolet Lumina, and supposedly he had the best car, he thought—at that time the Monte Carlo was just really coming into the picture. And A.J. was the type of guy that, just because Junior Johnson had one he didn't think he oughta have one. And, of course, if you were going to race those people with Monte Carlos, you had to have a Monte Carlo. Myself, at the time, I didn't really care, as long as it was a good car, that's all I cared about.

I didn't qualify quite as good as I should have, but I didn't change what I did because of the car. Once the race started, it was very evident that I had as good a car as was in the race. I think that probably was the farthest I ever came from, as far as where I qualified.

The reason that I picked that one was because, like I said, Bill Gardner and Di Gardner and I had a disagreement, and I left him, and I didn't have a Winston Cup ride, and they called me really in relief for A. J. Foyt at Talladega. And I did, I finished third in that race, and I got the opportunity to drive for Hoss all the time.

I would say that those . . . of course, any of the wins stick out, but I think those two would probably stick out the most.

The first one was very instrumental because I was a very young man at the time, without the background of being from up in the racing area, where North Carolina is. I had the opportunity to drive for Ford Motor Company, some people thought I could drive, and that proved that I could. The second one, I think I proved to a lot of people that I could still drive, and so that's why it's still pretty important to me.

■ *When stock-car fans think of racing families, the list usually starts with Petty and Allison and Earnhardt, followed closely by the likes of Wallace, Bodine, and Labonte. But there's a few other names from outside the stock-car world that have crept into the list in the last few years, and in this interview John Andretti talks about his greatest days at Indianapolis and Charlotte in the context of his family's auto-racing achievements.*

Okay, my greatest day, and it always has been and probably always will be, no matter what whatever happens, is when I qualified for the Indy 500. There are kind of a lot of things leading up to it.

It was my rookie year, obviously, and I was twenty-four or twenty-five. I went out for my first qualifying run—in Indianapolis you get three tries per car—and I went on my first run and blew the motor. So they worked all night and changed the motor and I went out the next day and I lost all my turbo pressure during the qualifying run. And we were really a pretty fast car, and now we had to wait a whole other week to get in. I had a backup car, but it was a backup car like I got another car at home that's sitting on blocks in its front yard with no wheels and tires on it. I mean they called it a backup car, but it was hardly even a car.

So I had one strike left on me, and my primary car . . . I went out and qualified for the race. I was pretty upset because I really wanted to qualify quick, but I guess the most important thing was getting into the race, so we ended up not being the quickest even on the day [of the race]. I think Greg Hall ended up being the quickest on the day.

I was pretty disgusted. I'm walking around, and when you get done qualifying for the Indianapolis 500, you stop and you stand on the car and you get your picture taken and all that stuff. But when I stopped I was really upset because I wanted to go quicker, and even though I was in the race, that wasn't the goal. The goal was to be the quickest rookie, to be the fastest on the day. Those were my goals, not anybody else's.

Then I looked over, and actually there's a photo of it—my dad was standing there, and my dad looked at me and he reached out and he had this look that I never had with my dad [*Editor's note:* Andretti's father is Aldo Andretti, Mario's twin brother.] It was like what I had just accomplished was something that not only he was never given the opportunity to do, but it was like I had accomplished it for both of us.

And people have to know . . . just how good my dad was and the fact that he was sort of denied the opportunity to be there. I looked at him, and . . . I just then realized just how fortunate I was, and all the other stuff was really meaningless, in the sense that I got to do something like everybody wants their child to accomplish something they want that's something that didn't happen for them.

It was like he knew how bad I wanted to be there. Certainly I would never claim that I have worked anywhere near as hard as he did, to get the same opportunity, but to me that was for sure the most important moment in my racing career and the greatest moment in my career. Because it was like . . . we did it, and it wasn't like I did anything all by myself.

I've never really sat down and said, "You know, Dad, you know how much that meant to me," because my dad is not a guy that sits around and says, "You know, boy . . ." He's the kind of guy, if you stuck a drill through your hand, he'd say, "Don't worry about it, you got another one." It's not like if you're bleeding to death he wouldn't take you to the hospital, but he's tough, tough as nails—he's been broke up, beat up, and nobody on this planet loves this sport more than he does.

That's the whole thing, when I looked at him, there was no way anyone else could have thought [that]. And the other thing is, he is not just my dad, you know, when I grew up we did everything together—I mean everything. I used to get up, we used to get up at five o'clock on Saturday morning, Sunday morning sometimes, we'd go into one of the Firestone stores he owned and ran, and I would be in there doing stuff like shampooing the carpet in the showroom and he could be out there washing his car and then we would wash whatever other vehicle we would wash—we just did everything together.

When I raced, we built the motors together every day, we worked on the go-carts every day, we did everything. So when I [qualified], it wasn't like somebody that helped me out, it was somebody who had been there the whole time. I think it really matured me a lot, quickly, because here I was rolling down pit lane, upset because I didn't get what I wanted, finding out that I really got what I wanted . . . so it made me grow up.

Also, in the race, me and Jack Debear, we had to start behind the first two-day qualifiers, we started twenty-seventh, and we were on fire. We were passing them everywhere, outside—and outside at Indianapolis is pretty uncommon at that time because the track was a lot narrower, and we were passing them outside.

We got up all the way up to seventh, a legitimate hard seventh, and the motor blew up. I had just passed my cousin Michael, which was another big accomplishment, because he'd been there for three or four years at that time, so you know it was important to get around him. . . . I mean I blew up right in his face.

I think he was already becoming one of the real superstars of the series, so I think he was in a little bit of shock. And also, Michael and I are really tight; when I went to college in Pennsylvania, he and I shared a room at my uncle's house. He was always happy for me when I did good, and, of course, I have always been happy for him when he has done good, so . . . I think he was like, "Where did you come from?"

And I said, "Well, I have been here the whole time, you just haven't been watching." It was an exciting day for me.

My biggest day in Winston would be when I won the Pepsi 400 because, when I came to Winston Cup, everybody had heard that I was going to be doing some races in 1993, and I heard, "You won't be accepted, you're an open-wheel racer, your last name is Andretti, you're from the North"—I mean, they piled up the whole list. And these are people that had some knowledge of what was going on, people that I know and respect.

I was thinking, You know, maybe I am biting off more than I can chew; but after driving a top dragster, I figured, What the heck, you never know what could turn up, right? And then I went to Billy Hagen, and drove there and unfortunately couldn't get a sponsorship, went to Petty Enterprises, made a mistake, and left Petty Enterprises for a new team. The new team had some really good people, the only problem is that new teams are tough to make go . . . and Winston Cup is just so competitive.

So really, I invested two years there, and then actually ended up really hurting myself in a lot of different ways, and certainly the ownership of the team didn't really help matters. So it was really a tough time in my career, and it had nothing to do with being accepted, it had to do with making the right decisions and getting the right cars. Then I went to Cale Yarborough, and Tony Fern and I hit it off in 1994, and unfortunately at Cale we lost the sponsorship, and I had to make another move.

But I went back home, I guess that's what I call it, to Petty—and that's really good for me, because that was what was good for me back at Yarborough's, because they were so much like Petty, when something goes wrong, nobody is there beating you down. And when something is right, boy, they are beating on you hard to do better . . . and that is what it is all about.

Well, when I made my move to Winston Cup, I was living in Indiana and wasn't making a lot of money driving other race cars because

I wouldn't sign a contract with anybody. I drove the Indy 500, and it wasn't like I wasn't making any money, it was just that I was spending considerable more than what I was making, sort of investing in a career change. But I'm making this investment in this career change that I'm not even sure that I'm gonna make entirely, but it made sense to me at that point.

So I did it, and when I got down there I needed to try to get back on my feet again. And unfortunately, when I looked at it, the team looked right, because it had a lot of really good ingredients to it. And they just kept on throwing more money until I said yes. So I made the decision for the wrong reason—and I won't make that decision again.

But the Pepsi 400, that was cool. It was funny because . . . you know, of course, we had a very, very, very good car and that is what it takes to win. I mean, Jeff Gordon is certainly not winning with a three-wheeled buggy, you know?

I know that the opportunities don't come very often, and that's what builds the championship team, when you could get those opportunities of having a very good car every weekend, but we knew the restrictor-plate races were the places where we could win at. So we focused 85 to 90 percent of our time on those races, because to me it is more important to win than it is to stack up a bunch of top fives or whatever—even though you get more credit for the top fives, I'd rather win.

And we were getting down to our last chance; we struggled for some of the season. And I said, "Man, don't worry, guys, we could get them at Daytona." And I'm thinking, "I hope we go there and get them, because we could use something good to happen to us," and it did. I guess the thing that I will always remember, I came into the pits leading and I went out and I was like ninth, because we certainly weren't as strong as the championship teams in the pit-stop area, and we kept losing guys, and guys were getting hurt, so it was kind of a mess.

And then when I came out, I passed people, but I got up to about fourth or fifth. And I started screaming on the radio, but, you know, "I'm not gonna get the cars, not gonna be able to pass them," and after I let go of the radio, I thought—you always hear the stories of Jeff Gordon, on the radio about how he's running fourth or fifth or even leading sometimes, he's all excited about the fact that something might not be right or he may not be the best, or whatever. And at that point I was like, "Now I know how Gordon feels. . . ." I knew that I should win that race, that I deserved to win that race, and yet I'm thinking, I'm not gonna win.

It was like at Talladega, I was running second, I would have easily finished second behind Mark Martin. But I wanted to win, and I ended up fourth. And when I was rolling in to get my spoiler checked, just before we had won, Cale said, "You did a good job, too bad those other cars wouldn't go with you." And I said, "You know, I'm really sorry because I cost you guys a better finish but I really wanted to win."

And Cale said, "You never take any chances, you never win any races, and that is what we are here to do." So he and I were alike, you know what I mean? That worked out really good because most owners would have got upset at you. And . . . you know Cale, Cale is like the king, winning is what it is all about, so I think I fit in best with him.

But when I got into victory lane—which I've been in before, but the other time I didn't drive there, it was a 24-hour race; I walked into victory lane and I knew where it was at, but I didn't know if I passed it. . . . So when I got there Cale had his hand out to shake my hand, and I asked him where victory lane was. And he walks up to me and puts his hand out and goes, "Are you lost?" because I must have had that look on my face like, "Where is it?" . . . I really didn't want to look stupid and pass victory lane, you know, nobody does that. So he said, "Don't worry, it's just down there, they'll find you," and I laughed and then drove on down, but it made me feel good that he came out.

He and a lot of the other guys came out. . . . I've always made good friends where I've been at, and I've really enjoyed it, even though Winston Cup has been tough and I've made it tougher than it should have been by my decisions. I think that was a key moment for me. The one thing that made me feel better is I fell back to fifth, but then Gordon tried the same move and nobody went with him. He ended up fifth, so I think I told him afterward, him and Ray, "You should have gone with me, you would have run second."

You've gotta remember, all this politicking before the start of the race, telling everybody that I couldn't hurt 'em during the points, and I could help 'em in the points. I was politicking pretty hard. Not a lot of believers, but a lot of hard politicking was going on.

I think that, first of all, it said that I knew how to get to victory lane. In Winston Cup it's really tough, and I think that with the budget that we had, and the way we did it, it's as big as other guys winning a lot of races, because . . . first of all, we weren't supposed to win.

Of course, the people that are my fans believed that I could do it, but there's more people that probably didn't. I always believed deep down that I could win, that I could win a lot of races. And I know I can.

That's why I'm so happy where I'm at now, because I know that I'm going to get my opportunities to win. They always say that winning the first one's tough, but let me tell you, the second one's no easier.

It was funny, because we came right home, and of course we got home and my voice mail—it tells you when you've got the calls, and within six minutes at the end of the race, somebody said, "Well, you just took the checkered flag" on one of the messages. So within six minutes of taking the flag my voice mail was filled.

So we emptied it, and of course you couldn't answer the phone, because then you would block everybody else out. We would answer them privately, but finally we let my office pick 'em out, because we figured anybody that was really close to us would call us on the private line.

Well, my uncle was calling—of course, I called my dad first thing I got home, and he was extremely mad that he wasn't there. Then my uncle kept calling, and it was funny because he was calling, and he kept getting a voice message, and you could hear that he was getting frustrated. We would pick up the call, and then he would end up on the voice mail, and finally he had my cousin Jeff call, and Jeff got through.

Jeff got to talk to me for about a minute, and Mario—my uncle—picked up the phone, and he starts right in, Yeah, it was great. And I come to find out that he's watching the replay of it that night on the Deuce [ESPN 2], and he's going, "Oh, oh, oh," and I said, "What, what, what?" I thought the place had caught on fire or something.

He said, "Oh, that's when you went on the apron and down three and passed him or something, so . . . that was a good move, that was a good move." [Laughs]

And then I got him talking about his Daytona 500 victory, I'd always wanted to know about it. My dad and my uncle—they will never, ever—I mean, you've gotta pull teeth to get 'em to talk about racing—you know, about their racing. Now they'll talk about racing, because they love racing. But to bring up a war story or something, they just won't do it.

And I lived with my uncle for four years, and, of course, I lived with my dad for a lot longer than that, and there's so much I don't know about 'em, that I'm just now pulling out. But you've gotta pick your moments, and that was my moment, and twenty minutes later I knew everything there was to know about the Daytona 500, and let me tell you something, that's a really interesting story.

It was cool, because, to me . . . I won my first midget race, and my dad used to call up and say, "Hey, this is Jackie Stewart," or, "Hey, this is Dr. Penske," and he used to goof around with me, you know? And this guy calls up and he goes, "Yeah, this is A.J., you know who I am, right?" And I go, "Yeah, right, yeah." And I said, "What do you want?"

He says, "You know, A. J. Foyt?" I said, "Yeah, yeah, yeah, I know who you are." And then, I thought it was my dad goofing around—well, when he said it was A.J. Foyt . . . I realized that it was him. I mean, who else could talk like A.J.?

And so we got to talking. . . . He said, "You know, I just called you up to tell you congratulations on winning your first midget race, it didn't take you long." And A.J.'s my godfather, but you know . . . those things are worth as much as the wins, that somebody that you respect so much took the time to tell you you've done something that's worth calling about. And that's what happened with my uncle, with the Daytona 500.

I mean, my dad wasn't gonna call me, because he knew that I would call him first anyway. I mean, I knew he'd be the first guy on my line, and he was.

You don't even realize it until . . . It's one of those things that you lose sight of, because you're so busy dealing with your own world. People don't have to remind you much, then you realize how much your uncle's done, or your dad's done, or your cousins have done. It's fun to be part of the family and at least add a little bit to it. I'd like to add a lot more, and that's what I'm trying to do now.

■ *When it comes to running at Daytona, Buddy Baker was the Dale Earnhardt of his era, leading the race a number of times only to lose the race in the final laps. Baker now analyzes the races for the national network, but in 1980 he finally closed the family racing circle by winning the big one in the legendary* Gray Ghost, *an experience that was capped off when he was met by his father Buck in the winner's circle.*

I've had several good days. I guess winning four times at my hometown here in Charlotte, and four times at Talladega, but the greatest day in my racing career was the Daytona 500 in 1980.

I can tell you that, just like Earnhardt, it took him eighteen years to win the Daytona 500, and it becomes a thing where everybody says, "Yeah, you've won all the big races, but you really haven't won the big one yet." And that race was . . . on I guess twelve or fourteen different occasions I had led the race down to fifteen or twenty miles to go, and I had mechanical problems with a huge lead on several counts. I think somebody said I won the "Daytona 475" eleven times.

It was one of those where I just felt, Well, I'm running right on the edge of my career now, because I've been in racing a long time, and maybe this is the one that I'm not gonna get. In 1979 I won the Busch Clash, the first-ever Busch Clash, [and then] came right back and won the pole position for the Daytona 500, I had been on the pole quite a few times. In 1979 the car was so dominant, I won the 125, I won the Busch Clash, I won the pole, and then, when the race started, I went down the back straightaway and it cut off on the first lap.

I had to come in, and we diagnosed it as being an ignition problem that could have been fixed. . . . I mean, as dominant as the car was, we should have won 1979 and 1980. We brought the same car back the next year—it was an awfully good car—but I think I ran like second or third in the Busch Clash, and I won the pole again.

I just ran so-so in the 125, so we made some adjustments on the car in the last practice the day before the 500, just made sure that it was handling the way I wanted it, and when they dropped the green flag in the 1980 race . . . this was almost the perfect race car, it was everything that it was in 1979, but this time it didn't have a problem.

We led the thing right down to the very end, and then there was the question as to the fuel mileage. And I went, "Hey, I'm not stopping, I can tell you that. The only way I'll stop is if it quits running." Every time it hit a bump we'd hear a surge and we'd say, "Yeah, there it is."

Lo and behold, we made it. It ended up we had enough to run a couple more laps, but I didn't know it. It still stands as the fastest Daytona 500 of all time; it was a car called the *Gray Ghost,* and that was because of the black sides on it and the silver top with the silver numbers on it. And the first year that I ran the car they made me put Day-Glo strips on the front of the car where the slower traffic could see it coming. That's why they called it the *Ghost*—all of a sudden they just felt this thing go by 'em. It had a lot of special meaning, and I was really well prepared.

To tell you how good the team is, it's the number 28 team that's still going. The main players have changed, but the number 28 car went on after I left, and Davey Allison started driving it after I was out of there, and I guess Cale drove it for a while. I guess he was the next driver after me—he or Bobby Allison, I can't remember—not that it matters to me.

It was just a group of people—pretty much like Jeff Gordon's group now, we just didn't know that we were ever supposed to lose. It was a very dominant car; that same car won at Talladega, it won Atlanta, it won in Michigan. It held the most poles that year, it was just a special car, a special team, it was well-prepared from the front office, all the way to the people who loaded the car onto the truck— everybody was just the best.

The race itself was pretty much like the batting [home run] title this year [i.e., Mark McGwire]—when the car was at full strength it was almost unbeatable. It was the type of car where I made up a 24-second deficit on Dale Earnhardt at Talladega: we had a jack break on the pit stop, and I come out 28 seconds behind and run it down past him with two laps to go, to win Talladega. When you have a car like that, you realize that you're just very fortunate to be part of a great team like that. Of course, if you look at my records at Daytona and Talladega, they're pretty good.

. . . I guess the team did a lot of celebrating. It was such a relief, and such a load off my mind, to finally say, Okay, you've won the Daytona 500. I was like Earnhardt, he looked like he was looking for somebody to share it with, and I was the same way. I had won the race, but hadn't gotten the checkered flag so many times, then when it finally happened, it took a day or two before it really sank in.

We had a race the next week, so it was like my being the first driver to break the 200-mph mark—that means more now than it did when it happened. The Daytona 500, I went upstairs, and sat down with the press. I mean, it was like, Okay, no matter if I was to die tonight, as far as a race-car driver, I have achieved that one special thing. I have more or less won the Super Bowl, or the World Series. I've done as much as a Winston Cup driver can do, as far as the magnitude of one event.

To have that happen to me, it was like the guy that really runs his [sic] best race of his life and all of a sudden he gets to relax. It was like the movie *Exhale*—all of a sudden I just went, "Ahhh . . ." You know? . . . All the other major races I won, they were very important, just like my first-ever win at Charlotte that was so very important, but it didn't have the same thing as winning the biggest of all events.

And no matter what anybody tells you, there's a couple of other events that probably pay as much or more, and a Winston Cup driver, there's nothing like the Daytona 500. Anybody ever tells you—I mean, I went to foreign countries after that, on several occasions, and they'd say, "What do you do?" and you say you drive a stock car, and they go, "Oh?" And they'd go, "Indianapolis 500?" And you'd say, "No," and they'd say, "Daytona 500?" "Yes." "Ohhh!!!"

Even today, I'm with CBS, I'm one of the broadcasters, every time they crank the motors up to leave the starting line to go 500 miles in Daytona, I feel like I should be in there. I still miss it. But I miss it in a nice way. I miss it because, hey, I'm one of those guys that won that thing. That's why I miss it, not because I'm not running—I love being on the other side of the windshield just as much.

I guess if I really had to come down to it, Charlotte is a very, very special place because it's home, and it's also the longest race of the year, 600 miles. I won it three times, but the other most special day of my life behind the Daytona 500, was my first major time in Charlotte, the National 500.

That's when the frog turned into a prince. That was the day that I stepped out, and my father was there, and my mother and my sister, and I look out and I see people that I went to school with, and people that helped me on my way up, worked on the cars. I looked out and saw people that I absolutely didn't have a clue who they are, and they're all there, and they're all cheering, and all of a sudden all the years of trying to get to that place in your life is there, and I don't guess there's any feeling quite like that. When you first win your first major title, that's just pretty, pretty special.

The other part that was pretty neat is this photograph that I keep pretty close at all time, and it's my father, at the time he had broken his leg, and he was in the winner's circle on crutches, and he was almost in tears. And he's huggin' my neck as I'm leaning over, with the roses and the trophy and everything in the background.

When you look at the photograph you hardly even see him, because you realize it's real—it's a caring thing, it's acceptance of a kid then. You always tell yourself, I can do this, but until you do . . . it's all talk.

■ *Back during the beginning of the 1990s, Brett Bodine applied the right touch at the finish to join his brother Geoff as a Winston Cup winner and help put the Bodine family on the map as a racing family. Pitting strategy was the key to Bodine's first career victory at North Wilkesboro, as he used a rather well-known NASCAR champion as his pace car and then applied the lessons from said master to take control at the end of the race.*

April 1990—I think it was April 11, no . . . it was the twentieth—North Wilkesboro, North Carolina. My first Winston Cup win, driving the Quaker State Buick for Kenny Bernstein, in our seventh race together as a team. We won my only Winston Cup race, in my first Winston Cup race.

That's a big day, when you can win at this level. You're experiencing a lifelong dream when that happens. What was really great was that all my family was there, my wife's family, and we just had a great day.

Larry McReynolds was my crew chief, and he made some great calls—the pitting sequence at North Wilkesboro was very critical: pitting at the right time on green-flag conditions, because of the drop-off in speed due to tire wear. Pitting at the right time is very critical to maintaining your track position, and Larry just made perfect calls all day, we had a great race car that was very competitive, and at the end of the day we were the guys leading the race.

It was a true, total team effort because the guys had wonderful pit stops, they got us in and out of the pits quick, and Larry made the right calls, and I did a good job driving, and things really worked out, it fell in place to win a race. And that's what it takes in Winston Cup racing, you've gotta have things go your way all day long.

We did test at Wilkesboro, and I had a lot of confidence going there, because Ricky Rudd, who had driven the car previously for the team, had always run well at North Wilkesboro. And I knew that the car was really good, and that Larry had a great setup for there. And during our testing I was very comfortable with the car, and I was very comfortable at North Wilkesboro—it was a racetrack that I ran well at.

. . . Ricky Rudd and I, our driving styles were very similar on a short track at North Wilkesboro. It was a natural fit for me to be able to drive that setup and make it work; Ricky had come close to winning there in the past in that car.

During the week we didn't qualify as well as we anticipated; we started twentieth, [and we were] a little disappointed in our qualifying. But Larry is a very thorough person, and he kept me focused on working on race setup, to make sure that we were good for the race. He kept focused on that, [he said], "Don't let the bad qualifying discourage our week."

We worked really hard on our race setup, and just got it perfect, our car was just awesome. That was due mostly to Larry keeping me focused. In 1990 I was a relatively inexperienced Winston Cup driver, and he really kept me focused and searching for that perfect setup.

I knew I had the best car I'd ever had at North Wilkesboro, and I needed to take care of it through the race and make sure it was around at the end of the race to be in position to win. It was funny, going to the track that day, I just had a real good feeling. I really felt confident, and that's hard to do at that stage of your career. If you haven't won a race, it's hard to feel confident that you're gonna win— sometimes that's out of the question. But I really felt good about our chances, because I had never had that good of a race car going into a Winston Cup race.

Larry's instructions on the pace laps were always the same—take care of yourself, and take care of that race car. And that's what I did. I made sure that I did not put the car in any position that it could've got ourselves in trouble or damaged.

We just methodically, through the day, with a lot of patience on my part to make sure that we just moved up through the field steadily. Not in a big hurry, and not in a way that we were trying to dominate the race; we wanted to make sure that we were in position at the end of the day to win the race. And Larry's strategy was such, that's what he had in mind, and he made sure that I kept that in mind throughout the day.

Through the race, Dale Earnhardt really took me to school. I mean, he taught me a lot about how to get around that racetrack during that day, how to drive the line on worn tires. I followed him, following his line at North Wilkesboro. At that time, he was really dominating racing at North Wilkesboro, and we had a car that we could really dog him, we really wore him out following him.

But he taught me how to run North Wilkesboro on worn tires, and that really helped me at the end of the day, to take advantage of that. I held off. . . . We got by people because of the chain of events in pit stops: [the fact] that we pitted at the right time, got our new tires on, and were able to be ahead of people by the time they changed their tires because of the track position.

And then we were able to hold off Darrell Waltrip and Dale Earnhardt going to the finish.

About halfway through the race we got ourselves in position to run in the top three or four, just depending on pit stops and how you came out of the pit. I followed Dale, Dale led the race, and I followed him for a long time running second. And he really showed me the line, and I learned the line from him, and was able to take that information and use it later on in the day to hold him and Darrell Waltrip off.

With sixty laps to go—no, excuse me, with forty laps to go— Larry pitted us a little early for tires. We were running third at the time, about a straightaway behind the leader. We weren't as good during that run as we had been in the past, so we had lost a little ground to the leader. Larry decided if we were gonna win this race, we needed to pit a little early, get our new tires on before they did, force their hand into pitting.

So we put our new tires on, and because you get the new tires on you can run much faster lap speeds. So we ran about five laps with our new laps on before the leader pitted—I believe that was Earnhardt. As he exited the pit, we went by him on the racetrack, that's what got us our track position. We actually passed him because we ended up with fresh tires on a little earlier than he did, and we were able to hold him off until the end.

The yellow flag came out, and they picked up the wrong leader, they didn't pick me up as the leader, this was shortly after the sequence of green-flag pit stops happened. The screwup was on NASCAR's part; they just did not pick me up as the leader, they had me at the tail end of the lead lap. They didn't realize what we had done, the strategy played out was phenomenal, and the pit crew had a great stop—I think it was like a second quicker than Earnhardt's people were. We blew 'em away in the pits, and that ended the strategy, and that's what got us ahead of 'em.

Everybody pitted, put their fresh tires on, and NASCAR realized, Wait a minute, the number 26 car's leading the race. And they straightened that out, put us at the front, and we held everybody off.

They were right on us, Darrell Waltrip and Dale Earnhardt were right behind us.

[I was thinking], Don't make a mistake. . . . Drive the thing the way you drove it all day, and just don't give 'em anything. You know, they contended, but we were that strong, we were strong the last run, and they contended but there wasn't ever a real threat, they never got alongside me or bumped me, or anything like that. We just held 'em off, we just had a good-enough car so that I could run my line and concentrate on it, we could bring it home.

They never got to the back bumper, as they say—they could never get to the back bumper.

It was great—your first race, everybody's thrilled for you, other drivers coming up, congratulating me. I remember my brother Geoff, he was the first in victory lane with us. Dale Jarrett—him and I were competitors in the Busch Grand National division, and had just got into Winston Cup kind of together—he came into victory lane to congratulate us.

That's what this sport's all about, having your competitors recognize your accomplishments and congratulating you for 'em.

Then, it was kind of funny, Kenny Bernstein was racing in his drag car, in Atlanta, and he went out first round, he got beat first round. So him and his girlfriend were driving from Atlanta to Charlotte to the shop while they're listening to the race on the radio. I can remember Cheryl, his girlfriend, telling me that the longer the race went and the farther we got to the front, the faster Kenny's driving down the highway.

They got to Charlotte, there was about fifty laps to go in the race, and we're in contention. And then the circumstance happens where we get the lead through pit stops, and she said they drove right on by where they were staying, they were coming to Wilkesboro. She said he was driving like a maniac, and when we won the race he was going crazy in the car. And he showed up at the racetrack about twenty minutes after the race was over. So that was really neat. And it was big for all of us, because I think Kenny had stuck his neck out with Quaker State to hire me as a driver. . . . It was a gutsy move on his part, and it paid off in seven races, very early in our season.

I think that's what Geoff was so proud of, the fact that he'd been a winner in Winston Cup, and now I had won, and that's a big accomplishment for any family, to have two brothers win at this level. And that was really neat, and of course our father was very proud, and just the fact that I was able to share this accomplishment with so many family members being at this race, because the track being close to the Charlotte area allowed that to happen.

And I guess I'm much happier that it happened at North Wilkesboro, instead of, say, in Sears Point—none of the family would be there.

Believe it or not, [the celebration was] nothing really special. Racers are kind of funny like that, once the experience of going up in the press box and doing the interviews [is done], and doing all the TV, and all the things that go along with the winner's responsibilities after the race is over, we just all piled in the van and drove back to Charlotte.

And it was neat, we got back to the house and our neighbors had put up banners and stuff on the street—that was all pretty neat stuff.

You work a long time throughout your career to just get in this league. And to have accomplished a win, your first win, that's what all of those 24-hour days of trying to make some short track, you know, put a car back together in New York State, that's what it was all about.

I learned that the second win is a lot harder than the first win, and I learned how I truly respect the guys and their teams that can go out and win consistently, because I know how hard it is. And I guess that's what I learned, that for me to get back to victory circle's gonna take an awful lot of work and dedication and continued just working at it.

I know I can do it, not because I won once already, but I know that my abilities are good enough to win at this level. We've just gotta get the circumstances right again, we've gotta get the people in place, and the equipment in place, and we can do it.

I think [Dale Earnhardt] . . . at the time it didn't mean anything to him that I'd won. It meant more to him that he didn't win it; that was really when he was dominating the sport, they won a lot of races that year.

■ *If you happened to be fortunate enough to be at the Daytona 500 in 1986, that guy selling souveniers in the K-Mart parking lot down the street from the speedway with his parents really was Geoffrey Bodine, the winner of the race that day. Working with a new team and new crew chief, Gary Nelson, Geoffrey Bodine used fuel strategy to outlast Dale Earnhardt, fulfilling his childhood dream by winning NASCAR's ultimate race.*

It's tough to pick your greatest day—they're all great. You want me to take you through my whole life?

It's hard to not say that winning the Daytona 500 is your greatest day in auto racing. Winning my first Winston Cup race, I thought then was my greatest day—winning the Winston in the number 7 car, well, that could have been my greatest day. But I'm gonna have to narrow it down to Daytona 1986.

We were in the Busch Clash with the same car, and it was a new team. Gary Nelson was my crew chief that year, so it was a whole new group of people, and new cars we were dealing with. That was when Chevrolet Monte Carlo came out with the slope-back window. I guess we tested there, so we tested well. . . . I think I was going for the lead, I know I just passed Earnhardt, and down in three and four, the car got sideways, and I spun out in front of everybody.

No one hit me, and I didn't hit anyone or anything—I just drove right down in the pits and changed four tires and went back out; I think we finished third or fourth. We had a great car, and I remember after the race, Bill France Jr. came down to the garage area and said, "How you doin', lucky?" I said, "What do you mean, 'lucky'?" He said, "You're lucky you didn't hit anything." I said, "Naw, it was all skill . . . aw, it was all luck." Anyway, he called me Mr. Lucky that day, and he was right, because we didn't hit anything, we qualified second with the car for the 500, Bill Elliot was on the pole.

I don't know what happened in the 125 race. . . . I might have won that race, because I have a Gatorade trophy and a Rolex watch, it might have been that year I won.

So anyway, now we're going to the Daytona 500, starting second, outside pole, knowing we have a good car, a fast car. . . . Gary Nelson [had] won at Daytona before, so I really felt confident that this should be a good chance of winning this race, and then, after seeing how fast the car was, we all thought we could win the race, and we did.

We all knew the competition was pretty strong: Bill Elliott just came off that super year he had, and the Chevrolets were better because of the sloped window, so we knew Earnhardt was gonna be there, Neil Bonnett—just keep naming 'em along.

They had one big wreck coming off of turn four, I remember. I think Bonnett had a transmission or something break, and a lot of cars wrecked. So that eliminated some competition, but still it was down to that black car and the other white car, your car, because we'd been racing up front all day, door to door, 200 miles an hour. It was coming down to him or I.

I just watched a video of that race before we went to Daytona this year, woke up in the middle of the night one night and put the video in. I wanted to make sure I knew how to win that race, and . . . I do.

We came down to a pit stop on the green, and he pitted, and [Bonnett] left a little early, he didn't get all the gas in his car. And it showed it on the video; I mean, it was pretty obvious he didn't get all the gas.

I came in, and being the kind of cool driver I am [laughs], I waited until they said go, and they filled me up with gas, and they only put two tires on me—I think they put four tires on him. And so I ended up with a pretty good lead when we went out of the pits, he didn't know they didn't get all the gas in his car.

But he caught me. . . . I mean, I slowed up, because number one, I was saving gas, and two, with only two tires, I was trying to conserve my tires for the last couple of laps because I knew it was gonna be a dogfight.

They interviewed Gary Nelson on TV, and they weren't really matched up with what we needed—I was wishing he was gonna change four, because it drives a lot better with four new ones than two.

But anyway, we're battling it out, and I'm saving gas, he drafting, and we're racing. With a couple of laps to go coming off turn four, he ran out and had to make a pit stop. I remember looking in the mirror, I was watching him in the mirror, and I remember watching him pull to the inside of the track and head down pit road. I yelled on the radio, "He's outta gas!"

And then I remember . . . really praying to God: Please, don't let me run out of gas. You know, this was gonna be the biggest win of my career, winning Daytona was what I dreamed about as a kid; I mean, I just dreamed about racing there. But then dreaming about winning, I mean, that, as we've all seen, even some great drivers haven't won there, it took a long time for some great drivers to win that race, that's how tough and how important it can be to your career.

So for me to be in a position to win that thing as early in my career as I was then, it was really, really special. And when it happened it was like, Uh-oh, this is what my racing career was all about—was to come here and win this race—now what do I do? Do I retire now? Is it over?

But after the race . . . my parents were selling souvenirs for me, they were parked in the K-Mart parking lot just down the street from the speedway. And so, you know, I think winning the Daytona 500 in 1986 wasn't quite as hyped-up as it is today. Things don't happen— as many things didn't happen back then as they happen today—they didn't fly me all around the country doing interviews and all this stuff.

So I drove down to the K-Mart parking lot after the post-race interview, saw my parents, and helped sell souvenirs and sign some souvenirs for some lucky people that happened by to see the Daytona 500 winner.

And then the next morning we got up and did . . . *Good Morning America* from pit lane, that was pretty special. But, I mean, the neatest part was going over with my parents and selling souvenirs from that parking lot. I always tell people about that, and they don't believe it. . . . You wouldn't go down there—you just won Daytona— you go get drunk, have a party, whatever." I went to the K-Mart parking lot and sold souvenirs with my parents.

They were smiles from ear to ear, and they were gonna stay open all night. They wanted to tell everybody that their son had just won the Daytona 500. By then I'd changed [out of the racing suit], and they were very glad to see me, of course, and like I said, the race fans that were there were very glad to see me, too.

There was a little mix-up putting the gas in, and [Earnhardt] left before they could get it all in—whose fault it was, I don't know. . . . On the video you could see it, they were struggling putting the gas in, and never got it all in.

I was gonna win anyway—or else there was gonna be a hell of a wreck. Back in those days he and I were battling it out every week, banging fenders, tore fenders off, every week just about. So there was no love lost between us, and he claims to this day he was gonna beat me, and of course, I claim he wasn't gonna beat me.

I was saving something. . . . I had more laps, I had a real fast car, he wasn't gonna pass me, and I wasn't gonna let him get close enough to run into me. But if he did get close enough, like I said, there was gonna be a hell of a wreck. We weren't the best of friends back in those days.

[Gary] brought strategy with gas, tires, when to do each, setup of the car, strategy throughout the race, to run long enough that when I gassed up the last time, we were gonna have enough gas, and to make sure it got all in the tank, that was the key. He was the crew chief, so he directed all that, and he made sure everything went right, and the crew did a good job, and I had to do the rest. You have to work together, and he did his job and I did mine.

Right at the end he said, "Save fuel if you can." So I drafted lap cars, I drafted Benny Parsons—actually, I never passed Benny at the end, I drafted him at the end and he was ahead of me when I crossed the finish line. And I was gonna use him as a pick if Earnhardt had stayed in there racing. Benny was gonna be a pick, but we never had to use Benny that way.

So I mean, I had a lot of strategy that I didn't have to use. But I did use the saving-gas thing, and by Earnhardt trying to catch me like he did, he used a lot of gas. They never told me on the radio—they saw it, but they never told me he didn't get a full load. So I didn't know he was gonna run out—they were pretty confident he was.

It's the most important—it is such an important race to win. My whole career in racing . . . my parents took me and my sister . . . to Daytona in the wintertime for the Daytona 500, pulled us out of school, we took our schoolbooks with us, and we'd go down there and watch the Daytona 500.

And on the way home I'd tell 'em, "I'm going there someday and race." . . . They'd laugh. It took us two days to get there; back in those days, that was neat, because we got to stay at the Holiday Inn on the way down and back—that was my dream, that's what I told 'em, "I'm gonna go there and race someday, I'm gonna win, I'm gonna race with Richard Petty," and all this stuff. And they just . . . you know, how can a kid from Chemung, New York, growing up on a farm, ever go to Daytona to race?

I'd race go-carts, my father built me a little racer when I was five years old, I grew up at the racetrack they had ever since I was a year old. But still, you know, the dream, it was pretty far-fetched in everyone's eyes, but when I started racing for real, my dream, my eyes, were focused on someday getting to Daytona. I didn't tell people that—I think they saw it, knew it, because I didn't just race for the fun of it, I raced to win. That's how I was gonna get there, was by winning—it wasn't just having fun. So I was pretty serious about my racing.

When it did happen, I mean, it just made my whole career come together, it made it all worthwhile, all those good days, all those tough days, all the time away from home, away from my family, all the times I went broke, had to borrow money, couldn't pay our bills. It made all that . . . worth it. It was worth it.

My two brothers are down here racing, my mother lives here, my sister—it given them something to shoot at. My son Barry, he's gonna win two Daytona 500s, he says, at least, before his career is over. It's opened a lot of doors for my whole family, my brothers, and my son.

It was definitely a confidence-builder. I'd won some races before that, with Rick Hendrick—he was the owner then, when I won Daytona. It just taught me and showed me that dreams come true, if you work hard enough at it.

It's still great . . . and unfortunately, I'd have to say I should have won it one other time, at least one other time. The following year we ran out of gas leading, so I know the thrill of victory and the agony of defeat—a year apart, it took a year to learn that Daytona. But no, I'm still proud of it. I've won other races at Daytona, but to be able to say I won the Daytona 500, that's something you can be proud of forever. Every year I appreciate that win more and more.

■ *Until he joins older brothers Brett and Geoffrey as a member of the Winston Cup winner's circle, Todd Bodine's greatest days will be his best runs as a Busch racer, particularly a memorable win at Michigan in which he took on the Winston Cup drivers and drove to victory. But his other two greatest days are equally significant in a completely different way, bringing the hometown angle into play in a pair of races at Watkins Glen.*

Well, I would say I've got two in Busch. One would be winning the first Busch race at Michigan, which was my first time there, and the first time for Busch cars, and the next eleven drivers were Cup drivers, so I kind of beat 'em at their own game, I guess you could say. [The date] would be 1992.

There's really nothing special for that one, just that the next eleven drivers [there] were Winston Cup drivers. At that time, it was only my second year racing, and to beat all those Winston Cup drivers at their own game was pretty incredible. I mean, nobody going there, none of the press or anybody gave Busch drivers an outside chance in the race.

In practice we were pretty much junk. Whether it was me getting used to the track, or the car, I still don't know—just terrible slow. And we qualified quite a ways back, I don't know where it was, twenty-fifth or twenty-sixth or something like that. We changed the car just a little bit for the race, and I think I adapted, and the car was better, and just went to the front and won the race.

I couldn't exactly tell you who it all was. . . . Well, Hut [Stricklin] was second, I remember that, but I don't remember the rest of 'em. I mean, it was all the top Winston guys.

You go to a new track like that, and you're up against all them Winston Cup drivers, you don't expect a lot. You just want to run all day, learn a lot, and finish the race. And actually we did a lot more than that, and it was a pretty phenomenal day.

I guess we steadily progressed all day, for the most part. I do think Earnhardt was third, and on the last restart I got a good start and passed him going into turn one, I do remember that. And that was with about twenty-five laps to go

Being the first time there, it's a pretty intimidating track, because in a Busch car you barely let off, so it's very intimidating. Plus it's an extremely fast track, and just the experience since then, you realize the limitations of the car are a lot farther than you think when you first get out there.

Hut was right there with me, he was like two car lengths back. I remember just telling myself not to mess up, you know, don't over-drive the corners, that's the main thing. That was the one thing I learned during the day, that you can't drive it in the corner real hard, you have to just kind of float it in there, and then get on the throttle real hard to get off fast, and that's what I concentrated on doing the last thirty laps or so.

Well, I got out front, and he just ran there with me, we had about equal cars, I think.

I didn't get to talk to him, or anything, or any of 'em, really—just the normal victory-lane stuff and press stuff afterwards. I think every-body in the Busch series was pretty happy that a Busch driver had won the race; nobody gave the Busch drivers any chance of winning that race. We ended up having a guy win it, and I think it made everybody in the Busch series proud of it.

No celebrating—just go back, eat dinner, go to bed, and get up and go on an airplane home. That's part of the job, there's work to be done, and you just have to move on to the next race.

Two years ago, Watkins Glen weekend, Mike McLaughlin, my teammate, won the race, and I was second. And it's pretty significant that we're both from that area, our cars are from that area, and everybody in the area considers that our hometown track. So I mean, the hometown boys and teams came home and finished first and second.

It started off Monday morning, Mike and myself rode our motorcycles from Charlotte to Mike's home in Waterloo, New York. We took two days, and just the two of us rode up there, we rode up on the parkway, and just had a really good time, enjoyed ourselves. It was pretty ironic later, that on the way up there, we said, "Wouldn't it be cool if we could finish one-two . . . and we really didn't care who won and who finished second, just as long we finished one-two.

We rode up there, we took two days, and enjoyed ourselves. And we got up there, and the town, the city of Waterloo, puts on a Mike McLaughlin Day, and we did that and had fun and went out that night with some of Mike's friends and had fun. I mean, it was just a really good week, an enjoyable week.

And then for us to come in one-two, it was pretty phenomenal. We both qualified around twentieth. I can't even remember, to tell the truth, neither one of us qualified that well. And it just played out we had top five cars in the race, we ended up going on a fuel-strategy deal, we just stretched our mileage out. We stopped at a certain point, and then everybody had to stop after us, which that put us in front of all of them. So it was a strategy race.

I mean, we didn't have the winning race cars, but we had top-five cars. It was late in the race, probably with about twenty laps to go or something, the caution comes out, and we had already pitted, and everybody else had to pit, so that put everybody else behind us.

On our pit stop Mike beat me out of the pits, so that put him in front of me. And then he got through a couple of lap cars a little quicker than I did, so I was a little ways back, and at the end I was chasing him down. I caught him at the end, but I ran out of time; we finished three car-lengths apart.

After we took the checkered flag, I pulled up alongside of him, we give the thumbs-up to each other, and we rode around the whole racetrack, and, of course, Watkins Glen's a road course. We ran around the whole racetrack, idling, you know, slow, side by side, with our arms out the window.

And that was pretty neat, because the fans were going nuts, and it was absolutely an extremely memorable moment. It was just our way of saluting our hometown, and showing that we had conquered everybody and finished one-two like we said. It was a victory not only for us, but for everybody in the area.

My experience there has always been good. I've never finished out of the top five in a Busch race, and I think I've run eight or nine Busch races. I just enjoy it; I love road racing, I love the Watkins Glen track, I'm sure that going home was kind of like home-field advantage also, with the psych factor.

Ironically, my Winston highlight is Watkins Glen also. We're from the hometown there, and my car owners are, too, and we had a hometown sponsor, Harner's Machine Tool. They like to run the Winston Cup race there, because it's hometown. They've run it before; in fact, the year before, they tried to make the race and didn't make it, with Mike driving.

And we went up there and ended up sitting on the pole, which was pretty phenomenal for a Busch team that only attended this one race a year, to come up there and sit on the Winston Cup pole. We were running pretty well, and the rear-end gear ended up burning up, so we didn't finish. But we had a good car, and a good race going.

Sitting on the pole, period, is tough enough; to get one on a road course is really tough. And for us to go up there and do that was pretty phenomenal, to be able to do that.

It's just three things that stand out. I've had a lot of good times and a lot of great memories, but those three stand out. They're special moments because of the situation, or the circumstances around them.

I think maybe the Michigan deal may have helped the Winston Cup car owners and the Winston Cup people take notice that I wasn't just riding on my brothers' names, I wasn't just out there riding around. I was a racer for real, because I beat the best of the best. I think maybe that made a little difference. The other two things are just special moments.

■ *This interview with Jeff Burton took place early in the 1999 season, shortly before he won a memorable shootout with his brother Ward at Las Vegas and led the Winston Cup points race through the first half of that year as this book went through the editing process. Burton's greatest day in auto racing may or may not have changed since then, but the Virginia native chose a memorable victory at Martinsville the year before, when he outran Rusty Wallace and triumphed over a unique physical problem that could perhaps be considered every driver's worst nightmare come true.*

My greatest day in auto racing ... let's see now ... would have to be winning Martinsville last year. The reason why is because the week before, two weeks before, I had a viral infection, and was so dizzy that I couldn't drive. Two weeks before I'd been at Loudon and didn't qualify the car, ran limited practice, ran the car for a little while, and then got out.

The week after that we went to Dover. . . . Couldn't drive on Friday; Saturday morning, couldn't hardly drive; Saturday afternoon ... felt, maybe can do it. Sunday, didn't feel good out of the car, but in the car I could halfway do it.

Preceding all that, the doctors had told me to count on being out for six to eight weeks. Count on not being able to drive for a minimum of six to eight weeks. So we went to Martinsville two weeks after being told, don't even think you can drive for another month and a half . . . and was able to win the race.

Martinsville, as everybody knows, is one of, if not the hardest racetrack we go to. It's physically demanding, it's mentally demanding, it's just a hard racetrack. And during the race, real late in the race, I was able to pass Rusty Wallace on the outside, which is all but unheard-of, to take the lead.

It was a big day for me, because I had to overcome, personally, some physical problems. We as a team had conquered one of the most difficult tracks on the circuit, and had beat the best in the process. And two weeks prior, I was told, "Hey, two months, man, you're out."

It was an anxious week, certainly, as all of those weeks were, because out of the race car you're convinced that there's no way you can drive a race car. I had been given some advice by some physicians that you could train your mind to ignore this problem. And to do that you had to simulate whatever it is that you wanted to do. So I spent many days in a car, going in circles, in a golf cart, going in circles; there were positioning things that I did, some positioning exercises I was doing. It was a constant barrage of trying to fix this problem so I could drive a race car.

I felt fine—there was nothing wrong with me other than being dizzy, but being dizzy is as bad as it gets. But the team . . . I think what was neat about it to me, in retrospect, was that the team just proceeded as if you're gonna be okay. They prepared the car, they prepared themselves, they did all the necessary things as if there were no problems.

I thought that was really neat, because they were saying to me, without saying a word, "Hey, we know you're gonna find a way to do it. So we know that if you can do it we'll be okay, and if you can't do it, by the way, it's okay, it's not your fault." I think that was pretty special.

All year long we'd had a chance to win a bunch of races, and that was actually one of three races that we won that year. We had gone there and tested about a month before, felt like we were very prepared for Martinsville. My history there was moments of brilliance, with finishes that were not so brilliant. We looked at the deal, and we always ran well there, we always had a chance to win—but we never won. We ran the car out of the brakes, or we had an engine problem, or . . . something, we always had something. I got us in a wreck, we always had something that we didn't need to do.

So we were confident in being able to perform, but we weren't very confident in being able to finish well. That's kind of the history of what we were doing at Martinsville, and what we've done since, as well: run real well but really nothing to show for it.

When I went after Rusty. . . . You know, Rusty is really good everywhere he goes, but he's exceptionally good on the short tracks. We were a little bit faster than he was, and he blocked the bottom, he was blocking the bottom pretty well. So I said, Well, hell, I'll try the outside. And it took about ten laps to finally inch by him on the outside, which is not easy at Martinsville. I knew when we passed Rusty Wallace on the outside at Martinsville, that we had something going on.

The race really went very smoothly; I mean, as smooth as a race at Martinsville can go. We sat there and ran third, fourth, and fifth, and saved the brakes, and stayed out of trouble, and no anxious moments, really . . . which is rare for Martinsville.

And actually, toward the end of the race, Rusty beat us out of the pits. We had a restart, and Rusty started real early, so on the next restart . . . NASCAR told him, said, Hey, you restarted too early. On the next restart, he started early again. And I was behind him, and . . . as soon as he started I'm thinking, They're gonna black-flag him.

And sure enough, on the back straightaway, . . . my spotter said, "Hey, NASCAR just said they're gonna black-flag the number 2." This was probably with twenty laps to go, which made it easier for us, because—and I kind of let my guard down, to be honest—somebody had blown an engine or something, there was speedy drop all over the racetrack, and the track was really slippery.

Bobby Hamilton came up, and made a real strong run at us. He was underneath me, and for three or four laps we ran side by side with me on the outside, and I was finally able to clear him, and then went on to win the race. It was pretty neat, because Bobby's a real good racer, Rusty is the king of the short tracks, I was able to beat those two in a real tight situation, and that was neat to me.

They were upset, because very rarely do you get black-flagged for jumping a restart. But when you do it twice, and they tell you not to do it, then you're probably gonna get black-flagged, and that's kind of what happened there. And I kind of felt bad for 'em, because, you know, it would have been okay for us to race him, we'd rather it come to a shootout.

But part of racing is not making errors, and when you don't make an error and someone else does, you've gotta take advantage of that, because I promise you when you make an error, they sure take advantage of it. You win these races in a lot of different ways, and one of the ways you *have to* win 'em is not making mistakes.

You know, I tell you, we don't do a very good job of enjoying the moment. Victory lane was fun, we clinched the Ford championship, the manufacturer's championship for Ford, winning that race. So that was fun, because years before, when I first started Winston Cup racing, I remember seeing Rusty clinch the championship for Ford, and he got to put the T-shirt on, and all that stuff, and I thought, Man, that's cool.

And we got to do it . . . so that was fun, that was a lot of fun. But I think because we had been through so much those two weeks before as a team, I think it was more relief than anything, that I did drive the car and that we did have a good day, and all the stuff that had happened prior was not over, but closer to being over. And I think it was as much a relief as anything.

The thing about winning is, if you take a whole lot of time to really enjoy the win—in all honesty . . . because work starts again Monday morning, you are letting yourself down for the week coming up. Racing's different than other sports, in that we work; basketball's like this too, but . . . in football, most pro football teams don't practice on Monday, you win a big game on Sunday, you can take Monday to enjoy it a little bit.

You really can't do that here, because the work that happens on

Monday and Tuesday and Wednesday is why you run well on Sunday—same way with football, but it's different in that we can't take Monday off, our teams can't take Monday off, we have to work Monday. So you can't stay up all night partying and having a big time, you've gotta go home and get some rest. Tomorrow's another day.

Anything less than that attitude and you can get yourself in trouble.

That race was, quite simply . . . it's a Virginia racetrack, it is a racetrack that most drivers don't like. And when you win in a place that most drivers don't like, the reason they don't like 'em is because they've never had good experiences there, or they've very rarely had good experiences there. So if you win there, you've won at one of the hardest racetracks. And when you add that to the fact that I was going through some serious physical problems, it makes it that much more special, because it's hard, and we made it harder than it ought to be.

I'm a little young to look at things like that just yet. I've got what I hope is more ahead of me than what's behind me. . . . We work hard to make that a habit, so I don't really do a good job of looking back on my career, because my career's too young to really look back on anything.

I like the racetracks that most people don't like, because . . . there are quite a few racetracks that most people don't like. If you run well at those racetracks, you have great chances at winning those races, because not a lot of people run well. And where it's difficult to run, that is an opportunity; there's opportunity everywhere, but there's more opportunity there, because there's not gonna be that many people that run well, because it's so hard.

So that's the way I look at it. I think it opens the door for opportunity.

WARD BURTON

■ *This interview with Ward Burton took place a few days after a memorable shootout at Las Vegas in which Burton finished second to his younger brother Jeff, which accounts for his query at the start of the session. Burton then turns to matters more positive, describing his success at Rockingham as a Busch driver and then in Winston Cup, closing with a brief account of the Las Vegas race and some thoughts about the value of his approach to teamwork with his racing team.*

So you're really not talking about this past weekend?

I'd probably have to pick my first Winston Cup win as being my greatest day.

I had only gotten with Bill Davis seven races prior to us going to Rockingham, and we had come off of a . . . Let's see, we had a top ten at Charlotte, and I'm not sure where we were at Rockingham, but we were running pretty good, a lot better than Bill's team had run, and a lot better than I had run with my Hardy's team. [The difference] was just mainly support group, him being able to sponsor a Bill Davis team, and they were giving him good financial backing. We were just having a real struggle with the Hardy's deal, just mainly because of where it was located at, and finance.

I can't say that the Hardy's team didn't have good people, 'cause we did. The other team probably just had more good people. And at the time when I got in the number 22 car, the car just was handling better. I mean, the car was just performing better for me, I was able to do more with the car on the track. The car would just turn better, it was just responding to the steering wheel a lot better that what I'd had, which is what we all need to have to run up front every week, is a car that basically responds to the driver's commands. It was probably just better suited to me.

They had just paved the track one race prior, so the track had a huge amount of grip. We qualified third, I should have been on the pole, and I just . . . I had to make a change right before we qualified, and it got a little bit too tight.

Everything was clicking at that time. My crew chief and I were working real good together, they were just giving me good cars. It was actually the old Pontiac style, that was probably like the second race before the end of that year that they were getting ready to go to the new body style that we currently have. The response of the car was just superior to what I'd had before.

I'd won my first Busch race at Rockingham also, so the history of the track for me was pretty good, I always seemed to get around there pretty well. But that particular day in 1995, we took the lead pretty early in the race, and we had a tire starting to go down and didn't know it. And so we made an adjustment, got the car off a little bit and fell back to like twelfth position for an average of fifty, sixty laps before a caution came out.

And then we adjusted on the car, and once they realized the tire was going down, they put it back close to where it was before, and had it boiled down to the closing laps. Rusty Wallace and I were going back and forth. And Rusty and I had had an incident in Martinsville where I felt like he had done something to me he shouldn't have, and he spun around.

And Rusty and I—he had had a real constructive talk with me, about two weeks prior to this race. And you know, him being a veteran, he was a little bit upset with me, but he really handled it very professionally and was really courteous to me. Consequently, we both raced each other as hard as we could race each other, but we never touched.

. . . He didn't really talk about the incident at Martinsville [that day], he just said, "Look I know you're gonna start running up here with us, and we need to show each other respect, and if I did something to upset you, I'm sorry, let's drive each other clean and hard, and good luck." I mean, he was really, really professional and nice to me, and I still to this day respect him immensely. He didn't even bring up the particular incident.

I was leading when we came out of pits, and he passed me on the outside, and there were two cars below him he was passing. And then I made it four-wide on the trioval and got the lead back going into one.

Six or seven laps later they threw a caution, and the reason they threw the caution is because they had wrongly put Dale Earnhardt a lap down because of [him] only having four lug nuts . . . and come to find out he had five. So here we are, now they threw a caution, we've got sixteen laps to go.

Well, what they told us to do was, "Everybody come in," they said, "Okay, nobody pit." Once they let Dale go all the way back, him being at the tail end of the longest line, he pitted for tires. So then NASCAR said, "Well, this isn't gonna be right, we're gonna let everybody pit for tires and line up the way they were at the caution time."

So we all went in for rubber, and of course Rusty beat me off pit road, and my team was yelling at me to go take back the point, which was very confusing for me, and everybody else, you know, [they were] doing the same kind of thing I was doing.

And man, that was . . . a blessing in disguise, because my car was completely awesome for twenty-five or thirty laps . . . and I just walked the dog. For those ten laps we put like four or five seconds on the second-place guy.

But at the end of the day, I mean, it was just very exciting for me and my family and the team, to come from mediocre seasons in 1994 . . . I did get a pole and finish second at Pocono. But in the second full-time season in Winston Cup there's not many guys who have won races that early.

Since then I've had somewhat of a drought, but I've got two second-place finishes with my new team in about the last seven races, so . . . what I'm doing is, I'm including Charlotte which is at the end of the season last year in October. Then we got a second at Vegas.

The support group I've got now is a lot different than what I had then. The communication between me and the crew chief I had in 1995 just broke down, it just wasn't working. And we brought Tommy Baldwin on board, and he's done a great job—not only working with me, but organizing the job and just getting really good job descriptions for everybody. It's a real focused effort at that race team now, and we had lost that in 1996 and 1997.

To be honest with you, you take 'em one lap at a time. And I was just running as hard as I could, and, of course, felt like I could win, but whether it was my time to win . . . I guess I wasn't questioning or constantly thinking about that, but I wasn't looking at the big picture—it was like, Hey, I've only got thirty, I've only got twenty, I've only got ten. But once they threw the caution with ten to go, I knew I was in the driver's seat. It was my race to give away.

Basically, Rockingham, after you pave it, in two or three years it goes back to the old Rockingham. And what I mean by that is that the place gets so abrasive that it just wears the tires completely out in twenty-five laps. So then all of a sudden you'll see a whole 'nother group of cars start running good on old tires. Some cars can run good on new tires when they've got a lot of grip, but not on old tires. And I'm still to this day struggling with a proper setup for that.

But once they put the new pavement on there, I mean, we were able to throw a right rear spring to it and come down to right front, take a wedge out, take nose weight out, and that car just responded to all of it, and I could drive it like it was. And that was just a very adhesive track, we just had a huge amount of grip.

I could drive the car almost like I was qualifying every lap. I could sink the car way in the corner, get back on the throttle quickly and the car still stayed under me because we weren't getting the tire wear like we do now at Rockingham.

Victory lane . . . well, it was a blast. I was lucky enough, when it happened both my children Sarah and Jeb were there. Sarah was about nine at the time, and Jeb was about four. So Jeb was up on top of the car, jumping up and down, my dad was there, he was actually spotting for me.

So that was a thrill, as much as my dad's helped my career, to have him actually on the radio, coaching me, and bumping me up. And then having my wife Tabitha and Sarah and Jeb there, and the folks with MBNA, I still have a great relationship with them. It was just a magic moment. [My dad] just kept me pumped up over the last ten laps, like he always tells me, easy in the corner, which . . . I wouldn't listen to him. He had some tears in his eyes when I saw him, and I did, too.

My dad, I can remember the first time he took me to a go-cart track, back when I was eight, and the heat race, I got spun out taking the lead in the last lap in the feature. Of course, they made start in the rear, and we won the race.

It goes all the way back to . . . my dad was support man, my mom supporting me when I was eight, to where all of a sudden I was winning a Winston Cup race in 1995, and he was still involved with the team.

[After the race] we actually went out to eat with Charlie Carley, the chairman of the board of MBNA, and the team—a place called Lobsteer, and we were driving to all the races then, so we drove on home. And I got home, and I had balloons, banners and all that stuff all over my house. It took me a week to get all that stuff down . . . but that was a good problem to have.

Las Vegas was a lot of fun. . . . Jeff and I finished one-two in Myrtle Beach in 1993, so it's the first time that we've been able to actually compete for the win in Winston Cup. I was happy for him, but at the time I was very disappointed that I didn't win. My crew did a heck of a job of getting me out, I came in third, went out first, that gave me the opportunity. But he was just a little bit better.

So it was very frustrating at the time, but now that I've had time to reflect on it and get away from it, I really like it that we drove each other clean, we didn't have any negative at all come out with it, and, you know, hopefully we'll have at it again. But next time maybe I'll be the one. [*Editor's note: Ward Burton finished second to Jeff again later that season.*]

I talked to him Monday morning—I didn't go over there, I had to go do all my PR stuff after the event. But I knew he was real happy, they've been running real good for the last couple of years, he knows my team is close to giving him a run for the money.

. . . Jeff was pretty much taking his time, I felt like he was in the driver's seat. His car was just a little bit better than mine, and, you know, not that I was giving up, but I was aware of it a little bit, just because of him being able to spin away from us from the middle of the race to the end of the race. But at the same time, I wasn't giving him an inch—I wanted to make him earn it.

Well, the success came so quickly [at Rockingham], I took it for granted probably a little bit. Now, this next win that we're getting ready to have happen for us is gonna probably be sweeter than the first one—I know to appreciate it more. I mean, the last time . . . Heck, I won a Winston Cup race in two years, I almost won my rookie year at Pocono.

So I guess it's just made me appreciate, and made me realize more than anything I can think of, how important a team is. I mean, I haven't gotten any better—I've gotten better, but I'm not that much different of a driver, so I can feel like I can win about any given week. But I cannot do it if the equipment's not under me. And I guess that I've learned that I do not take that for granted, and whatever I have to do for my team, any member of my team, to keep them on my team and to keep them happy, I'm always there talking about personal stuff with my team members, because I want to be there for them.

Because I know, not only do I respect and like these guys, but I know I'm dependent on them when I get in that race car.

Communication is a major key. Having a team philosophy, and team goals, instead of a bunch of individuals. Everybody having their job description narrowed down, everybody knows the proper chain of command . . . it's almost like the military, or running a company. You've got to have it very organized, and everybody knows what they do every day they come in the shop. That structure will, in the long run, make the team stronger.

DERRIKE COPE

■ *One of NASCAR's most articulate drivers, Derrike Cope, was thrust into the national limelight when he earned his first Winston Cup victory in the 1990 Daytona 500, besting Dale Earnhardt when The Intimidator suffered a cut tire on the last lap. In this account of his greatest day, Cope discussed the strategy that went into one of the NASCAR's more memorable Daytona 500s and his thoughts as the race went down to the wire; the family racing legacy (Cope's father was a champion drag racer); and the thrill of winning, and victory lane.*

You want me to tell you about Daytona? It was a good race car, we had a good test, and we had a good test leading up to it. Buddy Parrott was the crew chief, it was really early in the restrictor-plate program, and . . . surprisingly enough, I guess leaving the test we knew we had a good race coming back for the race.

The whole time, the car had shown signs that it was very productive, and we went through the qualifying race and had a good run there. I think we ended up twelfth, and I think we started sixth in the race itself—twelfth in the race, actually, we finished twelfth in the qualifier and ended up sixth in the race.

. . . You know, I think that the last practice was something that stuck in my mind the most. We got out in the draft, and we drafted with several of the fast guys, we drafted with Earnhardt, and I was able to stay with him. Actually, we passed him on the racetrack, we did some things in practice that I think showed a lot of people that the car was capable of being up front. Obviously I didn't have a lot of experience there, but I felt like at that point that if I could just be patient and stay out of trouble that I had a good opportunity to win the race or be up front.

I think that was pretty much the truth when I called my brother that night. You know, I'm not much to brag or boast, but I told my brother Darrin that I really felt that I could win that race. "I know it sounds crazy, but I really think I have the car to do it—if I can stay out of trouble, I can do it."

So, sure enough, that morning I had spoken to Davis, and I think everybody knew that the car was quick. We started the race, and primarily just started trying to stay out of trouble. The car was fast, we moved up relatively quickly, and I think we got to second place, and I was just being very careful. I was trying to correct the throttle, and lift here and there when we needed to, to be patient, getting me into second place.

Dale had put some ground between us, and the race unfolded and he seemed to be pretty much the dominant force. The race went without a lot of cautions, and I was trying to be real careful, and Buddy kept saying that it would come down to the end, that there would be a caution and we'd have a shot.

Sure enough, it happened. The caution came out, and Buddy elected to stay out on used tires. Everybody else pitted; I think I had Bobby Hamilton in front of me, and on the restart we were able to clear him. But Earnhardt had passed us with new tires, and I was able to get to his back bumper and take care of [Bill] Elliott and Terry Labonte—they were behind me. And for pretty much the rest of the laps remaining until the end of the race, they were right there. They tried me down the back straightaway together, and they really didn't have anything for me.

. . . At that point I knew I could resign myself to the fact that I really had to work on Earnhardt and worry about him, because the other guys really couldn't pass me. So if I could get to him, if they could help me, I'd have a shot. Every lap, he'd pull away, we'd get loose going into the corner—we were on used tires and Labonte was getting me loose getting in. We'd climb the bank, and Earnhardt would have three or four car-lengths on us, and by the time I'd get back to the start/finish line I'd be back on his bumper again.

And going into turn one, on the last lap, I was right on his bumper, and Labonte was right up mine, and I got loose getting in there. As the car climbed to the top of the racetrack he opened up about three or four car-lengths again. And going down the back straightaway, you could just start seeing chunks and pieces of tire starting to come apart, and the tire just kind of got real elongated.

At that point I went into the corner, and he got sideways, and I thought we were gonna pretty much wreck by the looks of things, because he was completely sideways, and then the car just drifted up the racetrack as I went to the bottom. And we came around.

I think the caution was with eighteen or twenty laps [left], and then we went around under caution with about thirteen to go, if I remember right. Up until that point he had had some ground on us, because, again, we had been caution-free, and we had just kind of pedaled the car. We were just hoping and waiting to see if there was a caution, because we had knocked the spoiler down some more, and made some more pit stops, and the car got freer. . . . We were just trying to do what we could to keep the car relatively balanced.

I remember that when the caution came out we were all pretty much overjoyed, everybody was—Buddy said, "I told you." And I said, "Okay, okay, what are we gonna do?" And he said, "We're gonna stay out, and we're gonna keep the track position," and at that point they all came in and put tires on.

So I knew that some of the guys were gonna go by us, but I knew that I had been lifting a lot, and I knew that when push came to shove in the last five to ten laps, I could run wide open—I thought there was something left in the car. So I was worried, but I wasn't that worried; I knew I had something left. I pretty much resigned myself that I was gonna have it flat to the floor, we were gonna hang on. The car was there, we were able to have some good people behind us pushing us, and I was able to stay right there and be in a position for something to happen if we couldn't have got [Labonte.]

My thoughts were that he was running the bottom of the race-track, and I remember thinking a lot about him. I was going into the corner, and I let the car have its head, and I was flat-out, never lifted, but I was driving a high line. And then Dale kept inching up the race-track, leaving the bottom and coming up, and he kept coming up, and I think he just kind of thought that I had used tires and I couldn't run the bottom.

My thought was, I could go to the bottom if I had to, and the last lap or two I was gonna go to the bottom of the racetrack no matter what, and hopefully, that Elliott and Terry [would go] with me, because I knew they couldn't do anything by themselves—we were that strong.

So basically, the last lap I was trying to do that, but Labonte got me really loose going into one, because he was right on my bumper—up the racetrack we went—and Earnhardt was in the middle of the racetrack. We were going up the back straightaway, and I was start-ing to close on him. I figured we'd be close to him by the time we got to the start/finish line, but I didn't know how close.

About that time, that's when things started to happen.

We had been fairly fast, and pretty much anytime we'd shake out, we could be up front and stay up front. And that's what really hap-pened: I had gotten by that hill in there, and Earnhardt had gotten by on the bottom side, and I ended up being in second place behind him. And then I had Terry and Elliott there, but we really kind of pulled away, and it was just a four-car race at that point.

As the laps unfolded—I want to say with four laps to go—Labonte pulled out with Elliott, and they had to pull back in line, they really didn't have anything for me. So I knew then that they were gonna have to help me, that they couldn't do it on their own. We were the second-fastest car at that point, and I felt like they were going to have to help me, so I didn't worry so much about what they were do-ing, other than the fact that he was getting me loose going into the corner.

So I waited until the end, to see if I could somehow decoy Dale to go high, and at that point I could stay to the bottom and have help. And it ended up with what I had hoped for on the last lap, going a white-flag lap.

I think that we had seen really early that Keith Dorton had a good restrictor-plate motor that year, he had a good piece for the manifold, it was a good motor. And we knew from testing that the car was fast in the draft, it was exceptionally fast; the car was good, it had tight fender wells. And it drove good all day, and we drove it free. I remember Buddy, I told him that the car had been a little bit on the free side, because I had been pedaling the thing, and I remember coming into pit stops, and instead of knocking it up, he'd knock it down. And I knew then that we were in for a hard-fought battle, because the car was free, and we had used tires on it, and Buddy had knocked the spoiler down, so it was gonna be freer yet.

So it was one of those things, where I think he just felt like, to keep us up there, he had to do something. And being the inexperienced person that I was at that point, I think that he just felt like I could handle the car freer, and he had to give me the choice. That's what happened.

I think that it definitely comes down to having a great race car there—I don't know any way around it. You've got to have a race car that's capable of running up front if you're gonna be up front. And at the same time, drafting does play a major role; even then, you have to be able to draft well, and understand the air and make the right choices.

But I think in that race, we had a good motor and a good car, and Buddy made a lot of the right choices on pit-stop strategy, and put us in a position to be there. And I drove with my head all day, and if you look back at those restrictor-plate races, they're not like they are now. Now the parity's there, even more than it was then, you don't see one guy being able to stretch out and pull away; that just doesn't happen anymore. The slingshot just doesn't happen, it was still different racing then from what it is now.

You have a good race car, I think you have to be proficient in the seat, but you have to have some good fortune and make some right choices, and I think collectively we all did that on that day.

I remember taking the checker flag, the screaming on the radio. I just remember going down the back straightaway and thinking about my dad. My dad was really the reason I was there, and I was thinking about him—he wasn't there—I was thinking what he would want me to do, and that was to get out of the race car and be as proficient out of the race car as I was in it. Knowing my father, that's exactly what was on my mind.

So when I got to victory lane, obviously it was pandemonium, everybody was so excited, and you were sitting in the car, and it's unbelievable. Coming down pit road, all the guys were out there, much like when Dale [won], all the guys came out to pit road, standing there in a line as I drove by, and I was just hitting everybody's hand.

I drove in, all the guys jumped on the car, and we drove in through victory lane—you know, you get out of the car, and it's just total jubilation. You couldn't believe it, what you had worked for all those years, what you dreamed about had finally come true. You get out, you do the interviews, you say the right things, you talk about the sponsor, you do the things that you've been groomed to do.

And then you just . . . After that's done, you're up in the suite and you're toasting champagne, you're talking with the press, you're doing all those things, even until eleven-thirty, twelve o'clock at night you're still doing live feeds from the racetrack. Then you go to a party afterwards, with all the crew and stuff—that night is just a reflection on the day and what had truly happened to us.

It's a great moment. . . . I've said a number of times, you can still close your eyes and feel the sun on your face, that's how much of an impression that that race makes upon you.

I don't think anybody ever gave [me] real credit for winning the race, there was stuff like, "It was handed to you," and all that—it was obviously not what you wanted to hear. But there's a number of races that everybody's had something handed to them, or been in a position to win and something else happened, a part failure or something like that—I think they could say that about Gordon's race right now, and to every other competitor. You want to be a realist about it.

I was not happy about it, but at that point you're young in your career, and you feel like there's gonna be more of those wins, and there's gonna be a lot of good things happening to you. . . . I think I was more upset about my guys having to listen to it. I told 'em, "Just stay within yourselves, and we'll stay within ourselves as a team, and we'll go and we'll win another race this year, and we'll solidify the fact that we are capable of winning more than one race, and that this was not a fluke."

And sure enough, that happened at Dover, and I think that was what so much of the excitement about Dover was. It was just very much of a reinforcement, that we really did belong on victory lane, and that we won races, and we weren't a one-hit wonder. I think that's really what my thoughts were.

But looking back, obviously I took a lot of heat, and I still take a lot. Prior to Dale winning, I still took a lot about it. I don't know, I try not to be very defensive about it, but it still bothered me. And I think the more experienced I got, I think the less tolerant I became about people telling me something, and I would probably have rebutted. I'd say basically that I didn't really feel that I had to take any more crap at that point.

Looking back, Dale won the race last year, and I felt like I had the best race car there, and I felt like I could have beat him, and I didn't mind telling people that. Because it's the same story, it's just a year later, or it's just the opposite of what happened in 1990. I got wrecked on pit road, but I think he was pretty glad I got wrecked there, because I think I'd have beat him.

I think that it elevated [my] notoriety extensively; that was a key at that point in time when you're young and you're trying become a stable fixture in the sport. It did great things for me there, because it thrust me in a position where people knew who I was, my picture, my face, those things there were well-known. The media tours, and *Letterman*, and all the things that come with it, did a lot for me from a personal standpoint.

And I think you ride that for quite a while. And then even when, after we won the race at Dover—you know, we won two races, and even when we started going through some difficult times, with changing rides and not having a ride, or trying to procure more funding to get to a better ride—you kind of ride that for as much as you could through the years.

I'm not one to reflect very much on what I've done in the past. I don't collect trophies, I don't look at things—I guess when I'm older and retired, maybe I'll look back. I'm just looking forward to what I can do. I feel like what we've accomplished has been great, it's been the best that I could do to this point, and that's the way I take it.

I think that I learned then that patience was a key, but I think I learned the thing that helped me the most is that I could win. Daytona's one of those places that eludes so many people, that I was able to be there, to make it happen, to see it to the end, and to win. And then, at a place like that, I just felt like that was probably a major accomplishment, because it think that people have a tendency, if they're really truthful, to say it's all about winning at Daytona. And I think when you do that, it just makes you really realize that you've reached a pinnacle, you've done something that not a lot of people have done, and you're capable of doing it, and you're capable of doing it again. Since then I've been in a position to win that race, so it's not like I've felt like I don't understand the craft, I don't know what I've been doing; sometimes I've done it with a lot more deficient equipment than what the competition's been. That's the way I look at it.

It's funny, I really don't look at the win as much as I look at 1991, and a race like this past race when Earnhardt won. I think I look at those races more, because next year, the 1991 race was the odd/even pit-row rule, and I had the field down a lap and they wouldn't give it to me. and Buddy made the right call on pit road, and we pulled out, we had the field down a lap, and they put us a lap down instead.

We had the whole field down a lap, and they ended up giving me my lap back, I had gone back around the entire field, lapped everybody except Davey Allison, and was getting ready to pass him, and the caution came up, and I was still a lap down, but they gave me my lap back. So with thirteen laps to go again, I'm at the back of thirteen cars, and I get a chance to go, and that's when Kyle and Rusty wrecked, and I ended up getting wrecked.

But I won that race, and I knew that, and I thought that would have been a back-to-back win. And then the year that Earnhardt did it, I felt like I was capable of winning that race again. So those are the things I reflect on, not so much the win, but the time I felt that I did a very proficient job getting the car in position to win the race, and maybe it just didn't happen. I look at those things more in a positive light than I do the actual win.

There's so many variables—people don't realize how many variables there really are. I mean, NASCAR's a variable, tires are a variable, luck—it all has to come through. That's why when you say, Well, you're given a race, or this or that. . . . No, not really, because it's just another one of those variables that didn't work out for him that day. But next year, 1991, that variable didn't work out for me, and I had the race won.

People don't realize that, people don't want to look at that, and people don't want to talk about it, but that's the true face.

■ *The greatest days of New England's foremost contribution to NASCAR and Winston Cup racing ran the gamut, from Ricky Craven's first victory at a unique and relatively obscure short track in Oxford, Maine, to a victory at Loudon in New Hampshire that helped propel him into the world of Winston Cup, to a unique finish at Daytona in 1997 when three teams from Hendrick Motorsports finished one-two-three, led by winner Jeff Gordon.*

Boy, that's interesting, because it's so hard to single out an event, a race. But I can tell you this, there was a race in Maine called the Oxford 250, which is very significant to racers of that area, and actually all racers in New England. As a child growing up, that was the first chance I got to see Morgan Shepherd and Harry Gant and Butch Lindley, Bob Pressley, the Southern drivers came and they usually dominated the event.

But anyway, it's the Daytona 500 of New England in terms of short tracks. And so we won that race in 1991, and I have to say, putting things in perspective, in a lot of ways that was as emotionally as significant, because of what it meant to me as a child, growing up and watching that race.

But I've gotta add a couple—how would you put it?—alternates. That would be the race, but my alternate would easily be winning at

New Hampshire, the Chevy Dealers 250, because the New Hampshire International Speedway, when that was built in the early 1990s, that provided us Busch Grand National North drivers and New England drivers an opportunity to . . . get some exposure to a superspeedway.

Although it was only a mile, and racing in Winston Cup now, I realize that in a lot of respects it's still a short track, but to us it was giant in comparison to the third-mile and quarter-mile tracks. And winning that nationally televised race was big for me, and then the one-two-three finish for Hendrick Motor Sports in the Daytona 500 in 1997. It was my debut for them and Budweiser, and with the circumstances being what they were with Rick being diagnosed with leukemia, it was unbelievable for the race to unfold the way it did.

The Oxford 250 had always been singled out from the other short-track races because of the purse, because of the winner's share. . . . fifty thousand dollars was the winner's share, or more. That was extremely important, because . . . you have to put yourself in the correct setting, which at that time, you've got all kinds of help, great help, great friends, but you've got no money. So you race week to week, almost.

Anyway, leading up to that race, we had had a good start to the 1991 season. That race . . . a lot of potential winners have fallen victim to what's called "lap money." The race pays a hundred dollars to lead each lap. I remember the early stages of the race, challenging Steve Grissom and Chuck Baum for the lead, and I couldn't get to the lead quick enough, because I knew that every lap I lead—and it only took roughly 16 seconds to make a lap—would pay a hundred dollars.

And so there was that motive, but as the race was unfolding and we had led 120, 130 laps, I realized, "We can win this race." The strategy worked out for us, and in the closing laps, we ended up racing Tommy Huston for the win. And when we won it, it was probably as emotional as any race I've been involved with—again, because of my childhood and having attended the race several times, putting such an emphasis on that one event.

I think the racers, the peers of my sport, are familiar with the track, because the event, the prestige, the exposure that it carried, it got quite a bit of attention. That was in contrast to the track itself—all kinds of glamour and prestige and exposure, but the track itself, it's a small third-mile track. . . . When I moved South, I realized that the attraction for the Southern drivers was the money. They went there; Tommy Ellis won the race and came back every year because of the money.

But they all laughed about the track that you could slide off of turn one, two, and three, and not hit anything, because there's no barrier around anything. You could slide out, spin out, and then drive back on. It certainly carries a little more weight, I think, if you're a member of that environment, if you grew up around that race. It was like the season was cut in half—the season was everything before the 250, and everything after the Oxford 250.

But it really wasn't much of a racetrack—it's a nice little facility, but not the type of facility that you would think you could win $50K in. They always had a great crowd, and obviously enough to support the purse. The track is a nice track for a third-mile racetrack, but again, it's not Daytona, or even Bristol, it's just a small little short track.

I can't remember. . . . At that time I was twenty-five years old, and had just gotten married. I desperately wanted to move South and be a part of this scene. And it provided me some momentum. But that particular moment, I remember—they give you the big check, you know, for display, for photos and stuff, the one you can't carry? I think it was like $51,230.

And before I left the track, I got a check for $47,583. And I swear to you, I had no idea what had happened. I thought, "How did I . . . What am I gonna do with this kind of money?

So we did celebrate—we celebrated and never went to bed. We were so happy, but the other aspect of it was, I didn't dare go to bed, because I had forty-seven thousand dollars . . . and I was the first one at the bank, I was actually there at eight o'clock, and I was just watching the small hand tick every second away, going, "Come on." Because I thought that I was gonna be mugged, I had no concept of what to do with forty-seven thousand dollars.

It's a little different now, and I must admit that that good feeling, you know, it's not the same—1991 was different than 1999. Each of those races, we won the Oxford 250 and the Chevy Dealers 250 the same year. . . .

I think the Chevy Dealers race paid thirty-something thousand. So anyway, I went from a poor broken-down racer to actually putting some money in the bank. I thought, Boy, what a wonderful life! I think I was real before, and in some respects happier, but I gotta tell you, it *was* a lot of emotion. It's more fun now to reflect on it, because there was a lot of apprehension, and honestly, some fear involved with carrying forty-seven thousand dollars back to New Hampshire with a crew of guys, team members and thinking, I've *got* to get to the bank, this is a lot of money.

I think the significance [in New Hampshire] was that it was the end of the season in what was easily my greatest year. It was our tenth win, and winning the championship that year, the Busch Grand National North, and the highlight of it was that Harry Gant, Mr. September, Mr. October—whatever he was that year—he had won four consecutive Winston Cup races and three or four consecutive Busch races.

And we were battling Harry and Chuck at the end of that race for basically the last fifteen laps door-to-door. So it was a pretty exciting race, and it kind of put an exclamation point on the end of the season for us. We weren't going to win the race, we were going to finish fourth, fifth, sixth, seventh, and a caution came out with maybe forty, fifty laps to go. And we were able to get four new tires, and with the new tires we were able to wrestle the lead from Harry Gant and Chuck Baum.

Otherwise we would have been a top-ten car, but we won the pole earlier in the week, and we were fast enough, but being young and inexperienced, I think that there were maybe some . . . Certainly I hurt my case a few times, maybe with track position or whatever. But the way it ended up, we were able to get four new tires, and I think we were the strongest car on new tires.

But it was an exciting event, and in large part because New Hampshire's home, and Maine and New Hampshire are home, and

I've always had a tremendous support group there. So Harry Gant was the hottest driver going, and to be able to race him for the win was pretty exciting was pretty exciting for a twenty-five-year-old.

I think it was, again, the exclamation point to an awesome season. We had run seventeen or eighteen Busch Grand National North races, and won ten of 'em. And then it was kind of like graduation, it was time to move on, the next year we were moving South to the Busch Grand National series.

And actually, the week after that race . . . I made my Winston Cup debut with Dick Moroso, a person that I'm very grateful to for giving me that opportunity. But I think that helped me win that race, I really do. See, Dick had contacted me a few months prior to that, and we were doing really well, and he had been through an awful lot of difficulty, losing his son. So he wanted to give a young guy a chance, so he called me and said, "Hey how'd you like to race Rockingham?" And I said, "Today?"

The race wasn't until October . . . and I said, "You just tell me when I've gotta be there, and what time I've gotta be there"—it was just awesome. That emotion and that excitement of being given that opportunity, I think, it gave me an extra boost, a little extra pop in my step for the remainder of the season.

The race in New Hampshire went *much* better than the one at Rockingham, but knowing that, "Hey, I'm gonna be racing Harry Gant next week in his league, so I'd better get it done here on my deal." It was pretty cool.

Dick actually was watching the race from his home in Florida—he loves to fish, and I know that he spent a lot of time doing that then, trying to accept what had happened to his son, the emotion of losing a family member. But he watched the race, and he called me immediately after, and he had tears. . . . It was an awesome time, really a great time in my life. And I'm grateful that Dick gave me that opportunity, but also very grateful that I had the chance to spend time with him, because of what the man means to our sport.

Daytona. . . . The opportunity of a lifetime, as I saw it—and still feel that way. It was just a tremendous opportunity to race for Hendrick Motor Sports. . . . I had just completed my second season in Winston Cup. And maybe the Chicago Bulls of NASCAR, teamed up with Jeff Gordon and Terry Labonte, and . . . a lot of expectations. I had fallen a little short early in the week, I crashed my car on the 125, so I had to start in the rear.

But I had a beautifully handling car, just a beautifully handling car. I was just dicing for position and I got together with Chad Little and just caught a piece of the wall, enough to knock us out of the race. Maybe a little bit of youth and a little bit of inexperience, but I think combined, on both Chad and my parts, neither of us gave an inch, and hopefully it didn't end up costing us. But I think that little incident, perhaps, prepared me better for the race a few days later, in that on Sunday it's gonna be a day of giving and taking.

So we started in the rear of the field, and we took what it gave us, and we gave a little back, we had to give a little, and at the end of the day, Jeff and Terry and I slipped by Bill Elliott for the lead. And we raced back off of turn four, to what was going to be the three-lap-to-go mark, and it was gonna get really interesting with the three of us leading the group. And the caution came . . . and it was a pretty big wreck, and they couldn't get it cleaned up.

So it ended under caution. Probably rightly so; it was the perfect scenario for all of us. I would like to have won the Daytona 500, obviously, from a selfish standpoint, but for what was going on in Rick's life, and the little boost that it gave him. And also, it was a nice entry into that group, my first race for Hendrick Motorsports.

I think it's something that a lot of the fans will remember, just because of the uniqueness of the three teams finishing one-two-three. I think there was [a strategy], we all had the logical or obvious idea of sticking together and drafting by Bill Elliott, because, hell, we're running second, third, and fourth on the restart. What better scenario? It's perfect, right?

Well, let me tell you, that went to hell. As soon as we got to turn one, Jeff, instead of going to the outside—and we're gonna push him on by—he goes down on the apron. And it's like, "To hell with that, I'm not following him." And Terry, he's like, "I'm not having any part of that," he goes high, and I'm like . . . "Uh, I'm gonna go with Terry."

When we were done, when all the shuffling was done, what could have been a mess coming off of turn two ended up being Jeff, Terry, and I, in formation. So it worked out, but not the way we all planned.

I love that race—that is the single greatest auto-racing event in the world. I grew up feeling that way, watching in 1976 when Richard Petty and David Pearson slid across the infield, and in 1979 when Donnie and Cale wrecked, and my favorite driver, Richard Petty, came through to win. And all of the races, every year—growing up in New England it was a long winter, but it got easier in February knowing the Daytona 500 was coming. So it's always been my favorite race, bar none.

So being that close to victory was a tremendous satisfaction . . . but at the same time, we didn't win. So that burning desire to win still exists. But it was nice, still, as an introduction for Hendrick Motor Sports, to run that well.

And then after the race, Jeff and Terry and I, in kind of an unusual fashion, Terry and I were invited to victory lane. So we got to be there, and the three of us celebrated, as we should, because of the scenario. It made for an awfully special moment.

Jeff's always been a good friend and a quality person—we've shared things regarding that race. I was disappointed I didn't win, but believe me, I was very happy, because, again, my very first race, and thinking, "Gosh, where do we go from here?" I was also very happy that he won—he hadn't won the Daytona 500, so that was his first 500. As we're speaking now, he's won two more, so if I knew then what I know now, I'd say, Well, why didn't he give me that one? He's just a quality guy, and he helped get me that ride, and I think we both consider that a pretty special day.

We all did—I don't think he or anyone else was prepared for that type of a finish. I think we were all thankful that it ended under caution, because it couldn't get any better than one-two-three, except for from a selfish standpoint of Terry and I probably wanting to win. But the reality was, it couldn't get any better than that for Rick and the teams, except it could have gotten a whole lot uglier if the three of us had to settle it . . . and . . . under the circumstances, it was fitting. It was awesome, it was a special day.

But I still would have liked to have won the race.

[Rick] is . . . I don't want to get off-track, but as you get older, you realize that there are people you meet in life that have an impact, and having met then, and spent time with them . . . and Rick is one of those people—he really truly appreciates what he gets out of life. He appreciated that, for why it happened, for whatever reason, whether it be because we had a competitive advantage, because we all worked the hardest, or because it was fate. And fate is important in his life, particularly under the circumstances, I think he obviously realized that even more. But he really appreciates what he gets out of life, and he gives a lot back. And he was awfully good to me.

I never had a conversation—this is an interesting point—I've never had a conversation with Rick where it didn't end better than it started. He's just a very positive person.

Obviously Jeff got to him before I did, but at some point in the day, we talked and he congratulated me and the team for our strong performance in our very first race for Hendrick Motor Sports. But he was thanking me—I think he probably was doing the same with Jeff and Terry and those teams; it's like that's worth as much as any trophy or any check, just being appreciated. That's so important. He had been through an emotional roller coaster, the three or four months leading up to that race.

[Winning Daytona] would be the ultimate greatest day. I think that when that happens, it will warrant you and I talking again so we can modify this a little bit.

WALLY DALLENBACH

■ *Before he raced in Winston Cup, Wally Dallenbach was the SCCA Trans-Am in 1985 and 1986, and he is a four-time winner of the 24-hour Daytona race as well as the annual 12-hour affair at Sebring. But Dallenbach's greatest day took him back to his first professional victory in the Trans-Am circuit, a win made sweeter by the fact that it took place on Father's Day in front of his dad, Wally Sr., a steward for the CART/PPG Series.*

[It] probably would have to be my first professional win, which was in a Trans-Am car. We were in Portland, Oregon, and we were in a support race with the Indy cars. So basically my whole family was there, because my dad was the chief steward, and the race actually was on a Saturday, which happened to be Father's Day. And I was driving for Roush racing, the factory Ford team, the Trans-Am, and at that time Trans-Am was heavily involved with the factory effort. So there were a lot of good teams and a lot of really good drivers in the series, and one of the hottest drivers at the time was Willy T. Ribbs, who happened to be my teammate.

And basically we raced each other's doors off for the whole race. I beat him to the line, I don't know, it was probably under a second, for the win, and that was my first professional win. And I did it in front of the Indy car crowd, on Father's Day, and . . . it was a big step, because that was the first one, and I had to beat one of the best out there. It was pretty exciting.

It was 1985, I was probably twenty-one—I started driving and racing when I was sixteen. I was doing different things, and I ran different types of cars, and kind of bouncing here and there. And then in 1984, I ran my own Trans-Am team, and it was a family deal. And based on my performance, I got the ride with Ford and the factory deal.

Basically it's probably the same as anything else as far as family deals go; we had a very small budget—it was myself, my sister, and my sister's boyfriend and the crew. And the three of us trailored this race car all over the United States, and we were involved in a series—Trans-Am being the road-race series—which I think you know about.

It was very competitive, I finished fourth in the points, finished second, and then when I got the phone call for a tryout from Ford, I stepped out of a family deal that was run out of our garage, into a factory effort that was a multimillion-dollar–backed effort—you know, the best people, the best equipment and testing, and everything—and actually a contract. So it was a big step. It was what you'd call probably my first big break in racing, was getting that ride.

That was actually probably about the third or fourth race in the season, and we had finished in the top three or four in every race. But that first win is always the toughest one, so going into Portland I was still seeking my first victory.

Willy and I raced really, really hard that whole race, and to beat the guy that was really on top in equal equipment, was really . . . It was a big day.

The car was good, we had lots of horsepower—I don't remember where I qualified. . . . It was pretty much a two-car race the whole race, you had factory Chevy, you had factory Pontiac, you had a Porsche factory team, Nissan factory team, you had a lot of really good cars in there.

We were making big horsepower, Jack was making a lot of horsepower back then, and Portland's got a straightaway that's about a mile long, so we used that to our advantage. The car was perfect, I just had to drive my butt off to beat Willy. The track is a two-, two-and-a-half-mile road course, very flat, but it's really a neat track, because it's more of a driver's track, you can't really set up a car for any particular place on that racetrack, because it's so different in different areas.

It was a nice day, and as far as using anything to my advantage, all I know is that I abused every part of that car. . . . I mean, I had no tires left, no brakes left, and probably no fenders. In the Trans-Am races there were no pit stops, it was basically hundred-mile races—when they threw the green flag you hauled ass for a hundred miles.

Willie and I were in traffic for the first eight or nine laps, and then we got out front. And then of course we got into lap traffic, probably twenty, thirty laps back into the race. We swapped the lead, and we were side by side, and sideways—I mean, it was a hard race, and it was a fun race, because it was so close. Our cars were very, very close.

We just kept swapping positions, and there were places on the track where he was stronger, there were places on the track in corners where I was stronger. And it just so happened, I think I passed him about two laps to go in one of those places that I was stronger, and I held him off.

"Don't screw up"—that's basically what I was thinking. It's really, really hard to win 'em, but it's really easy to lose 'em. I was just trying to make sure that I hit every mark just right. The track was good the whole race, there were some wrecks and stuff, but they were clear from us, so it was pretty uneventful that way.

It was pretty big—I did it in front of my family, and I know a lot of people in Ford and Roush had really gone out on a limb to get me this ride, and I was able to produce. So it was big, it was a good feeling that I was on my way, and actually that year, won the Trans-Am championship.

That first win is always the toughest, and getting it was a big relief. It took a lot of pressure off my shoulders. . . . It's a lot like what I'm trying to accomplish right now, which is to win my first cup race. It's like, boy, once you get that first one, it just takes a lot of pressure off. . . . It's very different now, but Trans-Am at that time was a very complicated series. You had a lot of very talented people in the sport, so it was an accomplishment for me to do what I did at the time.

Of course, it's so much different than where I am now. You're in Winston Cup, and it's a whole different league. But at that time in my career, that was a stepping stone that I had to conquer before I could move to the next step. It was really important for me to de well there, and it helped me—it helped open doors, to get actually it helped a lot where I'm at today, because of my relationship with Ford Motor Company.

The cars in Trans-Am handle a lot better. They're a lot lighter than a Cup car, probably a thousand pounds lighter; they have the same horsepower, but they also have a lot more aerodynamics, down-force, and they also have wider tires. So the Trans-Am cars, really even then, were much more advanced than the Winston Cup cars. The Winston Cup cars are a lot more difficult to drive. They're very heavy, a lot of horsepower, undertired, and you've got forty other guys out there that are very good drivers, instead of just seven or eight.

The biggest, toughest thing in the learning curve for me was having to learn oval driving and oval tracks. So it was a big step for me to go to racetracks I'd never seen, and race in such a competitive series as Winston Cup. It was difficult, and it's a lot harder even today, because it's gotten more competitive even than when I started.

It was a big jump—you really can't adapt a whole lot from a Trans-Am car to a Winston car. I feel if you have the tools to drive fast, you can drive anything fast, but say, "Well, I learned this in Trans-Am," really doesn't apply, because you're talking road courses to ovals, and really two totally different types of cars.

It was a good crowd, because it was a Trans-Am/Indy car weekend; there were a lot of people there, I don't know the numbers. It was probably one of our biggest spectator attendance races that year.

It was just nice to do it, whether it was Father's Day or not. It was nice to do it for my dad, because my dad obviously helped me a lot to get to that point. And I know that doing our own Trans-Am team had dipped into his retirement to get that thing started. So it was nice to be able to do that in front of him with him there on Father's Day. It was kind of nice that it all fell into place. I don't even remember what we did—I was a twenty- or twenty-one-year-old punk, so we probably didn't do anything but go back and have dinner. He was proud, I don't remember what he said, but he was proud, because it was as big a win for him as it was for me. And it was nice that we did it in front of all of his peers, too. It was just good for everybody.

You try to win every weekend you get in a race car—being your first one, it's gonna be like my first Winston Cup race win. It's gonna be something that you work really hard for, you put all your time and effort and your whole life into it, and then you do it for one reason— that's to win. And at that time Trans-Am was everything in the world to me. At this time, Winston Cup is everything in the world to me. So I think that, other than it being on a much, much larger scale, the feeling'll be the same when I win my first [Cup] race. It's just a sense of accomplishment.

The championship was great, there's no question about it—but I still think the first win is still the biggest. I just think that . . . you're out there trying to win, and winning the championship was great, and it's great on the résumé and everything, but to be honest with you, I'd rather win twenty races and lose the championship, than win one race and win the championship. That's the way I look at it.

BILL ELLIOTT

■ *During the mid-1980s, Bill Elliott had a truly memorable run, winning the first Winston Million in 1985 by taking three out of four of the "crown jewel" events—the Daytona 500, the Winston 500, and the Southern 500, and then winning the Daytona 500 again in 1987. But the man known as "Awesome Bill from Dawsonville" chose two other races as his greatest days—one of his two Daytona 500 wins, along with a race in which he finished second to Rusty Wallace in Atlanta, a finish that allowed him to cop the Winston Cup championship in 1988.*

Well, it'd have to be several, you know. I think winning the Daytona 500 and winning the championship was probably . . . Everything to me's a building block into the next stop, getting to the next point. But I'd say learning and growing and winning those races and winning the championship was a lot of what we're doing.

. . . We had a good season in 1987 in which we were able to build and expand on and come back in 1988 and win the championship. We led a lot of races, we won a lot of races, not as many as in 1985, when I finished second in the championship, because of falling out of several races. It was pretty tough, because I was racing Rusty Wallace, and . . . I didn't have a very big points lead on him going into Atlanta the last race. We had some trouble, and he ended up running well and winning the race. And it was a very tight, stressful day, because we knew what we needed to do to win the championship, and you know, I kind of got criticized about it, but it came back to next year that [Rusty] was racing someone else for the championship and he ended up doing it the same way.

So you've gotta do what you've gotta do to look at the whole picture. You may lose a battle, but you've gotta look at winning the war at the end of the day, and that's basically what we set out to do, and we accomplished our goal. And now it's totally forgotten—I mean, all it shows now is that we won the championship in 1988. It doesn't matter how you did it, but we did it.

. . . We qualified really bad. We ran the first day, we didn't rerun the second day—we probably should have done that. You know, we stayed about mid-pack most of the day, I remember having a flat tire on the left front that almost cost us, knocking us out of the race. And we were able to overcome that and finish plenty well enough to win the championship. I mean, we ran decent, but Rusty, he ran awesome all day long, he got a really good car, and it worked really well. He almost put it on us, but we were able to hold him off.

The track had been great to me, I won both races in 1985 and I won in the fall of 1987. And the track, I've really run well there, and I really enjoy running the racetrack. But it was just one of them deals where I was off a little bit and Rusty was on the money. He's gonna be hard to beat, and it was just down to me and him to either win or finish second in the championship.

I really wasn't thinking about it—when I get in the race car, I just want to run well. I mean, I felt like if we did what we needed to do . . . You see, Rusty was leading the points up until Phoenix and . . . he got into an accident sometime in the race, and then that's why I went ahead of him in points, down in Phoenix. So he had a cushion and lost it there. I mean, he could have easily done it in Atlanta, but I wasn't thinking about it, I was just concentrating on what I needed to do. I wasn't gonna worry about the rest.

It's kind of bittersweet—we had a really good winter; Ford changed the design of the Thunderbird over the winter, it was a lot of hard work. Went to Daytona and broke my arm right off the bat, so it was going from a great year to a not-so-great year. I ended up overcoming it by the end of 1989, but it was a tough season there for a while. Still, I look back on it—it helped you, it made you grow, it made you better, and that's what's a part of life.

I actually won Daytona the year before—you know, I won Daytona in both 1985 and 1987, and I mean, the first time I won it, it was like, Wow, man, I did this. Then we went back in 1987 and qualified at 210 [mph], which I'm very proud of, sat on the pole and won the race. And I mean, it was a great run, I think that was probably one of the best races we had run in a long time. The car was just totally awesome . . . both years, but we really had a good car in 1987.

I ran a lot of the day with Earnhardt. He was tough, he always is there. Benny Parsons ran well there, I ended up . . . I think we had to stop there late in the race and get a bit of gas, and I just barely beat Benny three or four car-lengths at the end of the race. The rest of it I can't remember a lot about it. We were able to run well all day, we had a really strong car, worked well all day. We overcame some obstacles—it was a great week.

The track always seemed to be a little bit slick, you know, back then we were running on the bias-ply tires, it was a little bit harder to get a hold of the racetrack—you really had to handle well; especially at the speeds we were running back then, because the cars were capable of running . . . Like I said, I qualified at 210.

And we just continued to work through that stuff, we kept working on the car all day long, we had a really great car, we had put together a really good pit crew of all local guys from around home.

It was a great celebration. Harry Melling, my car owner back then, he put a lot of faith in me, and I was really happy for all those people, you know, and all the guys that really worked hard over the winter to go down there to do and run as well as we did all day long. It was great, we had a great celebration, it was well-deserved for all the guys. It was more like, "Hey, guys, we did it again in 1987." We had run really so much better than we did in 1985 that it was pretty unreal. But in 1985 . . . Cale was my biggest competition . . . and he had problems and fell out of the race.

[My greatest race] would probably be the Winston Million from 1985. You know, winning the Daytona, Talladega, and then at Darlington. It was a great moment. We did well, we did a lot of things right, we weren't the best car all day long, but we were able to stay out of trouble. You know, Earnhardt ran well at Darlington; Harry Gant; there was Cale, he had a power-steering line go out right there at the end of the race, and I just barely held him off at the end of the day.

But I mean . . . it was a total surprise to me the way it all shook out there the end that I was able to do that and win the Million. I wasn't the best car, you know, all day long I was fourth, fifth, sixth, along in there. . . . I was there, but I still wasn't, I felt like, the best car. But everybody else had trouble.

I think it was more than I could handle at that point in time, because the sport was continuing to grow, there were a lot of things going on. We had a private party after the race, and it was totally amazing when I flew back home. I didn't leave and come back home until the next morning. And all the fans had showed up in Dawsonville, it was pretty amazing. Lord, there was no telling, it was a lot of people.

It's all a building block—but now racing's so much different than it was then. We don't run on bias-ply tires, we run on radials, cars have got more power, more aerodynamics, more down-force. It's just a total different world.

I think we had a really good group of people, and we were able to put several things together, keep it among ourselves, and work through it. And I think that's what . . . put it all together. We built our own engines, we bought cars, we were able to. . . . Everything just fell in place, and you just can't explain that. All the guys fell in place, everything else, it just worked out great.

It's all the same, because I had basically the same group of people in 1987. Nineteen eighty-six was an off-year, but we turned around and just kind of reorganized in 1987. The T-bird changed from 1986 to 1987, and we felt like that was a better change for us also. The car was better—I mean, it was just better, it just changed, the body changed.

Those were all building blocks to everythis else. . . . To me, it all leads up. . . . If you said the biggest ones, I mean, yeah, winning was big. But I felt like, to win the Daytona 500, win the championship, was probably the pinnacle of what we do.

■ *Harry Gant was named one of NASCAR's top 50 drivers, and in 1991 he electrified the sport by winning a remarkable four consecutive races, earning the nickname "Mr. September" in the process. But Gant chose his first Winston Cup victory as his greatest day, and in this interview he described that race along with his memorable run, as well as another, more obscure race in which he truly ran wide-open.*

I guess the greatest day would have to by [my] first Winston Cup win at Martinsville, Virginia, in 1982, driving for Travis Carter's Skoal car. The guy that I had to beat to win the race was driving in relief for Bobby Allison—his name was Butch Lindley, he was the Sportsman driver, which is what they call the Busch series now.

He and I were running all day, hard, but I ended up to be ahead on the last [lap], so it felt like I was racing him at Hickory Speedway or somewhere on a short track. It didn't nearly dawn on me that I was in a Winston Cup race until about a day later. But that was the first big win for us, and we had one of the vice presidents there from Skoal, everybody was there, and it was a pretty big treat for us, my dad and mom was there, it was her first race since the day I started.

If it had to be the best one, that would be it.

You know, I don't even remember, to tell you the truth, if it was the first or the second race at Martinsville that year. We'd been good, we were close to winning, I started driving the car in April of 1981, the year before that [race]. The season had already started, the fall race at Darlington was my first race; I think we qualified on the outside pole and finished second. I knew I had a good team, and a good car, and we continued to go on and do that. . . . Heck, I finished second a bunch of times. We felt like it would just be around the corner, the win would be.

And it came pretty quick there, so everybody was all pumped up. But I really had run Martinsville a lot of years in Busch, but in a Winston Cup I hadn't run that many times there, and I'd never won there in a Busch race, or a late-model race, and [I'd] been going there since 1969. And then, to win the Winston Cup race, it just felt a little strange. I was thinking, "We go to Martinsville here, I can get me a good finish outta here, I'll be really lucky."

We were running real high in the points then, and all the sudden you've got the quickest car on the racetrack, and you can't figure why. Everything's working for you.

I know I had a real fast car, a good car, and if we had just picked the right setup to last all day, I'd run there long enough to know how the track gets. It used to get gravelly and start coming apart, and you'd wade through that stuff—that's the key at the end of the race, is to be able to get through that stuff and make the car stick. And it just got better and better and better; before I won it, it was like I had new tires practically all day long.

It was just real good for us. . . . I lost the lead a few times on pit stops, came in first, came back out second or third, and I'd always get right back up to the front, and then I could run my own pace there, which saved all the brakes, saved the tires, and made it work real good. The only pressure I had, really, was Butch.

We were always good there qualifying; we were real, real close to the front, I think we were third or something in there, because I know I took the lead there at about twenty laps, to get in front. I don't know for sure, but we was always at the top in qualifying up there.

I pretty much was in front for most of the day, once I got in front after the pit stops, I was always gone. And then Butch, he'd be in front. . . . Butch had pitted, though, he got a lap down right there at the end, so I won the race with a lap lead, because he was one lap down. He got a lap down somehow or another on a pit stop and he came back out, and I think somebody else was leading the race, he got beat out of the pits, he was on the inside lane, and I took off and followed him and he motioned me by at the last there, because I was starting to slide [on the gravel] and he didn't want to hold me up with a few laps to go.

We just ran so good, I'd back off to save tires, and get farther ahead. So that was a good feeling when they tell you that on the radio, you're still pulling away and you're not running hard, that's when you know you've got a real good car. But sometimes you ran faster [when you don't run as hard] on a little track.

The caution came out a lot, you know. I wanted to get this thing over with because you had the feeling that something was gonna happen to the car. That was the biggest worry I had there at the end there when Butch got a lap down, it seemed a caution would come out, and then you'd run a little bit, and here you're getting down toward the end and a caution would come out. It come out two or three times and you had to restart, you know, and I didn't like to do the restarts, you can tear something out pretty easy up there on restarts; we didn't have the real good transmissions then that they've got now.

But that was the biggest thing, was to let this thing keep going green. The last lap, I knew I had it made, because I had a lap lead, so even when the white flag waved, I was on my way without even running the next lap. [Laughs.]

We had the vice president, and I think the chairman of the board was there, too—maybe just the vice president of Skoal, U.S. Tobacco Company, Hal Needham. We stopped on the racetrack then—they didn't have the one they have now, the winner's circle—a lot of people came by to congratulate us because I'd run a couple years there in Winston Cup and had done real good but not won. So a lot of other team people, and a lot of other drivers were coming by and congratulating me there when they were taking the photos and all that.

I got to spray the champagne bottle. . . . I'd seen that happen a lot, but I hadn't ever done it myself. We just drove home, and a lot of people in my county had put big signs up in their front yards and everywhere, congratulating me and all that. But nobody was here except the family when we got home.

Well, we had a lot of confidence, and that helped the whole team; we figured now we'd go on over to the next race after that and win again—which we did, we won at Charlotte, the first superspeedway win. I think I even took the same car down there—I'm not real sure. We won down there, and we ran really good down there. We had two cars on the lead lap, me and Bill Elliott. The last caution came out with just five laps to go, something like that, and they blew an engine, had Stay-Dry [all over the track], and we went down pit road, because we were the lead lap cars, you know?

So then we came back on the track. . . . I went in first, and Bill made another lap, and I said, "Oh well, I probably messed up here, because he was fast"—it was an old Ford Thunderbird he had back then when he was winning all them races. So we come back out on the track, and then he came in . . . that put him behind us, like he was to start with. So I felt comfortably, I just worried about that Stay-Dry wrecking me. We only ran about four laps, I believe, but I pulled way, way, way off. I turned the last lap of the race at exactly what I qualified at.

I'd won over three hundred races before we went to Winston Cup, so we were used to being up front, we knew what to do. We went to Daytona, won a modified race there, brought the car back Charlotte, won there before we went to Winston Cup. I always ran good at Charlotte in the Busch race they had—they just started having that kind by the time. . . . I think I only got to run three or four before I went to Winston Cup. Darlington, Rockingham, we were used to leading and being up front with the Busch cars that we had at that time.

You wanted to win just to get that first race down, so it seemed like that was the main thing. Like I said, we'd run a lot of seconds, even in Jack Beebe's car before I went to Travis's car and the Skoal team. We'd come close to winning doing a couple of races with Jack

Beebe—one being Dover—and we ran real good in that car, so we were used to running up there. . . . I just needed to get accustomed to running with the people that was in Winston Cup at that time.

I hadn't run with 'em that much, and I felt real comfortable by the time I was with the Skoal team, more than I was with Jack Beebe. Back then my biggest fear was to spin Cale Yarborough or Richard Petty, but I knew if I could just stay in there, I could finish second or third. So that's what I done, and then I built my confidence up that year. And then the next year, with the Skoal team, I was ready to charge a little bit, you know? We had a good team . . . a real good team.

The greatest one [in the September run] was winning Darlington. I think it was the first one we won out of those four in a row. We won Talladega before then, but then we won Darlington, came right back and won the Southern 500 at Darlington, and then came back and won the other three that month.

That stands out all the time—whenever I'm doing autograph sessions, everybody always says "Mr. September" when they walk up. That's the biggest thrill we had, that team, the Leo Jackson team, was winning those five races that year, four in a row and we lost a brake, a little plug in the brake at North Wilkesboro, or we'd five in a row, the car that day was the fastest of all the other races . . . by far.

We knew we were gonna be strong at Darlington—the first time I ever went there I run third in a Winston Cup car. Darlington was always easy for me, I really should have won several before then. I'd get too overconfident, slide against that wall . . . that stripe got to be a dent. You though you had it whupped easy . . . then I learned a little bit more, but the day we won it in that car, it was just real fast, just like at Martinsville that day.

That car was just real fast, and I led most of the race all day; nobody really could get close, and I didn't really have anything to race against except my pit stops, and that day they were just getting me out of them pits just like a clock, boy, right on the money. It seemed like the more I led the race, the faster the pit crew worked; they got us out of there every time in front, boogeying right on through there without any trouble. [I was] just trying to be cautious, and not trying to overdo anything, trying to concentrate on just the track. . . . I didn't even look in the mirror that day, I don't think.

That got us off to a good start then, it was a super race for us, when I was running out there.

I just tried not to really think about it, because I'd like to say, going back a little ways, I was used to winning a lot of races on the weekends before I went to Winston Cup. We never did talk about 'em much after the race, or celebrate or anything, we would just go on to the next night; you could win, like, three on the weekend.

We never really thought a lot about it. I mean, you're glad you won and everything, but we didn't do a lot of celebrating—and that's the same way I wanted to do Winston Cup when I won the first race. It might have been a big deal, but I just said, "Boys, don't be bragging at the garage area next week, something might happen."

It was the same with winning those four in a row, I said, "Let's just leave, do our deal in the winner's circle," and kind of block it off [your minds] and start again next week, because it seemed like the more you brag about it, in the past, I'd have more bad luck to do that, you know, in the next race. We had a little agreement, among myself and my two boys, that helped me here at the shop all the time—we won, we just left.

Now, even when I won the last couple of races I won in 1992 . . . you know, you've gotta do a lot of radio, TV shows, and so on. You can't forget it now, because there's too much sponsor involvement and everything and . . . you've got a lot of people on the car, and we had a lot of different people's names on the car, [so] that you have to do things for [them] after you've won, photo sessions now, and everything. So that's the way it is now with the guys that win, they can't just leave like I did, and take off, because they've got so many commitments.

We won a Busch race at Martinsville. Along about the same time I was winning Winston Cup, I was winning a lot of Busch races. In fact, I won every Saturday that we ran, and won on Sunday, too, when I was winning the four in a row. We won Martinsville the last race of the season, and we weren't gonna run that race; our sponsor was Skoal, we were only gonna run fifteen races, and we'd already won five races out of the fifteen. Ed [Whitaker, crew chief] said, "We've gotta go run it"—and qualified on Thursday 'cause the modifieds come in and had the whole track on Friday.

So I practiced a few laps and qualified eighth, covered the car, and said, "I'll see you on Sunday morning." And I went up there on Sunday morning, and the crew chief was in a panic—"Boy, the track's changed, everybody's changed springs," and all this. And Bobby Labonte was running Busch, and Dale Jarrett was running Busch . . . you had some tough cars, I said, "We'll just do what we can do, we'll be okay."

We won that thing going away so easy, because we didn't touch the car—only practiced ten laps on Thursday in qualifying. We took the lead and won the race, and I was really wanting to leave, so I had to go up to the winner's circle on top, but at the same time, that was the last race of the season in Busch, and I think Larry Pearson had won the championship, so they got to do a big deal with him.

So they gave me a trophy and snapped a picture and said, "Wait a minute. . . ." I had my hat on, and I'd already changed clothes, and I had parked my truck outside. I was standing around looking at that ladder behind me on the building, and I just kind of eased down. I was going across the track with my hat turned backwards, and a handkerchief hanging in my mouth so they didn't see me, I didn't even do the winner's circle, I just got in my truck. I was the first one out of there, and that was that.

But I came on back home, and the next day Skoal called, and they said, "What happened? Where was you at?" And I said . . . "I left."

I had another great day, and a lot of people didn't know about it except the crew; this was is in a Busch car at Darlington. Darlington is a tough track to run, and you got to learn the timing—when you come off the fourth turn you use the throttle to keep the car cocked. Back then with the bias tires, the radial tires stick a little better. But even the Busch car, you couldn't run it flat wide-open then.

I was leading the race, and there was ten laps to go in the race, and

I've got, you know, a couple hundred yards' lead, I think Morgan Shepherd was running second that day. I go down the third turn, the throttle hangs to the floor. I grabbed the switch real quick, and then I tucked my toe, I couldn't get my toe under the throttle, and so I switched the car back on to get it to come on around and get out of Morgan's way. And I get to the flag stand, and he just . . . *voooom-mmm,* by me he went.

And so I switched the car back on to get around the pits, see what we can do. I switched it on and went around the first turn—switch it off, switch it back on—and I could see that I was staying with him. So I thought, "Well, I'll try it for two or three laps. I'll hold my hand up on the switch and drive with the right hand and my left on the switch." And I went to the corner and switched it off, and I went a couple of times and I caught him, coming off the corner. And I figured, "What am I gonna do now?"

I went through three and four and everything, patting the throttle and cocking the car. I almost . . . See, I had to leave my foot on the throttle to keep my body in sight sequence, you couldn't drive with something where it's not supposed to be. But sometimes I'd lift my foot and I'd forget to switch it off, and I'd about run into him.

Anyway, I passed him down the back straightaway, and I won that race just switching it off and on; the throttle was still stuck when I went to the winner's circle.

The first one I told was Ed Whitaker, because he was looking at the throttle that's been hung wide-open for ten laps. The biggest thing is there would have been a wreck if I hadn't switched it off quick enough. But that was . . . I was just pretty proud of that there, because that being Darlington, to win the race with the throttle stuck and just using the switch to switch it off and on.

When you switch it off, it's not like backing off the throttle, the car stops real quick a lot quicker, and you didn't have that free motion through the turn, when you let off you kind of touch it back a little bit. . . . All I had was nothing, or throttle. So that made it a little tougher to do, but we done it pretty good, we got back in front then, and Morgan brushed the wall pretty hard, and I think he knocked his toe-in out with about four laps to go, and then he started falling back. . . . Well, then I could do it a lot easier.

They just laughed and laughed [when they found out]. I didn't say nothing on the radio, I was afraid word might get back—I told him the throttle was stuck, and then I didn't tell him no more. He said, "Come on in." I just kept running, I knew they wouldn't talk to me if they knew I was winning the race; they didn't say nothing, and I didn't say nothing else. I knew people would pick it up in a pinch, and with Morgan running second, if they knew the throttle was hung wide-open they might have put more pressure on me, just like I did at North Wilkesboro when I was trying to win my fifth race in a row.

I really couldn't say nothing on the radio, 'cause they all monitor you, and then NASCAR, too, [they'd] black-flag me for sure for running laps without a brake to my name out there.

It helps you [going back and forth between Busch and Winston]. I was needing to run all the races I felt like. I felt like I could run seventy-five races a year, that'd be better, running the Busch car, too. But the Busch car helped me more than anything I ever did; then I sent through a real bad spell a couple times the last couple of years with Travis, winning five or six Busch races, and that would keep you up.

It was the same way with Leo Jackson. When I wasn't winning any of Leo's, I could win the Busch races in Ed Whitaker's car. That kept the team up, too; they knew they were gonna have to do a little more hard work on their car and things like that, so it was just a big tremendous help to me run that Busch car.

The Busch car feels like a go-cart after getting out of that Winston Cup car. We didn't have any power; they had the V-6s [in the Busch], . . . they still have about the same amount of power as the ones they're running now. You hear the interviews now from Sadler, driving number 21, he says the power and all is so much different, and in reverse, you hear Tony Stewart—they asked him why [he didn't] do good in the Busch car he run that year, last year; and he said, on the TV he was used to the Indy cars with so much more power, it was hard to run a dead car.

Well, that's the way it is with Winston Cup—to step down to it, it's so easy to step down to run that Busch car. But now they've changed the wheel base a little bit, and the weight a little bit, they're trying to get 'em closer together now, so the boys won't have a big transition to make. When I started running the Winston Cup car, I said, "Well, I'm not gonna run any more Busch, get settled in on it," and I didn't run any [Busch] there for probably about four or five years. I guess 1985 or 1986, somewhere along there, I started running for Ed Whitaker, because Earnhardt was running and I wanted to race him.

Ed had been calling and calling and calling, and finally I told him I'd drive it, but I had already got set in for several years, maybe five or six years in a Winston Cup car without running any Busch, and that worked good, the way I done it was a pretty good way to do it.

We beat [Earnhardt]—we beat him more than he beat us. We were running fifteen races; we'd always win five or six, we had a good average right there that last year. We'd only won one race in 1994 when I quit racing, we won Atlanta in a Busch car, that last race. But up to that point, that was my only win that year, we had to do a lot of changing over, going to V-8 motors and stuff. I guess we had a V-6, we had some help with the factories in the Buick, but we lost that deal somewhere on about 1993, and that really hurt us a lot. We were underfinanced because we had trouble getting a good sponsor with enough that we could go out and get those good motors, like Buick was really having a lot of.

They all were great, all the races, you know, every time you win. The thing sometimes was that you'd have a real bad car and finish third or fourth and it should have finished tenth, and you feel pretty fair after the race. And if you have a real good car and something happened in the race, and something breaks or something, or you get spun out or you get in a wreck, you'd be mad till the next week. I know one time I won a late race at North Wilkesboro, and Hal [Needham] said, "That's the best race I've ever seen you drive since I've been a car owner."

I said, "No, Hal, a couple weeks ago at Nashville was the best race I ever run, and the car finished fourth." Anybody could have won in the car that day [in the earlier race]. The one we won at North Wilkesboro, it was just a super-handling car that day, just to a T. That's the way things go like that, it gets to be a pretty discouraging and disappointing business to be in sometimes, but you've got forty-three cars out there running, the guy that win's gonna be happy, and then somebody had a car that wouldn't run good and finished good, he's gonna be pretty happy, too. But those other forty-two people are gonna be like I used to be—aggravated [until] the time they get to the next race to qualify.

There's a lot of mental stuff you've got to think about the whole time. We were always running for points, we finished pretty good all the time—never did win, but finished second, third, fourth or fifth all the time. That's the back of your mind, you think, "Well, I've gotta finish this race"—you know, you're thinking that, plus winning points and all . . . it's a pretty tough deal.

■ *Joe Gibbs knew exactly how to handle and enjoy the fruits of victory when he coached the Washington Redskins to a pair of Super Bowl championships during the 1980s. But as a race car owner, he found himself in a slightly different position when he experienced his greatest days in auto racing, particularly during Dale Jarrett's memorable Daytona 500 victory.*

It's easy for me. There were two days that we had, one of 'em . . . well, we hired Bobby Labonte to go to work driving our race car. He had not won a race, a Winston Cup race, and we were racing in Charlotte, the Coca Cola 600, and I can remember the last 30 or 40 laps; it was finishing up at night, because that was such a long race.

And I can remember everybody standing there, the last 30 or 40 laps Bobby was in the lead, and I think everybody was crying. Everybody was standing there: Donna, his wife was there, everybody was so emotional, because we're thinking, hey, he's gonna . . . he's got a chance to win his first race, and it's in a great place, so it was one of the most emotional nights that I've had in sports.

The second one was obviously Dale Jarrett winning the Daytona 500, and that was in our second year. That was our first win in NASCAR, and all of us were there, me and Pat and all of our family, and Dale and all of his family in the winner's circle, and Norm Miller from Interstate.

That was . . . those two are set right at the top for me, and two of the more emotional experiences and two of the greatest experiences I've had in sports. I think Bobby had shown great talent, and we felt good about that race, because we had qualified extremely well, we had a good car. And we have always, as a race team, raced good there. So you have . . . lot of times you have high expectations, we had high expectations this year at the Daytona 500, and lost both cars with a motor problem.

You're always having those kinds of expectations, but in auto racing, it's so hard to win. So, you know, I thought . . . we were positive, but you know how it is for a driver like that. You know he's never won a NASCAR race, and you know that he's got the potential and is gonna do it, it's just a matter of time. But to actually be there, and be a part of it, it was a great experience.

I think the thing I remember most about the winner's circle was Bobby had Tyler, his son, in there, and Donna, and, as a family, they were very emotional. And I remember Bobby's mother and dad were there, and they were all—you know—it was like a giant family deal. Then all of us with the race team were so excited, because it meant so much to us. I don't remember a lot about what was said, or anything, I just remember all the emotion. The emotion at Daytona was similar, but I had never been in that position before. I knew a lot about the tradition and the history of the race, of course, but when the victory took place I almost felt like I didn't know quite what to do, how to handle the emotion of the experience, being in the winner's circle and the celebration and all.

I remember being with Dale in the winner's circle with my wife [Pat], and the rest of the team, and Jimmy Makar making great calls during the race. It was almost a shock because I was so new to the sport. I just remember being overwhelmed by it. Then there was Ned being there, and hearing the [television] call later, and that just made it that much more historic and memorable.

People ask me about what I do different in auto racing compared to football, but to me what's similar about it is the people, having and finding good, quality people, and then creating the conditions and giving them the freedom to do their jobs. As a coach my job was to put together and execute a game plan, to put players in the best set of conditions that would allow them to do that.

In that sense what I do now isn't all that different. You put together a team the same way, and when you have people like Jimmy Makar and Dale Jarrett and Bobby Labonte involved it just increases your chances that much more. So many things can go wrong in this sport that you can't control, but people like that are going to have success because of the dedication with which they go about doing their jobs. My job is just different now. I'm responsible for taking care of the sponsors, making sure their needs are met, and I leave the game plan to people like Jimmy and Dale and Bobby on Sunday.

■ *It is perhaps the ultimate challenge faced by virtually every red-blooded American male on an annual basis: finding the perfect Valentine's Day gift. Spending early February in Daytona with a serious strong chance to win NASCAR's biggest race gives Jeff Gordon a bit of a leg up on most of us, but on Sunday, February 14, 1999, he gave his wife Brooke the perfect Valentine's Day gift—winning the Daytona 500 in a 25-lap, bumper-to-bumper shoot-out with Dale Earnhardt.*

That might be a tough one, you understand. Actually, you've caught me at a good time, because right now, you know, after coming off the Daytona 500 win, I . . . without a doubt can say that that's my greatest day in racing.

To win the Daytona 500 is one thing itself, but then you throw all the other factors in there. . . . I didn't have any teammates that could help me out a lot, so we had to do a lot of battling on our own. I got shuffled back several times, and never really led a whole lot. But then we come down to the finish, and we've got a 25-lap shoot-out, we come in and get tires and then we've gotta come through the back of the field to the front.

And then we get there and we're battling with Rusty [Wallace] and Earnhardt. I mean, it was just an unbelievable day for me, to be able to be able to keep that number 3 behind you. Because I know how difficult that can be, especially at Daytona. And to pull that off, and then you look at the million-dollar bonus, Valentine's Day, you know—I got to celebrate that with my wife. And she said that's all she wanted. It was just . . . I don't know how a day could get any more perfect at the racetrack than that.

Everything was a surprise. We sat on the pole, first time we've ever sat on the pole for the Daytona 500; that one really caught me by surprise. I mean, we'd had a good test down there, and we were running good in practice, but we'd run good at Daytona for qualifying before and just seemed to come up a little bit short. It's like maybe we didn't have quite what it took to pick up that little extra bit of speed that all the other guys would pick up when it came time to qualify.

But this time we found it. And we drew the right number, we drew a late number to go out, and everything just really worked out well for us. It's not really anything that you find, it's just catching the right cloud or the right gust of wind, it's getting the car to the maximum performance that you can, and tuning the engine. We do a lot with springs and shocks now, where we really get the car down very low—everybody does that, but it's just trying to get the car balanced just right where it's as low as possible on the racetrack.

I think the thing that sticks out in my mind the most is . . . how many drafting partners I did not have. I absolutely had no friends out there whatsoever. We were in the top five all day long, and we had a great race car, and I knew we had a great race car, but I never was able to show how good it was, because I'm battling with guys that have teammates—Rusty Wallace, and Jeremy Mayfield, Earnhardt, Skinner . . . Who else is up there? Maybe some Roush guys, Dale Jarrett, Kenny Irwin, so I was kind of fighting a battle that I couldn't really compete with, and I remember being pretty frustrated with that most of the day.

I'd be running about third or fourth, and I'd go, "Okay, I'm gonna make a challenge and go up there and try and lead some laps." And I'd dive down there thinking, "I've got enough momentum to make it, and this guy'll go with me," and sure enough, they leave me out and I go back five or six spots. That went through my mind most of the day.

But at the end, when we finally got to the front to win, the guys didn't have a choice; it was like, "It's time to win this race, whether we've got a teammate or not. It's time to get to the front, and we've gotta do everything we can to get there."

And I happened to be at the right place at the right time, when Earnhardt was pushing. I know that he didn't necessarily want to push me to the front, but he didn't have a choice, either; he knew that that was gonna be the best opportunity for him to be there and challenge for the win.

. . . I've had some teammates—Terry [Labonte]—and I had Terry working with me this year, but what happened was he got caught up in that wreck. And then something happened to the number 25 car, I think they got shuffled back or something. So I had teammates at times, but not very often. In the past, yeah, I've had the teammates, and they helped me win the 500 in 1997. At Daytona, it's important to have a drafting partner. It doesn't have to be a teammate, but usually it is your teammate.

Ray [Evernham] did not think the car was as fast as some other cars. I think that was more Ray, because I felt like we were just as strong as anybody out there. We just never were in position to show it until the end.

I took the lead with like ten or twelve laps to go, it was that big exciting pass on Rusty, and that kind of got exciting there for a little bit. But once I got in the lead and Earnhardt was behind me, I literally watched my mirror more than I ever watched what was going on in front of me.

Because . . . there are ways that you play around with the air in the draft and things so you can make passes happen. With the restrictor plates these days, if you just stay full-throttle on the gas, you're just gonna follow the guy in front of you all day long and you're never gonna make a pass. So you've actually kind of gotta get on and off the throttle and try to utilize the air to kind of give you a little bit of a slingshot. And [Earnhardt] was working me over every lap, to get that going and try to make a pass on me, so I was just trying to block his every move.

There are certain guys that know how to do it—it's not quite the slingshot that maybe you saw without the plates, it doesn't happen as fast. But you can still gain momentum and get a run on a guy and get underneath him, and he can't block you. And that's what I was trying to prevent from happening.

It's funny, because [in 1993] I'm sitting there riding behind Earnhardt, and there were like five laps to go, and I was thinking, "Oh, nobody's gonna make a move yet, they're gonna wait until the white flag." And then all of a sudden, *boom,* Jarret's up beside me, and I'm like, "Uh-oh" . . . so I guess he decided he was gonna go a little sooner than that. He had a strong car, and if I could have kept him behind me, I might have had a shot at winning. I kick myself every day because of that—a lot of that was just inexperience.

I think that a lot of my success . . . you can directly relate it to that Daytona 500 in 1993 and take that as an example of what happened basically for the next two years that led up to us starting to have a lot of success. And that is, that right out of the box, we had a good team. Maybe we weren't as consistent back then as we maybe could have been, because of our lack of experience, but we basically came to Daytona with a car that was capable of winning the Daytona 500, and here we were in position, so, you know, I finished fifth in my first Daytona 500. But that valuable experience that I gained in that first Daytona 500 helped me learn from mistakes, or things that I did right, for the next time we came back.

There's a lot of rookies, a lot of young guys, a lot of veterans, that are in our sport that don't always get to be in that position. Once you're in that position once or twice or even three times, you know what's gonna happen, and you can anticipate what's gonna happen. When you're not in that position, you don't have that experience, and usually you're gonna get caught by somebody who is experienced.

That's specific to Daytona . . . definitely. Restrictor plates, and especially Daytona restrictor plates, is unique to every other track that we run. You've gotta have your Daytona memory log going, and say, "Okay, I've been through this, and done this, this happened to me." Once you leave Daytona, you can throw that out the window, and you've gotta have your Rockingham memory log.

Every track, you take notes, and you have mental notes, and your crew and your team, they take all their notes with the race car and the racetrack. And you've gotta make sure that you keep track of those things and know what to expect the next time you come back.

Well, you know, anytime you win the Daytona, it's an exciting victory lane. It was very exciting, and it was like disbelief at that time, just totally overwhelmed with joy. Because with the way the day went, and having nobody really help me out much, and not having any friends and partners out there, I was the last guy that . . . I never really dreamed that we would have run that race. So victory lane was just a huge celebration of that.

I think when you put everything in . . . See, in 1997 when I won the 500, I won under caution. And, you know, as great of a race as that was, and as great as a win as that was, it was a little bit of a letdown to win under caution. So to be able to do it under green and hold off Earnhardt, who I consider, and most people would, as *the* best there is, especially at Daytona . . . I think that's what contributed to make this an even more special 500 for me.

The race was over when he tapped me, that's . . . you know, Dale has a funny way of congratulating people.

We always celebrate Valentine's Day at Daytona. . . . I think nothing's any cooler. You know, my wife, she's my biggest supporter, and she loves racing and loves to be a part of what I accomplish, and I love for her to be a part of that. And for me to do something like that on Valentine's Day, I think that it was very special. Luckily I had plans regardless of what happened. So that was only an added bonus—we finally got home late at night, I had dinner planned, and roses and candles, and a nice romantic dinner for the two of us.

I know people laugh, and go, "Yeah, right," when we say this, but we really do, we leave the track and we look at each other and we just go, "Wow, I can't believe it. I just can't believe that we won this race today, and what an awesome feeling for us to accomplish it."

To me, when you win a race and you win a championship, like we did at Rockingham last year, that was a big day. But if I've gotta just pick one day, this is just the ultimate, I feel like it was this year's Daytona 500—just the way everything happened.

You know, if I had to list a top five, then I would have to throw in there winning the championship last year, in the fashion that we did it. Because we won championships before, but we'd never run strong all the way till the end of the season and won a race and the championship, and we did that and then some last year by winning Rockingham and winning the championship and then going to Atlanta and winning Atlanta.

But the championship, it's not like it's just one big victory, you know, it's spread out throughout the whole year. And when the whole season's over and you're the champion, it's like you've had a complete year, it's not like you just had one great day.

Then I would go with . . . It's a toss-up for me between the inaugural Brickyard 400 win, and the Coca-Cola 600, which was my first win. But then I've got days back in open-wheel races that were huge moments for me, too, that I'll never forget. Heck, I could go all the way back to being seven years old racing quarter-midgets and winning my first Grand National event. You know, it's hard to say. They all have so much meaning, and that's why I would not be disappointed if my career ended today. I've accomplished a lot of things, even before I got to Winston Cup, I wouldn't be disappointed, because I've accomplished a lot of things before I ever got here.

I think the most surprising and overwhelming thing, to me, is that we've had this much success at this level in Winston Cup. I mean, sure, you expect it on the short track before you ever make it to this level. A guy can win a bunch of races and be real successful there, because the competition's not tough. But once you get to this level, everybody's got money, everybody's the best at what they do. You don't expect to pull into victory lane on a consistent basis.

I think you've gotta look at the whole team and where it all started. I knew that there was something special between Ray Evernham and myself the first time we ever worked together. You know, he drove a race car at one time and he was the first person that I felt like

I could relate to and they understood what I was saying, because he drove a race car.

So I'd say, "Hey, the car's a little loose or a little tight here," and he'd say, "Does it feel like this, this, and this?" I'd go, "Yeah, it feels just like that." And he'd say, "Okay, I know what you're talking about, let's try this, and tell me what you think." So we clicked right from the start when it came to that. Plus, I never met anybody that wanted to win as bad as I did—maybe even more, at times. He's a very organized, very focused, a very hardworking person. It's great to have a person like that on your side.

And he started this team up, and he didn't go into this saying, "Okay, I'm going to go get the best of the best from every different team and hire 'em for this job. What I'm gonna do is I'm gonna get the people that I think work well, have the same work ethic that I have, that maybe don't have experience, but are people that I feel like will learn, and learn the way that we want them to learn."

So . . . when he built this team—I mean, luckily we had Hendrick funding, and Hendrick resources made that a whole lot easier—but he went and he picked from a lot of different areas, from the Northeast, guys that he used to work with and race with, and people he worked with at IROC or different things. Or people would bring in résumés, and he'd say, "Hey, this looks like a kid that's gonna put his whole heart and soul into it."

And we built this whole team around that, and now what we've got is the growing of these types of people that are now probably the best at what they do. But they've all done it together. And that's why the chemistry is there, because they all came into this together, it's not like you have to deal with a lot of egos and different things like that. Because everybody feels like, "Hey, we've worked hard, we've worked together to do this, and it's a special thing."

Also, when you're winning, it builds that—when you're winning, the confidence level goes up, the chemistry gets better. Those people believe in one another and believe in the teamwork even greater when you have that success. I mean, there are teams out there that could have the same situation and the same chemistry as we have, but maybe they don't get to go to victory lane as much, or maybe they've missed on just a few of the little combinations. And so they're not getting to experience it, the team's not saying, "Hey, we've got that chemistry." Where my team, they're like, "Hey, we've got it. We've won two out of the last four races." And they don't second-guess themselves—my guys don't second-guess themselves.

■ *Back in the early 1960s, a not-so-obscure driver from California by way of Manhasset, New York, took the Left Coast of the NASCAR circuit by storm, co-opting Riverside as his personal racetrack for the better part of the decade. In this interview, Dan Gurney reminisced about the five victories at Riverside that constituted his greatest days of NASCAR, capping it off with a description of the Belgian Grand Prix that he considered the other major achievement of his long and amazing career in racing, which took him from drag-racing to Indy cars to Formula One as well as the stocks.*

I've been asked that question before, and I always sort of shy from it, because it's just very difficult to pick. First . . . I won the Belgian Grand Prix in our car that we built here in California with our own V-12 engine, which we did in England, that was 1967. So in terms of uniqueness, that's pretty good, because it was the first time that was done with a car built in this country and the same driver and everything, since Jimmy Murphy did it in 1927 or something earlier than that. I did have a very fortunate run of 500-mile stock-car races at Riverside, and that maybe would be more significant. I mean, that's also a pretty tough one to beat, especially 'cause they don't run races that long anymore. . . . I'm almost safe there.

In the end, I'd say just the stock-car stuff, because that was a span of probably six, seven years. The first stock-car race I drove in was . . . I went to Daytona in, I think 1962. The track hadn't been opened that long, I think it opened in 1959, there's still some of the old buildings there, but in those days that's where you'd go for breakfast, it would still be dark. It was just every bit as much . . . like a foreign country, as it would be going to Europe, it seemed like to me. It was a completely different culture, this was kind of a very special place in terms of the stock-car racing at that time, the first real superspeedway for them, and everybody was dealing with drafting, things that were more of a mystery than it is today.

And it was the deep South, and there were a lot of what they call "good old boys," I guess, and they didn't welcome someone from elsewhere easily. But in the end, the minute you got down to it and finally broke through that veneer, why, I made some good friends, and liked and respected them, and enjoyed it very much. But it was a pretty good stretch for me, too—so there you are.

My first stock race was at Meadowdale, Illinois, which was a road circuit, around 1959 or 1960. That ride was arranged between Troy Ruttman, and Jerry Unser, the oldest of the Unser brothers, who was a friend of Troy's, and I had met Troy in 1958 in Europe, we had traveled around together, he and his wife and I, in the same car.

When Jerry Unser couldn't make a race, because of some other engagement . . . it was being married or being at a wedding, I don't know which, and they said, Troy said, "Well, why don't you offer it to Dan?" And that was when I first did it, and it was a great experience for me.

I went there just sort of helmet and gloves and that was it, and then was met at the Chicago airport by Lou Seyboldt and Bob Rose, who were the co-owners and mechanics on the car. Went to their apartments, and outside, under a kind of lean-to, was a stock car. And it had recently run in a dirt-track race, and it was all tilted to one side and everything.

We had it converted in a period of about three days into what we thought a good road racer ought to be. So I helped them work on it, and we tried to plan things together, and we ended up with what I thought was a doggone good car—I think it was about a 1958 Ford.

And in the race, we got there late, and I didn't get to qualify, although in a practice session I turned in about the fourth-quickest time. But I started twenty-eighth, and in the race worked my way up to second place, behind Freddy Lorenzen, who was leading it.

I think it was partly a NASCAR-sanctioned event, and it also included a bunch of USAC guys, so Jimmy Bryant was in it, Marshall Teague was in it, Chuck Stevenson was another USAC guy who was quite good, Sam Hanks, Paul Goldsmith might have been there, a lot of the old names that had run in the Mexican road race and everything, as well as did all the USAC or stock cars.

It ended up, Freddy had me off the road when I first tried to pass him, and then I dropped back a couple places and then worked my way back up to have another go at him. And then the center of my clutch tore out, and that was the end of the race. But I felt like, "Oops, maybe I can do this."

In the meantime, I had made some connections at Ford, and Holman and Moody was the big Ford outfit at the time in the South, and I drove Daytona in a Holman and Moody car. In fact, I ended up finishing fifth in a race that Tiny Lund won, the Daytona 500, and I finished fifth. I raced with Tiny all day, and in the end he drove off and left me in the last couple laps.

The size and weight, and the smells, the people . . . I mean, I was there kind of alone. It was intense, and yet I felt like a pioneer, I thought it was fabulous. The element of drafting was certainly something, but also I learned to help each other, we could actually . . . I could pull up from behind, push the other car ahead, and we could end up going a little bit faster, and all that kind of stuff. Just about everything was different. . . . The weight, I mean, the cars seemed— what's the word—ponderous; just big, heavy kinds of things. Can you imagine trying to dock an aircraft carrier?

I used to say, with the car, if something was gonna happen, it could write you a letter and say, Look, by the time you receive this . . .

That didn't make it one bit easier to drive, or to do well, but yeah, it was just a different animal. So I felt like a fish out of water in many respects, but still, it was a thrill to sort of be there with Junior Johnson. Actually, the first time, I think Lee Petty was still running, I don't think Richard had started yet. Fireball Roberts, and Freddy Lorenzen, Joe Weatherly, and I met some of the mechanics—but Ralph Moody helped me a lot, he sort of was like a father to help drivers that were coming along, he could still outrun most of us.

Happy [with the race]? Yeah . . . one never knows, you get in the pit stops, and you almost lose track of where the race is, although you've got time to look at the scoreboard. Actually you'd like to run a little better, but on that occasion, that's not bad for your first time. So I was kind of pleased, just to get it under your belt.

Now, when it came to Riverside, why, same kind of car, but that was more sort of my territory. So that was also good.

In the end, I ended up being very fortunate, the first year I ran with a Holman and Moody car, and all the desperate characters [showed up]. [Laughs]. . . . We had a good race, ended up winning it. And then the following year . . . it was arranged that I would drive for the Wood Brothers. And boy, that was really a great experience for me, I drove for them for three years or something. Well, you know, they professed, or they acted as though they were hillbillies that didn't know anything, and in fact under that kind of facade was a very close-knit, well-run team, with some doggone good engineering behind it. And they were, if anything, often one step ahead of the next guys. Often on a pit stop, I'd end up gaining on the guys I'd been running with, that sort of thing.

It was a great team—they were very, very good. I would say, I was fortunate enough to be with the Wood Brothers when they were in their prime, which lasted a long time. Both Glen and Leonard and all the other brothers and cousins from Stewart, Virginia, it was really very, very special. I think they were the class of the field at that time.

Not that there was anything wrong with the Holman and Moody guys that I ran with before, but I think if you look at the total package, the Wood Brothers . . . I don't know, I don't want to say like the New York Yankees, but I think they were the best guys in the business at that time.

That was great, I almost felt like I had an advantage that I didn't deserve.

I ended up winning five of those things. I think, except for the first one, the rest of them were with the Wood Brothers. All the top guys in those days, David Pearson, and Cale Yarborough, and Junior, and Freddy Lorenzen, Fireball Roberts and Petty, they were all there. Banjo Matthews was still driving, I think; later on he was building cars. It was a terrific group, and Curtis Turner was another one that was a superstar, and very, very talented.

Most of those races included seven or eight pit stops; it took roughly five hours, usually. In those days they didn't have the brakes that they have nowadays, and if you were not careful, you could easily end up racing toward the end without any brakes, or very, very down on braking power. And you couldn't do much racing that way, not at that place. You had to kind of pace yourself a little bit, just try not to take much out of the car, and still go fast.

Just exactly how you do that, I don't know. . . . [Laughs.]

They were great races, and gradually I think it was starting to get to them after a while. After winning a few of them, they started wondering, Who is this clown from out West? . . . I really have nothing but great memories of things out there; of course, we had one or two bad ones out there—Joe Weatherly was killed out there. . . .

I remember . . . one time, Curtis Turner—Curtis was a great driver, just oozing natural talent everywhere— He . . . I think his buddies and his supporters were saying, "Curtis, can't you go out there and blow this guy off and stop this?"

So, naturally, that's the kind of thing that Curtis would rise to. I think what he did was on his way out he stopped and saw his friend in Las Vegas, Betty somebody, and when he arrived it looked like he had been on a binge for about a week or ten days. . . . [He had] the beard, and just eyes all bloodshot and everything.

I guess that that was his way of training. [Laughs.]

I think he also wanted to make you think that, Oh, he wasn't gonna be much. He wanted desperately to smoke this guy, and finally the race comes, and I find myself ahead of Curtis—I don't think I was leading at the time, I was probably running third or fourth—he was just behind me.

And it was early in the race, and I'm trying to find a pace where you don't get left behind, but you're not just using up the car big-time. And because of that, it probably looked as though I wasn't really going hell-bent for election. And he got a little impatient finally, we may have been held up a little bit in traffic or something, and the next thing you know he kind of loses his cool and just decides, "Hey, I'm tired of this, I'm gonna blast by him."

Which he did. And he arrived at the next turn, and he was going so fast there wasn't any way he was gonna make it. He took off across the . . . it was kind of desert there, and hit a pothole, and the thing is . . . all four tires were probably four feet off the ground. He came down so hard that both front wheels were kind of splayed out, and it was the end of the race for him.

And I thought to myself, "Well, I know what he was thinking beforehand, but . . ."

In a way, that was too bad, I was a big fan of his anyway, but he couldn't contain it, I remember that.

I remember going there once when I was driving for Bud Moore in a Mercury, and Parnelli Jones was driving the Wood Brothers car. Bud Moore had this Mercury Cyclone, I think they called it, and it had the McPherson strut suspension on it, and the Wood Brothers were with the conventional double-wishbone kind of thing. And Moore thought maybe that the McPherson strut was better.

Well, when you looked at his car, it was about a minimum of a foot higher than the one the Wood Brothers had. And pretty soon it became apparent. I said, "Bud, this thing is slow down the straight-away. I mean, they're driving by me so fast it's ridiculous."

And he didn't want to believe it, and I didn't blame him, but I said, "Well, look—we ended up qualifying pretty damn well with that car." I said, "When it gets to Daytona, you're gonna see what I've been complaining about." And of course, when they got it down there, it was probably a minimum of ten, probably fifteen miles an hour slower at Daytona, and there was no way you could run with it. So they didn't even run it.

But in the race, just by luck, I ended in a situation where I had a lap on the field—it was part of all kinds of things involved there.

They were kind of tired of me, so they corralled me right near the start/finish line, just held me with the flag, you know, and they made the whole field go by me until they made that lap up again. I got hot under the collar about that, too, and I ended up running into somebody who gave me a brake check before I got to turn eight, I think they call it. . . . So I didn't make it to the finish of that one.

But during my qualifying, I'd run a pretty good time, maybe good enough to be on the pole. And the NASCAR guy said, "Well, your time was a little over a second slower than that." And I had about twenty different guys that had the same time that my guys had. And NASCAR just looked at me, one of the head timers in NASCAR, and he said, "Well, boy, we're sorry about that. . . ."

When you're there, and you've sort of transgressed or done something, why, they're gonna punish you—and that was kind of interesting to me.

Well, [when we won] we didn't have any champagne to spray. I mean, they were good, a lot of that was *Motor Trend,* and I remember Bob Peterson was there, and his wife, Margie, she gave me the trophy one year. The year that Joe was killed, why, that was a very somber victory celebration—that wasn't so good.

Otherwise, it was a great event. I was leading in Riverside at the time, and they just went ape over the whole thing. Those are some great times, and in the end the NASCAR people couldn't have been friendlier, and I had some real lasting friendships there.

Later on, when you do sort of go from one form of racing to another, you realize that if you're running against the best guys in that form of racing, it's just as tough, or maybe tougher, to win an event in whichever form it is on a given year. When these Formula One guys call themselves world champions, that may be true on one year, but it may not be true on another. It depends on who you're up against. And generally if you were fortunate enough to sort of cross over and run in some of the other guy's things and everything, you end up with great respect for them, and often vice versa. That was a great situation.

In terms of my career, that's a record [five victories at Riverside] that hasn't been busted yet, and I think drivers like to do that. It certainly meant a great deal to me, so it's right up near the top of my career. You never know, but it's fun to be mentioned in the record books.

A.J. was there, A.J. and Parnelli were both there. I ran against A.J. quite a few times there, and I ran against A.J. quite a few times in the Indy cars and NASCAR. I even ran at Atlanta, I didn't last long, but I remember Lorenzen was on the pole, and A.J. was second, and I qualified a day later because we were having some carburator problems or something, that was where the work was.

He had three laps that were the same, and two of my laps were equal to his, and so I was very, very proud of that. I think at that time A.J. was one of the hard runners, but not a bit more so than the established NASCAR stars. I think later on in A.J.'s career, he became a better and better road racer.

That particular [Belgian Grand Prix] circuit was about eight miles around; it was right there where the Battle of the Bulge took place near the end of World War II. I think Stavolo was the name of the little village at the far end of the circuit in front of the pits, and they had a lookout point with concrete maps that showed where the various routes that people took. It was one of the famous battles that the Americans fought in, in World War II. And it also happened to be the granddaddy of all high-speed circuits in Europe, Formula One circuits. It was quick.

They no longer run on that today, they run on a few portions of it, but they only run on about one-third of it. It had a hairpin that was more than 90 degrees—it was more like 120 degrees; it darn near came around on itself, just before the pits. I ended up with a lap record there, I think it was around 148 miles an hour, including the hairpin, so you were cooking a lot of the time. The top speed there was around 196, it was the car we built here in Santa Ana, except for the engine, which we did in England, we were the only ones that ever had that engine, which was 12 cylinders.

In the race, Jimmy Clark was the quickest, but he had a problem.

I was going along, I had some kind of misfire, I couldn't tell you what it was, but it seemed like it wasn't doing the engine much good.

I was trying to nurse it, although I don't know how you do that, other than just slowing down.

Gradually, Jackie Stewart caught me in a 16-cylinder BRM, and when he went by, I kind of was still wondering if I could make this thing last the distance. I kind of waved him by with a big flourish like, "After you"—he knew very well that I was letting him by.

But then I noticed that there was a little wisp of oil coming out of the back of his car. And I thought, Nobody'll believe me if I said I was trying to nurse this thing, and I don't know what's wrong with it, but I might as well go for it. So that's what I did. And I got back by him, and in the end I think he was having some kind of problem. But I ended up with the lap record, which was set during the race, and I ended up winning it, and historically many people would say that was my biggest achievement. But in the race itself, I felt that if things had been right, I could have done it even better.

After the race . . . I've never seen this before, and I haven't seen it since, but they put me in a Belgian military helicopter, and we took off, and I went for forty-five miles, quite a long time, and came to a stadium. And we hovered down and landed inside this stadium, and there were people there, and they popped me out of the helicopter and I went up to a podium and waved to everybody, and they announced that this was the winner of the Grand Prix at Spa Fuchshafen.

And then I waved—I couldn't say anything in Belgian, and that was it. I got back in the helicopter, and they flew me back. So that was an interesting and different way of doing that.

I was very stoked about the whole thing, and . . . it was a great feeling. We flew low in the helicopter, you could see the cows in the pastures, and the forest. And I couldn't have felt a whole lot better, because once you get one of those things under your belt, it's something that's . . . irreplaceable.

I was a fairly good driver, and the drivers were probably not so specialized as they are today. And it was just an era where you could [go from one circuit to another], and I had that sort of curiosity—I just wanted to know what it was like in these different areas—and I had enough interest.

In the end you have to believe in your own ability—I'm sure a lot of drivers would love to do that today. But it's probably much more difficult to be competitive with all the technical crutches that you have today. Nowadays, often the drivers do more testing in one year than I did in my whole ding-busted career. Therefore you can't make comparisons. But I had a passion for it, and I just enjoyed the lore and the history of each of the places that we went to. I think that the circuits were far more varied, and, yeah, they were a good deal more dangerous—we were going a lot slower than they would go today—but . . . it was just a different era.

I ended up realizing that a four-wheel vehicle, they all end up driving somewhat the same. If it's a big heavy one, why, you have to adapt your timing to it, and if it's a superlight one, it skitters around like a waterbug or something, you know, changing directions very quickly. And in between, the whole spectrum, it's still four-wheel vehicles, and they still have much the same characteristics, just different timing.

■ *Like his father Ned, Dale Jarrett chose the 1993 Daytona as his greatest day in auto racing . . . but it was a close call (no pun intended). In this interview Jarrett talks about having his dad call the race, comparing that experience to his other win at Daytona in 1996, and he also recalls his other most memorable victory that year, a win at Indianapolis in the Brickyard 400. A caveat: This interview was conducted in the spring of 1999, before DJ won his first Winston Cup championship.*

It would certainly be hard to pick one day, as just saying, "This was it, this was everything my career really is about." But if I got to pick one, it would certainly be the 1993 Daytona 500, that was winning our biggest race, having that opportunity, passing a guy that I consider to be one of the best of all time, Dale Earnhardt, on the last lap to do it.

It was just a tremendous feat. And then having my dad on national TV calling the race, it was just everything that, if I were gonna sit down and write it out, that's kind of the way it would have happened. And bringing Joe Gibbs his first victory in stock-car racing, to make it our biggest race, was quite a thrill. Because for someone who had accomplished as much as he had, to see the thrill that he had in him to win this race, was just a tremendous experience all the way around.

It was our first season for Joe Gibbs Racing, and it was kind of out of character for me, because I'm usually one that doesn't say an awful lot, and I really didn't, to anyone other than . . . When we came back from our last test session at Daytona, my wife and I were going to a wedding, and I told her I felt really strong that I was gonna win the Daytona 500. Of course this was coming from a guy who had only won one Winston Cup race in his career at the time. So she—as she's apt to do—laughed at me. . . .

You know, we got to Daytona, things went well, and qualifying for us, I believe we qualified second that year. We ran well all week long, and it just so happened that when we got there, also—something that kind of gave me a little bit more confidence—was that . . . on the first day, when we pulled into our garage stall, we were in garage stall number 11, which had seemed to be somewhat of a lucky number for me when I won my first race and, at that time, my only race in Winston Cup racing—I had started eleventh at Michigan that day.

And, of course, eleven was my dad's number, and with his career, we consider that a pretty good number. So things were looking up, and again, we ran well all week, and the 500, we ran well all day among the leaders. When it got down toward the end, we were sitting in fourth position after the round of pit stops, and I just had to kind of bide my time.

We had a great-handling race car, and what we were waiting for was a longer green-flag run, which was what we got at the end of the race. And there was a young rookie running second to Dale Earnhardt—I worked my way into third—a rookie by the name of Jeff Gordon, who was running second at that time.

I kind of used some experience and got by him, and got myself into second, and on the last lap was able to get a push by Geoff Bodine to get by Earnhardt going into turn one. And I think that's maybe the only lap I led in that entire race; I'm not sure of that, but at least I led the main one.

I'd been working [Gordon], he had an awful strong car, and I could see that he was watching a lot in his mirror, as to what I was doing. And handling, again—I could see Earnhardt's car starting to get a little bit loose, and Gordon's car starting to get a little bit loose, too.

And I got to the point where I was running a higher line through turns three and four, and that was enabling me to get a run off the corner and down the straightaway. And so I tried him low a couple of times right through the trioval-oval, and I could tell he was really protecting that line.

So I made the move a couple of times just to get him thinking that way, and then the next lap, which was with just a couple of laps to go, I faked a move to the inside, and went to the outside of him. And that kind of hung him down on the inside, and I think he ended up slipping back to fourth or fifth.

It was just the idea of having him look and getting him comfortable and thinking that was the only way a pass could be made, and then making it to the outside. Again, my car was awful good, where their shocks were starting to . . . having to lift a little bit in the corners. I was really able to get a good run, so I was able to lay back, and once I got him committed to the inside I was able to go to the outside.

After I passed Gordon I got to Earnhardt's bumper, and as we were coming to get the white flag going down the backstretch, I got as close as I could, because I knew that he had gotten loose, I could see that. And so I wanted to get as close to him as I possibly could, to try and loosen him up in turns three and four. And I was able to do that, and he had to chase his car up the racetrack again, and when he did that I was able to get to the inside of him.

And then once I got to that point I knew that I needed a little bit of a push from somebody, and Geoff Bodine was behind me. He followed me and then pushed me by Earnhardt just as we got down in turn one and two. And Geoff tried to make a pass on me then, but he'd given me enough of a push that it got me out front, and they raced side by side for just a second.

Then it was just a matter . . . I knew down the backstretch that he couldn't get to me, but I knew if I just kept it on the white line in three and four that there'd be pretty much no way that he was gonna be able to pass me. And, you know, we're talking about a guy that, at that point in time, had tried for maybe fifteen years, and had the 500 won a couple of times. I knew he was hungry for it, but I was able to have enough handling to get me through three and four and to get to the start/finish line.

When I got right to the trioval point I knew that I had the race won—it became the biggest thrill of my life. It was just something that a race driver dreams of. I mean, I literally had sat and thought about what it would be like to win the Daytona 500, and I was able to experience it.

I was trying to get my thoughts together, who I needed to thank, and wanted to thank, and as I came off turn four then, down onto pit road, I think probably the thing that almost makes it as special as anything, really, beside being able to beat Dale Earnhardt, was, when I got onto pit road—I won't say it was a hundred percent of the crews from the other teams, lined up on pit road to congratulate me, but there were probably at least ninety percent of 'em that were out there.

As a driver and a competitor, that's a special feeling, to know that the people that you compete against and with, week in and week out, thought that much of you to come out instead of just taking off, and, you know, a lot of 'em had had bad days with their teams. But they took the time to line up out there and congratulate me.

And probably the biggest thing I remember was, the guys that I left to go to Joe Gibbs Racing were the Wood Brothers, and their entire team was there congratulating me, and that really meant a lot to me.

Then I had to find my way to victory lane, I didn't really know where it was. They pointed me there, and just to see the excitement and the thrill on Joe Gibbs' face, he and his wife Pat. And the entire team, Jimmy Makar, and having my entire team there to be a part of it. . . . . It was just a big thrill.

Actually, I believe they played [Ned's call] back on an earpiece for me, but I couldn't hardly hear it because it was so wild in victory lane. And so they were having me talk to my dad, and they played the sound back, but I couldn't see anything. So it was actually on Monday, when I got back home, that was the first time that I saw that and actually knew what took place with him calling the race, the last lap like that. I heard a lot of people talking about it, and say things about it for probably about eighteen hours after the race was over, but I never got to experience really seeing it until Monday. When I did, it was a thrill, to know that he had had that opportunity, and as a parent myself, you know, the excitement that we have with our children's accomplishments.

When we finally got to just see each other, . . . to see how thrilled he was, because he knew how big a race it was, being a driver. . . . Even though he never won it, he came close a couple of times, and you could tell that it probably thrilled him, and he said it—it probably thrilled him more to see me win it than if he would have won it himself. It was quite a special day.

At first [Joe Gibbs] didn't really know what to say' you know, he got involved in a sport that he basically knew nothing about, he told Jimmy Makar and I that from the very beginning. And here it was, someone that had won Super Bowls and many, many football games and been in many types of different situations, but he was almost speechless. He really . . . We were in victory lane. He wasn't sure exactly what to do and how to handle it all, but, as he has in so many other ways, he found the right things to say. But he was genuinely thrilled to have the opportunity to be in victory lane at Daytona.

I thanked Glen, Eddie, and Len Wood, who were really instrumental, Eddie especially, in getting me into their car back in 1990 and giving me that opportunity, and getting my first Winston Cup victory in 1991. . . . . As much as they didn't want me to leave, they knew that I was trying to better my career and they truly were thrilled. And certainly, if it wasn't for them and the opportunity that they gave me, I would never have had that opportunity to be in victory lane in Daytona.

I think that it was just a combination of things—we had a good race team, and a good race car, which is something you have to have, to win there. But I think Daytona was a place I had always done pretty well at; I felt like I knew a lot about drafting and getting in certain drafting situations, and how to handle those. And I always tried to watch people like Dale Earnhardt, the moves they made and how they handled that, and I think that all of that just came together in one day for me.

Well, you know, when you come back in fourth or fifth after a round of pit stops and things, I knew that I had time, and I think that I didn't rush myself and didn't show my hand too quickly, so that I would get myself in a position where I could be passed later on. I tried to just bide my time and be patient, and I think that it was that patience that really paid off and enabled me to get to the front at the right time.

I guess that was as much of the story as anything, you know—that here Earnhardt had been denied once again his opportunity to win the Daytona 500 when it looked like all the way down to the closing laps that he was gonna get that victory. So it was just another chapter that all led up, obviously, to 1998 when he did win, but we didn't know all of that at the time. It was a thrill for me to be able to do that. I think it enhanced it for me; it certainly didn't take anything away.

Well, I think that certainly there have been more victories since then, and another Daytona 500 in 1996 is one that I rank right next to the 1993 Daytona 500. Winning at the Brickyard in 1996 was also just a huge thrill. I never even felt like I'd have the opportunity to race at Indianapolis, much less win a race there and be in victory lane there. So those are certainly the three top victories that I look at in my career. As I look back, that was a defining moment in my career, that no matter what else happened, I'd done something in winning the Daytona 500 that not a lot of people get the opportunity to do, to visit victory lane and say that they were a Daytona 500 champion.

Things in my life and my career changed dramatically at that point in time—it was a deal where I was always gonna be known as a Daytona 500 champion.

I denied Earnhardt once again in 1996, but I think there were things that I learned there in 1993 in winning that race. Even though things changed a little bit, because I felt like in 1996 it was a situation where I needed to get to the front as quick as I could to make him pass me, because I did know more. But it was still some of that drafting that I was able to do that got me to the front in 1996 and enabled me to win then, also.

I knew a little more what to expect and how to enjoy it a little bit more, because in 1993 it was total chaos, you know—you didn't know what was coming and what all was getting ready to change in your life. And even though the sport changed a lot in just those three short years, because then 1996 brought all new opportunities and different things happened. I was a little bit more ready to get into victory lane and help our guys enjoy it.

But once again, I was with a brand-new race team. We'd just put this team together, the second team at Robert Yates Racing in 1996, and our first race was the Busch Clash, which Ford Quality Care and Ford Credit sponsored. We won the Busch Clash and then came back a week later and won the Daytona 500. So we'd made a huge hit in a short amount of time with this new race team.

Man, it's so close, knowing that the Daytona 500 is our biggest race, and it always will be, regardless of what else happens, but the total thrill of winning a race at Indianapolis is just incredible. It's just an experience that's hard for me to put into words, because . . . Todd and I were so thrilled with that, I mean, you couldn't get the smiles off our faces. To be in that victory lane, that I've watched many drivers be in, was just a great opportunity and a great thrill for me. Again, it's really hard for me to put into words what it means, but . . . because of the history, the enormous impact that just the [name] Indianapolis Motor Speedway has on people . . . To say that you've won there did a lot for my career. I mean, there are probably . . . almost as many people that bring up that victory as they do the Daytona 500.

The pass of Ernie Irvan, with just a few laps to go, is what stands out for me. Of course, we were teammates, a great day for Robert Yates Racing; we were gonna run one and two, however it finished out, we just weren't sure who was gonna be in victory lane. And I was able to make a pass on him as he slipped a little coming out of turn one, and then held him off for the last seven or eight laps. That's the one that that I'll always remember, is just battling Ernie and realizing that it was gonna be a great day for Robert Yates, that his cars were gonna run one-two in Indianapolis.

There again, handling came into play, and I knew that we had a good-handling race car. And it seemed that our car was a little bit better as the tires got worn, than what Ernie's was. And, you know, I just tried to take care of my tires, and Ernie passed me late, and I saw that it was gonna be a battle. But knowing how tight it is, I didn't know if I could get by him. With each lap passing, I could see the possibility of it not happening, because Ernie was good at protecting his place on the track. But I got that opportunity, and then once I got there I knew that I didn't want to let it go.

The thrill of being in that victory lane and riding around when the race was over—you've got over two hundred thousand fans standing there screaming. We were in one of the pace cars riding around. Probably the thing I remember as much as anything with Todd and myself and my wife Kelly riding around, was just her screaming as loud as him. It just seemed that it thrilled her as much or more than it did me, to have that opportunity.

■ Millions of NASCAR fans have come to know Ned Jarrett through his role as a racing analyst for both the major networks and ESPN, but during his memorable career Jarrett gained a reputation as a gentleman's gentleman and a savvy driver who nonetheless competed hard on his way to a total of fifty victories. Jarrett offered two greatest days: the first as a driver in the Southern 500 in the mid-1960s; the second as a broadcaster when he made the call as his son Dale won the 1993 Daytona 500, a highlight that's become one of the all-time great moments in NASCAR history.

Well, there really have been two days that stand out. One was when I was driving, and the other was Dale winning the 1993 Daytona 500 and I was broadcasting.

The first one, 1965, was the Southern 500, in Darlington, South Carolina. I was leading the points going into that race, Dick Hutcherson was a very close second. . . . But as a result of winning that race, and Hutch having problems in the race, I opened the point lead up to the point where I didn't have the championship sewed up, but it was a very comfortable lead and I went on to win the championship. So that set me up to win the championship, not only was it the biggest win in my career.

That race was on Monday back then, on Labor Day, and on Sunday night, and at the request of Bob Callman, who was president of the Darlington Raceway, I traveled from my home, at the time was in Camden, South Carolina. And we went over to Darlington to speak to the youth fellowship group at his church.

So I went away with a good feeling, I asked them at the end of my talk . . . for their prayers, for all the drivers, that everybody would be kept safe. And I asked them to say a little extra prayer for me, that I might be able to win it, because that was one of the goals I set for myself in racing, was to win that race. And so I went away with the genuine feeling that I had their support.

The next day, I was in the pit area going over the strategy with my crew, and a gentleman walked up and introduced himself as a minister—I don't know what his name was, I don't remember. And he said, "Ned, I want you to know that I've got a very strong feeling that you're going to win this race today." He said, "I had the same feeling two years ago, and I told Fireball Roberts before the race, I felt he was gonna win the race, and Fireball did win." And he said, "I just want you to know that my prayers are with you, and I'll see in victory lane." And he walked away, and you had to pull me out of the sky to get me buckled into the car.

People would say, "Hey, I'm pulling for you to win the race," or "My prayers are with you," something like that, but as far as those two particular situations—no, it had never happened. I had spoke to other groups, and maybe asked them to say a prayer for us or something like that, but this was just . . . different.

So, anyway, during the race, we were running along, ran good, led the race for a little while; there were three cars that it looked like they were going to have a shot at winning, Darel Dieringer, Fred Lorenzen, and myself. And my car started overheating, so I had to back off.

So they were still going at it for the lead, and we got under a hundred miles to go, and my car was overheating . . . in fact, I didn't think it was going to live the rest of the race. All at once I came down off of turn four and I looked over and Lorenzen was in the pits with the hood up on his car, and the steam was coming out from under the hood, and so he was finished for the day. So that left me only one competitor.

And bless gosh, about three laps later I came around and there was Dieringer going into the pits, and the rear end was burning out on his car. And he was driving a Mercury, Lorenzen was driving a Ford, and the reason we had a heating problem with the Fords, Ford had brought some new aluminum radiators there for that race. Heating is always a problem, overheating is always a problem at Darlington. One of the reasons is that the track grinds off the tires and then you pick that rubber up and it throws it into the grille and stops up the airflow. And so, they brought these new aluminum radiators, had more water capacity, so they said, that'll cure our heating problems. Well, it didn't, because whoever made 'em didn't think about the rubber part going on it, and they made the vents too close together, so the fan would suck the rubber right on through the radiator, so it just knotted up on it. And so every Ford car in the field blew up.

It was only discovered on race day, because you couldn't simulate race conditions. You've gotta have other cars out there picking that rubber up and throwing it, a lot of rubber being put down, first of all; a lot of cars grinding rubber off and then picking it up and then throwing it into the grille. So it'd be hard to simulate that in test.

Anyway, I was the last hope for the Ford drivers. And the officials of Ford Motor Company came down in my pit, and I had, at that time, a fourteen-lap lead over the second-place car. They had plenty of time to come in and get the car cooled off, obviously everybody had trouble that day. And they gave me the blackboard then—we didn't have radiators then—in the pit, to cool the engine.

Of course, I was saying a prayer every lap, to let this thing finish. I'd learned a little trick, it popped in my mind, I don't remember if I'd heard it somewhere before or what, but it popped in my mind to cut the switch off and don't decelerate. You have to back off, of course, going into turns at Darlington. Instead of decelerating, hold the accelerator wide open and cut the switch off, and let the raw gas run in there, and it should have a cooling effect.

And it did.

It would cool it at least 20 degrees, every turn. Of course, it would make a big backfire and pop when you heard it, but you had to do that. I'm sure the fans enjoyed that, it was a boring race at the end, so that was little bit of an extra something to cheer about.

So anyway, they kept giving the signal to come in, and I saw those Ford officials over there, knowing that it could cost me my job if I didn't listen and come in, if that thing blew up.

Something more powerful than the officials and Ford Motor Company told me to keep going, and I did, and I won the race. And I always felt that between the prayers of the kids, and the prayers of that minister, and my own prayers that I was saying that day, that that helped me win that race.

Naturally, [the owners] are all happy once you win, and I told 'em what I had been doing to help cool it. They accepted that maybe I knew what I was doing. It was certainly the biggest win of my career. They figured I would blow up, too.

Going into the race . . . Darlington's the type of racetrack you have to drive very carefully, and . . . you need to be aggressive, but you almost need to be conservative at the same time, because that track'll jump at you—it'll still do it, it'll knock you back down and it'll still do it. So I figured, always, my philosophy was that you've gotta finish the race before you can win it. So I did what I felt I needed to do to finish a race first, and then if I was in position to win near the end, then I would do it.

Certainly, with the points battle, that was in September, and getting down near the end of the year, I went into it with some part of a conservative mode. But I had lead the race some before that, and there were no bonus points for leading back then. I make that point just to illustrate that, you know, I was not stroking, I was running good, but at the same time I was very careful to try and finish the race. That's where the points consideration would have come in.

Actually, I had a better car and ran a better race in the spring race at Darlington that year, [and I] . . . should have won that one, but we had a sway-bar bolt come loose in the last hundred miles. I finished third . . . but I really had driven a better race that day, the engine was strong all day and everything, but that [bolt] kept me from winning. And I had finished fourth one other time. It seems like I finished third one year.

Usually I ran good there, at Darlington, and one of the reasons that I ran and finished good was the way I approached the race-track—I respected it. There were so many drivers who would go out there and charge, use up, abuse their equipment. Back then . . . the equipment simply would not stand running hard, start to finish. Every once in a while you might get one to finish, but must of the time you'd be sitting on the sidelines.

. . . If we would have had the type equipment with the technology they have [today], we could have driven a lot harder from start to finish. I mean, you have to do that now, but at the same time still respect the track. The durability was just not there back then.

It was certainly our best year, that year, and that was the climax to a very good year. Not a total climax, because I think we won some races after that, but that year Ford went from their stock cars, of which you were required to run their concept—they went from a leaf spring to a coil spring. And we did a lot of work in the winter, preparing those cars; in fact, we were ahead of most others with the coil-spring concept.

Of course, I had run Chevrolets in 1961 and 1962, and they had rear coil springs, so were accustomed—I, as a driver, and our team, was accustomed—some of the members of our team were still the same. So that put us a little ahead, we felt. We experimented with some various concepts of locations of the springs, and we really hit on a combination pretty early in the year that worked very well. So we felt we were going to be hard to beat for the championship and perhaps destined to have our best year ever.

It's well-documented about Dale winning the Daytona 500 [in 1993], passing Dale Earnhardt on the last lap to do it, and, of course, I was working in the booth with CBS. When I got to Daytona that year . . . the producer—at that time it was Bob Stenner . . . but we sat down and we'd talk about who the major threats were going to be to win the race, who the favorites are.

And I mentioned Dale in that conversation, I put him close to the top of the list, and he asked me why. They had tested well there, they had run extremely well the first year that he drove for Joe Gibbs in

1992, but not many people knew how well he ran if you were not particularly watching him, because he didn't lead that much. He got about a half-lap behind on a bad pit stop, and Davey Allison was leading the race, and Dale's gaining over a half-second a lap on him. At the beginning, he was a half a lap behind and he cut it down to about a quarter of a lap, then got caught up in a wreck.

Anyway, drawing from that, and [Dale] ran good in the Pepsi 400 that year in 1992, and the testing of 1993, I just felt he was really going to be strong. And so he said, "Well, we'll keep an eye on him." Of course, I told him Earnhardt would be strong, and I guess Elliot—Gordon was not in the picture then, I guess that was his first Daytona 500.

During the race, Dale, he was there in the top five most of the day. So in the last ten laps he was sitting there running third, behind Earnhardt, and Gordon was just drafting Earnhardt, he was along for the ride, doing a whale of a job at it for being a rookie in that race.

So Dale sat there and sized 'em up, and I hit my talk-back button—we had the ability to talk to the producer—and I said, "Start watching that number 18 car, he's gonna make a move here in a little bit." And so they positioned—I didn't know this, that they were doing this—they were positioning. . . . He did actually say, "Have you got a shot to win?" And I said, "Yes, he does have."

So they stationed a camera that found Martha [Ned Jarrett's wife]—she was sitting in a van behind pit road—they stationed a camera behind her to get her reaction. And of course, it's not that unusual that they bring one to the booth; I guess it is at the end of the race, normally he wouldn't bring a camera to the booth, but they did that day.

The producer has the ability to speak to each of the individual announcers, on their headset, and he told Ken Squier, who was the anchorperson, he said, "Okay now, on this last lap, if Jarrett takes the lead," he said, "back off, we're gonna let Ned call him home."

And Neil, the late Neil Bonnett, was working with us that day, and he told us the same thing. But see, I didn't know that he'd told them that. So . . . he got by Gordon, and then the very next lap he was coming around to get the white flag, and he got a run on Earnhardt. He was making the pass, so when he went into turn one, they turned me loose [Neil] said, "Okay, Ned, call your son home and be a daddy."

So that's when I just turned form being a supposedly professional announcer and started being a dad. It has turned out to be one of the most replayed pieces of tape, I guess, in the history of NASCAR. And certainly, as we travel around the country and I talk to fans, that is mentioned more than all other things put together.

So it was a very special moment for us, and after I saw how it had played out, that camera that they stationed with Martha . . . They were shooting through the side-view mirror, she didn't know they were there—I doubt she'd have known they were there if they were sitting right in front of her.

Anyway, it was interesting how quickly they were able to put together a human-interest story that was about to develop and to capitalize on it. Because it was a unique situation, that someone was winning one of the major sporting events in the United States, and his dad was in the broadcast booth.

That meant more to me than anything I ever did in the sport. I never won the Daytona 500, but I did through Dale. That was better, for me, than winning it myself. . . .

I had some good runs at Daytona—1963 I was leading the race with about three laps to go, and ran out of gas. . . . And that was one of the biggest disappointments that I had in the sport, but I knew that Dale was okay that day as far as gas was concerned, because of the pit stops and where they fell. So that didn't worry me.

I had seen Earnhardt have so many of those things [almost] won, and then something happened, and here it happened again, somebody passed him this time. He had run out of gas once before, and he cut the tire down in 1990 when Derrike Cope won it, so many things had happened to him along the way.

You wonder—those things'll flash through your mind, but you don't really think of it, because I was just concentrating on helping him drive that race car. It was interesting. . . . I've got a little plaque up here on my wall, word for word, of what I said, on that last lap, I said a couple of times: "Keep it low, don't let him back down inside you," and every time I'd say that, he'd turn the steering wheel to the left, as if he was hearing me.

Just the whole thing together made for a very special moment, and it is still the most outstanding thing that ever happened to me, as far as driving or broadcasting or whatever.

I've talked to Bobby Allison and Richard Petty about their sons winning and the feeling they got, and they tell me that it was at least or more meaningful to see their sons than it was for them to win themselves. And certainly it was as far as I was concerned—it meant a lot more to me than if I had won the Daytona 500. You want to see your children well, and you want to see them do better than you did. And that gave me an opportunity to live, through Dale, something that I did not accomplish.

■ *It was, of course, one of NASCAR's most historic days, a race that literally changed the sport itself and the ways the races were run. The year was 1960 when the man Tom Wolfe called "the last American hero," noticed something funny about the way the air worked at Daytona. Junior Johnson used that knowledge to outrun a slew of superior Pontiacs in the 1960 Daytona 500—the race that marks the beginning of drafting as a stock-car race tactic.*

That's easy—the last day when I raced. (Laughs.)

I would probably say the greatest day, and the greatest thing in my racing career to happen to me, would probably be winning the Daytona 500. I had several other great moments with other drivers winning in races here and there, but to me, that's probably the greatest thing that ever happened to me in racing, as far as personally, you know?

. . . One of the big things about [it] was simply a situation where I didn't have a chance to win the race to start with. I went down to drive the car for Ray Fox; the car was very, very much uncompetitive. This was a Chevrolet, and Pontiac was in the factory and built this, at that time, and they were dominating the sport. We were off its speed a lot, and then, as time went along, we kept working with the car, and every once in a while we'd run real good. And we thought we'd fixed it, and we'd go back out and run by ourselves—it was running with other people at that particular time.

Well, I picked up Cotton Owens one time, he was in a Pontiac, he was very fast, and all of a sudden I was able to run with him. He came by, and I ducked in behind him and I started running with him. And I fixed it myself, and I'm thinking to myself, "There's some reason why I'm keeping up with him, I know I ain't got a car fast enough to do that."

So I got to thinking about it, and I says, "Well, it's gotta be the aerodynamics of the thing." And I said, "Well, I'm going back out there," and I didn't say nothing to Ray Fox about it, 'cause I didn't know exactly what was going on at that particular time. So I went back out again, and I told Ray—you know, he's all excited about how fast I could run, I could run with the Pontiac and all that stuff, and he thought he had really fixed the car.

So I went back out, and I sat out there on pit road for a little bit. One of them fast Pontiffs came out, and I went out and I was riding around the racetrack, and I come up and when it went by me I just ducked on in behind him, and sure enough, right away I just picked him up right there.

And I knew right then it was the aerodynamics of the thing, there was a slipstream of air coming off this thing that I was able to run in, which was a vacuum. And it would drag me along with him, all day long.

So I never said anything more about it, except when I went in the pits. I told Ray Fox, I said, "I figured out a way to run with these people." So when the race started, that's what I did all day long. I drafted Cotton Owens, Jack Smith, Joe Weatherly, and just anybody that had a Pontiac at that particular time. Paul Goldsmith had one, there was several of them there.

And when the day was over, about four or five of them Pontiacs had had trouble, Fireball Roberts, and different ones had had trouble. There was only one Pontiac left, and that was Bobby Johns, he was in a Smokey Yunick Pontiac. But I had a long lead on him at the time.

Well, Jack Smith, he had a front hub burn out in his, and they came in and they fixed it and went out, and he hooked up with Bobby Johns and they hooked up together. And they ran me down. And, of course, Bobby didn't have any trouble outrunning me, and when they ran me down, Jack Smith went back in the pits and dropped off, and left me and Bobby there to finish up the race, and there's only about thirty laps to go or something.

About ten laps after that, I was drafting him, and coming off the second turn, and his back glass blew out, he spun out and down through the grass and stuff, and by the time he got back up north, I had like a 20- or 30-second lead on him. And I went on and won the race. But there was no way, statistically-wise, without luck, that we would have won that race.

During the race, I thought that if all these Pontiacs go down, then I'm about equal to everybody else, and I've got a good shot at winning the race. But, you know, there was so many of them that you didn't figure every one of them would tear up, or that something would happen to every one of them.

But it did, it happened to every one of them except that one—the one that Smokey Yunick had in there, and he would have won the race if it hadn't been for the back glass blowing out.

Well, from that point on, everybody picked up on it and went with it and made sure that they was in a position like on the last lap, to draft down the back stretch and win the race, it become a big factor in how you raced at Daytona Beach, and Talladega, and places like that.

That was the unique thing about it, they didn't know. I didn't ever hear anybody say anything about it until after the race was over with, you know; they got caught off-guard. And it was something that I just picked up by myself that was able to let us win that race. Well, it's a known fact that that's what happened, and it was a thing with the press and everybody that knew how I had won the race. That was a big to-do because nobody knew anything about it but the fact that it was like a new invention, really.

They couldn't believe we'd won the race, you know, it was like,

How in the world did he win the race with that piece of crap he was driving? [Laughs.]

It was kind of a unique thing for me. I had my mother and one of my sisters with me down there. They had never been to a race, you know; coming from where I come from, it was just kind of like we was a long ways from home. And the three of us, it was a real joyful thing when we went out to eat that night with my mother and sister, with what had happened to me.

That was the second year of the Daytona 500, it was so highly recognizable all over the world, as far as that goes. And to win it the way I won it, and being as new as it was, it's probably one of the—I'd say—*the* highlight of the Speedway.

I pick that one basically because of the age, the disadvantage that I had, the stuff like that, it was just so exciting to me to have won the thing.

After that one, I'd have to say probably Lee Roy Yarborough beating Charlie Glocks back on the last lap at Daytona in 1959. We didn't have a shot at winning that race, either, because we stopped with twelve laps to go and changed two right-side tires, and he got a good lead on us, but the tires made our car so much faster than his that we ran him down. Everybody had sold us off at that race.

But Daytona's the World Series of our whole sport, and winning the championship and stuff like that is a great thrill. When you come home with a flag from Daytona Beach, you've done that best that you can possibly do in NASCAR.

■ *His name gets mentioned a lot among the young guns who are shooting for Jeff Gordon's spot at the top of the Winston Cup heap, but to get to that level, the twenty-eight-year-old Buckshot Jones had to make his way through the ranks like every other future Cup racer. Along the way Jones won what he considers the greatest race of his young career, a memorable run at Milwaukee in which he capitalized on the experience of crew chief Ricky Pearson, the son of NASCAR legend David Pearson.*

For me, it would have to be Milwaukee. You know, we started running Busch back in 1995. We were new in the sport, it was just me and two guys I had from Georgia, and Ricky Pearson was crew-chiefing another team, the Alliance team, that Dennis Setzer was driving [for]. It so happened that they were getting out of racing, the gentlemen that owned the race team.

So we found out about it, and we went and talked to Ricky, and Ricky came on board with us in 1995. And then he continued in 1996, and a lot of people were surprised to see him go with a rookie and not a more veteran driver, [because] looking at it, you're gonna have a long learning curve.

I mean, 1996 was tough for us; we ended up going out in that race at Milwaukee, the second time I'd driven there in a Busch car. Early in the race, got spun out, was at the tail end of the field. Ricky came up with some wild idea in the pits, and we came back and won the race.

It was exciting, me being in a team like we were. The thing of the day was just listening to Ricky say, "Don't give up, just be patient," and it all came right back around. Ricky said he saw that I really loved the sport, and he knew from talking to me that this is what I wanted to do, and I always put in 110 percent, whatever we had to do. He said he kind of would rather work with a rookie that he could kind of teach things to, than maybe with a veteran that you can't change things. Ricky's really taught me a lot, how to be patient, to learn about these cars, what makes 'em run besides just turning the wheel to the left. I guess that's the biggest reason.

I still had a lot to learn going into that race. That race was the middle of the year, and we'd probably already missed five or six races that year. I was learning a lot, but I would say we were about middle-ways on the learning curve. Ricky kept us in the back when we got there, we had a good car, but he kept saying, "Be patient, be patient."

We were patient the whole way through. Listening to him and doing what he said paid off that day.

I tell you what the deal was about that day—they had just got through repaving the racetrack, and I remember we were real fast in practice. And we went out to qualify, and the track was starting to tear up, and we got real bad loose and qualified thirty-second. Nobody went back out for second-round qualifying, but the only way to get around that track was to run on the bottom.

And a lot of people—I wouldn't say they got impatient, but they slipped up out of the groove just a little bit and ended up hitting the wall. That's where the patience came in, to really focus, no matter what you have to do to stay right there at the bottom. And I guess by the time the day was over we'd stayed on the bottom the whole time.

You know, we almost spun out one time. Dick Trickle was leading the race; he got up just a little too high and he spun. It was just one of those deals where everything went our way that day, with the exception of spinning out early in the race.

I didn't think we really had a chance to win there at the end, because Dick Trickle passed us and he pulled on away from me. I said, "Well, we're gonna end up finishing second unless something bad happens to Dick Trickle." But I never gave up, and I don't know, his tires must have started going away, I started catching him, and then finally we got some lap traffic and got right on his back bumper.

I don't know, he either got in a little bit too hard or something, and he slipped up. And when he did, I was just like, "Well, hey, we didn't give up all day, here's our shot." Our windshield was so dirty that when they dropped the checkered, I still thought we had a lap left—all I could see was a little bit of white.

And that's where Mike McLaughlin came up underneath me to congratulate me, and I thought we were still racing. I pinched him down, I said, "Well, I'd rather spin out here than take a chance on losing this race." I didn't know until I got on the back straightaway that I had won the race.

That was the best feeling. . . . I wanted to always be there, thought there were times that we had a car that was capable of winning, but me being a rookie at it, made a lot of mistakes, going through a learning curve.

I don't know. . . . I mean, words can't describe your first win like that, it's unreal. Just listening to what Ricky said, being patient, it kind of showed you that, yeah, you had a tough year, but when you get a good car, and things go right for you, you can win, you can still beat these guys. Sometimes during the year you kind of wondered, because you missed some races, you didn't have good finishes. But you say, Heck, if I've got a good car and everything goes right, you don't have any bad luck I can't run with these guys. So it was a big confidence booster—not just for me, but for the whole team.

To be honest, it really didn't hit you, because we had had such a . . . We had missed so many races, like five races, before that one. Had some times we finished good, some times we finished bad, so it didn't really hit me until we flew back in—we flew back that night.

My dad, sister, and a bunch of people in my family and a bunch of my friends were at the airport waiting on us. I don't know, it kind of all hit then, but there were so many good things that happened that you can't remember all of them.

We celebrated right when we won in a way, but kind of the whole week until we went back to the next race, we celebrated just about the whole time. It was about the best week of your life. You did a lot of stuff, radio stuff, did some interviews, like on *RPM Tonight* for winning the race. So it was a very exciting week.

You never give up, no matter what—I've always thought that. If you're gonna give up because you got booted in the back, or you got spun out, or your car's not running good, you might as well just pack it in and get out of racing. You can never give up.

Sometimes things change around. You can have a terrible car . . . You watch people like Mark Martin or Jeff Gordon, if they have a problem where they fall to the back, or they qualify bad, they work on their car, they don't give up. They just work on it, keep working on it, and by the time the day's over with, they're up front. If you kind of watch people like that and see what they do, they never give up.

But you can't [give up], you've gotta keep digging. We were in Loudon, New Hampshire, last year, and at the very start of the race, someone missed a shift, and I got in the back of Dick Trickle just a little bit, somebody hit me, and we hit the outside wall. We had to come in—we're dead last now, and we haven't even made a full lap yet. We never gave up the whole day, and kept getting closer and closer to the front, and we ended up winning that day.

It was kind of like we first moved up, with Busch Grand National, ran with a different group of people, probably more experienced people than what the series had run before. Everything goes right, you have a good car, you don't have a lot of problems, and you don't give up . . . you can win.

I was racing against the Mike McLaughlins that have been around, David Green, stuff like that, now you're moving up into Winston Cup. I think the Winston Cup's a lot harder transition than the transition I had to make from All-Pro to Busch. But knowing, hey, you're gonna have a lot of hard times, the first year or two you're gonna learn all over, but things can go right. . . . I don't know, you just don't give up.

I guess [my Winston greatest day would be] the first race we tried to make . . . in Atlanta, on our first try. After that, I would say Dover. We were patient all day, and I learned a lot, I learned a lot in racing that day, to see how much different it is from Busch racing.

You learn in these Cup races—they're so much longer, that the first half to three-quarters of the race, you're not really racing other people. You're more focused on getting that car exactly the way you want it and getting yourself in contention, so that last quarter of that race, you can race.

I learned that when you catch people, and you were faster than them, they just wave you on. They don't race you, they let you go. In Busch racing, our races are shorter, so you really can't give up a lot, so a lot of it's a matter of just learning things like that.

■ *For the last few years Bobby Labonte has been working his way up the Winston Cup ladder, putting himself in a position to make a strong run at the championship this year. One of Labonte's greatest days was the Busch championship that was a key stepping stone to his Winston Cup run, and the other was a unique run at Atlanta where he was able not only to win a race, but help his brother Terry win a Winston Cup championship.*

Well, I'd say one is when I won the Busch Grand National championship—the other would be . . . when Terry won the Winston Cup championship and I won the race.

We came down the wire for the Busch Grand National championship with Kenny Wallace at Martinsville. We were just a few points ahead, it was the last race of the season for us. Kenny had problems throughout the day, but I think the biggest thing was that my dad was the crew chief on the car, my wife's there, we finished fourth in the race—it was just neat that my family could be there. I don't know if Terry was there, I don't think he had a race that week, I think he came up.

Kenny and I are really good friends, and he had gotten hurt a couple of weeks before that. And he was still kind of injured, and it was like, man, you wanted to win, but it was it would have been nice if he hadn't been hurting a little bit, too. He broke his ribs at Loudon, New Hampshire, a few weeks before that.

As far as during the race goes, I mean . . . we had a real good car, it ran real good the whole time, we didn't win, but it was, "Let's win this championship."

I think he was having brake problems or something, and just struggling, just nothing went right for him for the most part during the day. We knew that they had problems; when they started having problems, we started backing up a little instead of taking any chances, as far as just trying to finish the race.

Well, I mean, we knew that we had to finish in the top "X" to . . . We had it all figured out where I finished tenth and he won, then we would win by two points, or whatever the number was. You know, when he started having problems, we knew that we could finish farther back, not that we were sitting out there stroking around, because we still were competitive enough to finish fourth or so, either fourth or sixth.

We knew where he was running, and we just knew that we needed to finish in a good safe spot to win the championship. We were pretty much out there running enough by ourselves to where we could take care of our own equipment without worrying about anybody else.

I have won there—I won the next year. I didn't win at that point in time, but we always had a pretty good setup there, we run pretty decent. . . . I think we ran two races there in 1990 or 1991, and I think both races were fairly decent. It's had its good points and bad points. At the time, Terry's car and my car, both of 'em ran pretty new.

It was a deal where, I'm sure it was a few laps before the end of the race that we were like, in position to win, because of the fact that Kenny had problems, and if we finish—thirtieth right now, then we still win, and there might not have been but thirty-two cars left on the racetrack.

I was just thinking about finishing that race, not having to worry about all the pressure before the race because you had to finish in

"X" position, it was like, whew, you kind of get to the point where it's kind of a relief toward the end, because we weren't having to be quite so careful about everything.

Well, you know, [afterwards], I think . . . we had a lot of fun, it was a good deal, my mom and dad and my wife, and Terry was there. It wasn't really too eventful, two days later I was at Mike McLaughlin's picking up a car. But at the same time, we were pretty excited that we were able to win, and the guys that I had working for me . . . actually about two or three of 'em left right after that. I think I knew that they were going to leave or something like that, they went to work for Jack Roush, so that took everybody [away]. It was kind of a deal where, yeah, it was all fun, but I had a few people leaving, and I felt like if everybody stuck together like I thought they would . . .

When [Kenny] got hurt at Loudon, I went to the hospital looking for him, and he'd already left. But, you know, when you run with somebody all year long, and you battle back and forth, you become friends, or enemies, and in that case we became friends. And he went to Rockingham and Rusty drove the car, and it was a deal where . . . I mean, I just feel bad that that had to happen to him, because we were having a good-spirited battle throughout the year, it was real close and everything.

I called him and told him, I said, "Well . . . I hope you do good, get better."

We went to Atlanta, he needed to finish. If Jeff [Gordon] won, he needed to finish sixth or better to win the championship. And we got down there, and we needed to win a race, because we hadn't won a race; we'd won three the year before. So we were looking for our first win of the year, Terry's looking for the championship. . . . We were pretty much on a mission to win that race, because we don't have anything to lose as far as points-wise, stuff like that. And we get down there, and sure enough, we blister 'em for a pole—not blister 'em, but we win the pole.

We go out there, and what happened before the race on Saturday night is, I think Terry qualified third and Jeff was second. And Terry made the comment to me, he said, "Man, I sure do need to lead at least three laps to get five points." . . . [I said], "No problem, if I can do it, I'll do it." And the night before the race, we had made comments about, "Hey, it sure would be neat if I won the race and you won the championship." Yup.

That's kind of far-fetched in a way, and it's like it was all in conversation—"Yeah, that sure would be neat, okay, see you later"—we both went our separate ways for the evening, and that was that.

And then when it came the next day, his PR guy said, "Hey, you know, we want you to come to victory lane if Terry wins the championship." And I said okay. And I've never said this before in my life, I'm never like this, but I said, "I hope I'm already there." I mean, I would never say that on any occasion, but we just felt good about the race.

It's probably one of the few times . . . I mean, I've won races I didn't have a feel for, you know, until you get out there and you're on your own. But I've never done it like that. So anyway, I said, "I hope to be there."

We took off, I got the lead from Jeff, and Jeff had a little problem with the wheel or something like that. And we were going along, and I let Terry go, he led a couple laps, I got back behind him, and we just ran our own race, and it was there toward the end.

We outran Jeff, ran real hard—outran Jeff, I think he finished third; Dale Jarrett finished second. Just a deal where we were able to hold on there for a win, and Terry was able to hold on to fifth or sixth. . . . I mean, when it was all over with and done, it was like, "Wow, this did come true, didn't it?"

Never would have thought that—you know, you want to think it, but there's so many things that are going against you to do something like that. So . . . anyway, we did it.

Well, I really hadn't done [much at that track]. . . . I think I finished second there the year before in the spring race, that was about it. I had never won a race there yet. And . . . like I said, it was the last race of the year and we hadn't won a race, and we felt like we'd kind of gotten better, the second half of the season was a lot stronger for us. We had to go for it, "go for it" meaning just nothing different than what we had done before. Just, "This is the last race, it's gonna be a long winter if we don't win," and we were fortunate enough to win.

I was on the radio, and they were telling me the whole time. I knew he pitted for gas and tires there at the end, and he had to get back up to fifth or sixth . . . man, it's close back there. I just felt like— I mean, being I knew where he was—I felt a lot more comfortable, that's for sure.

We were concentrating on what we were doing, but it was kind of neat to know exactly what Terry was up to and how he was doing and everything.

It was a deal where Terry and I didn't talk about it, but we ended up riding around that lap together, and that was like . . . that just happened. I was coming up on pit road, and he was outside on the racetrack, that wasn't something we thought about, that just happened. That made a lot of headlines, and all that stuff, and that was awful exciting. But we didn't even think about nothing like that.

Again, it goes back to, we're pretty quiet when it comes down to it, and we just talked about . . . "Man, I just can't believe that happened." That was the neatest thing, I think, for our parents more than anything, because their two sons won the same day, which was awful hard to do on a family deal like that, win the race and win the points.

It's just the fact that Terry and I were together, our families were right there, our wives, stuff like that, more than anything. The championship, because my dad was crew chief on the car, I owned the team, paid all the bills and everything, and Terry helped me get started a couple of years before that, my dad working there. . . . [T]here's a lot of people out there that work father-and-son on things, and that's not the easiest thing to do, and especially be successful. And we were successful at it, too. We were digging, we were trying, both of us, we were focused on winning.

I guess you can just say that they were highlights of my career, even though I've won more races than that, but those are ones that'll always stick out as being the most special, because I think Terry and

I, our age difference makes us better friends, especially as we get older. It goes back to when we were younger, he had different friends because of the age difference—eight years—and now it's just like we're good friends. So that's what makes Terry's championship special, and my win, is that we're good friends.

TERRY LABONTE

■ *This interview took place shortly before the man they call "Texas Terry" won at Texas Motor Speedway in 1999, but the betting here is that Labonte's greatest day is still his second championship, which came twelve years after his first one in 1984. Terry clinched the deal at Atlanta, during a race in which he got an intriguing assist from his brother Bobby.*

You know, it's probably hard to pick one, but I think probably the one I would pick would be on a day in Atlanta—it was a race I didn't win, 1996. But we won the championship.

We went to Atlanta and qualified third, third-fastest—my brother Bobby had won the pole. And we started off there and Bobby led some of the race, and then I led some of it. At the end of the day he won the race and I finished third. We clinched the championship that day. . . . For me, personally, that was probably the most exciting day that I ever had.

We had to finish eighth or ninth or something like that—that was if Jeff [Gordon] won the race . . . he might have finished second, I don't know. I finished fifth, and Jeff maybe finished third or something. And so we won the championship.

We knew that we were gonna have to run good; we couldn't just go start the race and ride around. So we knew it was gonna be a pretty tough race. I mean, you really just went out there and ran it like any other race, and really tried not to think about the points deal.

Of course, we were always aware of where [Gordon] was at, you know. At times during the race we were ahead of him, and he was ahead of us, so it was a real satisfying day when it was over and we had won our second championship.

At times you had to be aggressive, but you also had to be cautious, too. One time late in the race, I think we were running twelfth or thirteenth, and after a pit stop we had to get back up, work it back up front. It was like, "Oh, man"—we had to pass several cars, and we had to be careful doing it.

It was kind of a race that was a combination of everything, I thought.

I went in, and I had actually broken my hand down in Phoenix. And so I went to Atlanta and felt like I was gonna be okay, and went out and made the first lap in the car, and I knew I wasn't, my hand still hurt too bad. So we practiced for three laps to qualify and qualified third.

Then we ran a little bit in the practice on Saturday afternoon, and we ran pretty good in it. . . . And then I had Sunday morning, a doctor flew in, gave me some shots in my hand to kill the pain, we ran the race like that. So it was kind of an intense week, we didn't practice, we went down there and had a couple laps and qualified third, probably twenty more laps, and then raced. It was an unusual week. There was no choice. . . . I just hoped the painkiller didn't wear off until it was over.

We started third, my brother was leading the race, and I had talked to him the night before, and I needed to lead the race to get five points. So we had discussed that—"I don't need you passing me when I caught him"—because he was wanting me to win the championship; and then we just ran the race. It was kind of a typical race, there wasn't too much out of the ordinary in it.

The car was good—if I hadn't had a broken hand, we probably wouldn't have been as cautious. We probably had a top-three car. We had run good at the first race there that year; we actually finished second, led the most laps. We really lost the race on a pit stop late in the race . . . so it had been a pretty good track for us, we had run pretty good at it. We were pretty confident going in that we were gonna run good.

It was pretty exciting. I think it was a big relief, though, when we won it, because we had led the points there on and off during the year, then passed . . . or tied Jeff at Charlotte; we won the race at Charlotte, just came within one point of him. Then we were able to go beat him out there at Rockingham, and beat him at Phoenix—we won the championship there—so it was pretty exciting.

It was exciting for Hendrick Motor Sports, because we finished first and second in points. That's the first time that that's ever happened, as far as a team owner finishing first and second in the points standings. So it was a pretty good day for us.

I didn't even talk to Jeff, he pulled up beside me and waved, and that was it. But of course Rick and everybody was there in victory lane when it was over. Really, we didn't do nothing, we went through all the victory-lane stuff there, and actually we stayed over, and went to the motel and kind of had a little party at the motel, Sunday night after the race. And then I guess we went back to the track for a little activity on Monday, as far as some things that were going on back at the track.

Right then . . . I knew it was a pretty big deal winning the championship. It had been twelve years since I had won one, so I set the record for the longest time between wins, as far as the championship goes. But on the other hand you feel real fortunate, because if you look at how many guys have been champions, there's not really that many.

It really just meant a lot to me personally, because during those twelve years without a championship, I also went for like four years and didn't win a race. So it just meant a lot to me and my family, and then to have Bobby win the race too, was really special.

Actually we had some photos in victory lane together, Bobby and myself and Rick Hendrick and Joe Gibbs—it was pretty neat to see them have a good day like that, also. We congratulated each other, and hugged each other. . . . We were all smiles. And, of course, my parents were there, it was a pretty exciting day for them.

A race that I won? That's really hard to pick one over the other one, because anytime you win a race it's a great day. I don't know if any of 'em . . . I've won some races that have been really exciting, I've won some races that have been boring. I've won some races that have meant a lot to me because I've come so close to winning in a few places and then I've finally won there. I could tell you a story about every one that was pretty good.

That was the championship thing that makes that race stand out. That was definitely the most memorable day I've ever had in racing.

You know, it's the same thing—you really had to do the same things in 1984 to win the championship that you do today. And you can look at it and all the pieces are the same. The people are different that you work with, but it's really so similar, it's not surprising, but you've gotta have good people. You've gotta have a great engine program, you've gotta have good cars, you've gotta be consistent, you've gotta be competitive every week—all those things. And they all add up the same.

You've gotta have the top tens, you've gotta have the top fives, you gotta finish the races. You look at those two seasons, and you can lay 'em on top of each other, and they're the same, they're just the same.

The feeling for the second one is much better for the first one. You know, I didn't realize how big a deal it was to win the championship in 1984—I was, like, twenty-eight years old. And I thought, man, this is pretty awesome, but I really thought we'd win it again the next year. And I didn't really think it would take twelve years to win it again. And then, plus, the sport has changed tremendously in those twelve years. There were people that are fans today, probably the majority of fans today, that weren't fans back in 1984 when I won that championship. Just so many things like that were different.

Things have changed a lot since then, but some things remain the same. It takes the same thing to win the championship today. I think . . . equipment today is today than it was back then, everybody's made advances, everybody's got bigger teams, everybody's got bigger sponsors, you've got more people working for you.

. . . It's all the same. You start out the year, there's gonna be ten guys in the points deal. You know, I can go down there and I can pick out the top ten. And you might miss it by one or two, there might be a couple of guys that surprise you, a couple of guys that have trouble, and then halfway through the year you're going to be able to pick out the top four or five. It's the same thing.

It comes down to . . . you're gonna race one or two guys at the end of the year.

DAVE MARCIS

■ *If Junior Johnson is the last American hero, then Dave Marcis is definitely one of the last of a dying breed—the independent owner/operator. While Marcis may or may not have picked a single greatest day, he did offer a wonderful journey down memory lane, covering his early days driving for Harry Hyde against David Pearson and Buddy Baker, some of his runs as an independent, a race that included an impromptu concert by country singer Marty Robbins, and driving as a relief driver for Richard Petty. After this comprehensive tour of his personal highlights, Marcis closed with some thoughts on the future of the one-man band in NASCAR.*

I guess . . . it's hard, you know, because there are so many of 'em, and I enjoy it so damn much, been doing it for so many years. But I guess number one, just being able to be out there and be involved in it.

Of course, when I drove for Harry Hyde, K and K Insurance, the first time I drove the K and K Insurance Dodge was when Bobby Isaac had the kidney stones at Talladega in 1971. I was leading the race with five laps to go when we lost an engine. That's certainly one of the most memorable days. I guess that kind of proves that I was capable, just jumping in that car as a relief driver, and we were basically going to win the race if that didn't happen, because we pretty much had a half a straightaway on the field.

And then, in the K and K Insurance Dodge again at Atlanta, Georgia, when we beat David Pearson. We had a great race that day, we led the majority of the laps—I don't remember how many laps we led, but we led the most. And Harry would keep coming on the radio and he would say, "You've gotta watch that Pearson, you've gotta watch him, they don't call him the damn Silver Fox for nothing."

And I said, "Harry, I'm telling you, this car is just working so good. I am not having any problem running here, and I'm not overusing the car or the tires, I'm taking care of it." [He said,] "I'm just telling you, Dave Marcis, you've gotta watch that damn Pearson, he's got something up his sleeve."

He said, "I want you to go up there and run high on that racetrack," so I'd go up and run up against the wall. And we'd run up there, eight, nine, ten laps, and he'd say, "I want you to go down and run low. You show me you can run down on the bottom of that racetrack." So we'd go down and we'd run on the bottom of that racetrack.

And he said, "Now, you've gotta watch that Pearson, he's got something going on." And as the race got toward the end, the last ten laps or so, of course David was right on my tail. And Harry, he just never gave up on that "you've gotta watch Pearson" deal, and he had something up his sleeve, but our car was just so good that day, I mean, we won that race.

It was an enjoyment racing with David that way, all day long, racing that hard, it was really a spark. Harry was under the impression that he was just sitting back there following me, and he was gonna pass us one way or another, high or low. And Harry was making me demonstrate to him during the event that I could run high, and then he would also want me to run low. I guess he was wantin' me to show him that our car would do either, and that I could hold David off.

He just didn't have it that day—our car was better, and we had him covered. He never made the move, he couldn't, our car was just that good.

David was always a good guy to race against, he always had a good attitude, he was always happy, we never had no problems with

David. I think he was happy for me to be able to win the race, even though we beat him. . . . He congratulated us on a good day and on a good-running race car and everything, so, yeah, it was pretty incredible.

That was a big highlight, because that was the week after he had won the Talladega race that fall, also. So it was two 500-milers in a row. We spent a lot of the evening just talking about it, and of course I stuck around there while they inspected the race car and tore the engine down for NASCAR and stuff like that. It was just a pretty good time.

Harry's cars were always strong at Talladega, and we basically always won the pole; if we didn't, David [Pearson] did. It was like the Harry Hyde and Woods brothers deal in those days at Talladega for the pole. We ended up racing Buddy Baker at the end, and of course I was drafting on Buddy, and Buddy'll tell everybody that the reason we won was because he ran out of gas.

But Harry Hyde kept telling me on the radio, "Just don't even worry about passing him, they cannot make it on fuel. They're telling everybody they can, I'm telling you they can't. You just sit there and draft with him." Our car was capable of passing their car, but Harry didn't want me to. He said, "We don't have to pit no more, I assure you of that," and we don't have no problem.

Buddy and them ran out of gas, they didn't even come close. If I recall, they probably ran out of gas fifteen, twenty laps before the end of the race. Basically we were dealing with Buddy at that stage of the race, in Bud Moore's car.

Talladega's been a good track for me for my whole career, but basically it was always just a flat-out deal—Harry Hyde's preparation for his race cars always excelled at Daytona and Talladega. We were strong every time we went there right off the truck, he never had to work on his car; basically we would practice either three or four laps and qualify and be on the pole or the outside pole. We just always had good strong race cars, they were fun to drive, they were comfortable, that was just his approach to that racetrack every time we went there.

I was gonna sort of tell you [my greatest day as an independent] next. I would have to go to Richmond, Virginia, when we won the race there. It was rain-shortened, in 1982; that day we were running well, we qualified decent. But Joe Rutland was the guy who was really running that day, and Joe had just gotten past me, in the third turn. . . .

And Joe spun out coming off of the fourth turn, just lost it, and spun around backwards and kinda went down the straightaway backwards, but never crossed the start/finish line. So I immediately passed Joe right back. So therefore I wasn't down a lap, because he never crossed the start/finish line. So it was sorta almost like he really never passed me.

But anyhow, out comes the caution flag. It was right close to pit-stop time, and I was struggling too, that's why I was losing ground to those guys, because I'd had my tires out for so long. But everyone, when the pace car jumped out there, everyone was lined up behind the pace car and dove into those pits. It was very cloudy, we had had a few minor sprinkles, and you know, that race was 75 to 80 percent over with when all this happened. So what I'm getting at, we were pretty competitive all day anyhow.

I, of course, knew the weather conditions, and we were short-handed on the pit-crew situation anyhow. It was two things: It was important for me to get and stay behind the pace car and keep it closed up; and secondly, you know, I had to give my guys time and all to get ready to pit. But then the weather was bad, and so we were gonna try and stretch it anyhow, we just said, Let's just stretch it out.

I don't know at the time how many cars were even left running on the lead lap, but not that many. . . . I guess you'd have to check the records on that. . . . So, had I stayed out, they would have went back green, and at the worst I would have been at the tail end of the line. But I believe I was still in the top ten.

So we decided to stay out there. . . . It started to sprinkle, and it started to sprinkle more. Well, Dale Inman is the guy that realized that they made a mistake. And Dale and them only took out right sides, and they sent Richard back out. However, he did not beat the pace car out, they held him at the end of pit road.

So I'm in the lead, and now it's starting to rain, and all the other people took on four tires. And Richard came out behind me, and the rain just continued to increase and increase. And we went on, and they waited, waited, waited waited . . . they just rained it out. So Richard was sitting there second, because they realized that they had goofed up, and tried to get it back, but they just came up a tick short. But everyone else threw on the four tires, and they just . . . Richard beat 'em out.

For an independent operation—J. V. Stacy's name was on the car at the time—I was the only one that had won in the race at that time. And we had spent all that money, and [he had] all those other teams plus his own in-house team. And he was only giving us $5,000 a race. And here we are winning for this guy out there, no pit crew, only had about five guys up there or something like that, and we end up winning the race for him.

They did everything they could to get that race restarted, it just wasn't gonna happen. . . . We had to tear that car down at night, and by the time we got out of the buildings there at the fairgrounds where we tore the car down, it was like nine-thirty at night. And we started heading back here to Asheville.

It was just a great day, just the three of us in that tow truck, riding home, being able to talk about it. . . . We're the littlest team, we got this little bitty truck, we got this trailer, the car's not even enclosed, and we won the race. It was pretty neat.

That win probably meant more, because we built the engine here ourselves, it was our own car, our own crew—it probably was the biggest win of my career. In the K and K Insurance car we were expected to win, but still, you know how competitive this deal's always been. Today it's worse than ever, but in those days it was competitive, too; you just didn't walk in there and win races.

Maybe there wasn't thirty cars and as close a group then as there is now, but there was fifteen of twenty of them that were all capable of winning that were factory-backed. So it was no cakewalk, but that was a big win that day, as a little team, and no money, and we built the engine right here ourself in our shop. Ben Barnes out here in Asheville, he done some machine work on the block and stuff for us, so he was involved in it, too. But we really did the assembly and all here at our place.

I guess it was just kind of a bunch of old backyard guys, and come home with the big check. It was enjoyable, I tell you. It meant a lot to all of my guys, and me, and it meant a lot to a lot of people in NASCAR, too, I think.

I guess my philosophy there is, the reason it's been this long is because I enjoy the sport, and it's my job, it's the way I make a living, just like a man that works in a factory. It's been my job, my way of making a living, it's just what I've had to do, it's what I chose to do when I was about sixteen years old. I just continue to do it.

The purses are getting better, I like that. It was tougher to make ends meet years ago, but again, you didn't have the labor costs that you do now, the tires didn't cost as much, the engine parts, so it sort of, I guess, balances out. But I think NASCAR's realizing that it costs more to compete today, so they're constantly on the promoters to increase these purses. And that helps.

Years ago it was a little bit more laid-back, a little bit more relaxed. I think we socialized more among ourselves as a group in the garage and all, because we weren't bothered as much in the garage, we were left alone more in those days—there wasn't as many people, news media, fans, whatever.

So now, when guys got out of their cars they'd immediately head to the trucks. Before, they basically stood around in the garage, everybody shot the bull, they'd go in the cafeterias—we used to have a lot of great cafeterias on a lot of the racetracks. Today . . . there's only one left that I eat at, that's at Rockingham. The rest of 'em ain't worth going into, and plus, Christ, you've gotta go get a loan before you can go in 'em—you can't afford 'em.

But years ago it wasn't that way. We'd all go in the restaurants and we'd eat and all the guys worked on the cars; and, of course, fans were in there, we talked to them, too. But now the guys hop out of the car and they beat it right to the truck, because they just don't get left alone. There's no time at all, really, so I enjoyed that more back then. It was more of a pleasure to be involved in the sport then, as well as a job.

The best I've seen? Richard Petty, David Pearson—those two guys—and their records speak for themselves. Richard was so dominant, in short tracks and stuff, with them Chrysler products, but then David was so dominant on them superspeedways. And both of them, the accomplishments they did in those days, of course, that was always the rivalry, between them two.

But then Bobby Allison would come along with that Chevelle of his in some of the little-bitty old short tracks, like up there in Islip and Thompson, Connecticut, and Augusta, Georgia, and Macon and all them, and he'd beat them guys. So I can't take anything away from Bobby, either.

I drove with a lot of great guys in those days. Those old race cars, they weren't like today, we didn't have the shocks, we didn't have the power steering, the cars weighed thirty-nine hundred pounds—those things would wear you out; you know the relief that people had to have from other drivers in those days, versus today. And it was because the cars, they steered hard, they were hotter—we were not allowed to duck fresh air into those cars. Today we are.

We didn't have nothing. In those old days we had to have windows in the cars, and we had to run with 'em closed up. Them babies were hot—we could not run with the windows open, they had to close 'em.

I've been in some great races. . . . I guess Daytona stands out, the year that Buddy Baker won it. I had a problem early in the race, got down a lap, but I sat there and ran and drafted with Buddy all day long. However, I was always that one lap down, and Buddy ended up winning it. But that was a great race there, that day, for me. Buddy and I drafted a lot together; it's just so heartbreaking, I was down that lap all day. There I was, but I wasn't.

The day I took over relief for Bobby Allison at Bristol, and won that race. I ran like the last 112 laps or something. I won the race in Bobby's car, he had to have relief; that was a great day too, winning at Bristol, and in those days everybody would get tired and wore out and had to have relief.

I've got some really great moments. I mean, like all the times I drove relief for Richard Petty at Darlington. Just to be asked to drive Richard's car, in itself, meant a lot to me. Because Richard was always my idol, growing up in Wisconsin, and when I followed NASCAR racing, the only way I had to follow it was through *Hot Rod* magazine, and Richard was always my idol. I followed Richard, and my race cars were blue because Richard's cars were blue.

Running with Marty Robbins . . . and Marty at night. One year we were in Texas, we sat around that swimming pool, probably two o'clock, two-thirty in the morning, Marty sitting out there singing for us, me and Pearson and Richard and Cale, a bunch of the drivers. That was something, too. Marty really liked us guys, and we all liked him, you know? I'll never forget that night, that was great, we sat by that swimming pool, Marty just kept singing and telling jokes. I mean, you could hear a pin drop there, everybody was quiet, everybody was listening, and everybody enjoyed.

Multi-car teams makes it tough for small guys to get involved. They need to try and control costs, and that's difficult. I don't think there should be provisionals anymore today, I think you should qualify straight-up. The purses have to go up; I don't think there should be a winner's circle anymore, I think it should go in the purse. I think that would invite new competitors, because if all the money's there and it's available for everybody, and a new competitor comes in and he has got good equipment and he is competitive, he can make enough money to make ends meet and stay in business. The level the sport's at today, you don't need winner's circle—all the money should be up for grab for every competitor that qualifies for the event. And I think they should qualify straight-up.

I think the system can stand it—the money's there, the purses are there, the people are paying big bucks to see these races. They need to see the fastest forty-three or forty-two or whatever cars it is that's going to run in the event that came to that racetrack that weekend to qualify. That's what they're paying for, they need to see that.

. . . Right now, there's a lot of money in the purses that's not available to all the forty competitors. I don't think it should be that way. We don't need to close the door, we need to keep the door open for competition, that's what makes the sport as great as it is. But in order to get that competition, people have to be able to see where they can make ends meet. And if you've got a fourth of your money tied up to where they can't even get to it, how can you expect 'em to come in and make ends meet and stay in business?

I think that's some areas that things need to be done in—just control costs. I would like to see cars go back a little bit more to stock cars, like they are in the showroom. Get rid of this exotic air dams and noses we've got on the front on these cars, get back more to the production car. That would cut costs. . . . It would make 'em harder to drive, but hey, that's what you're supposed to be as a driver, that's what the mechanics are for, you gotta get it fixed, gotta work it out.

And when people bad-mouth individual racetracks, I don't think that is right. Again, my philosophy has always been, if a man built a racetrack, he built it the best he knew how, and he had no intentions of building it to where it wasn't a nice racetrack. That's what's you've got the driver for, springs, shocks, and all that stuff, fix that car, work it out, get it going.

All the bad-mouthing Texas got? I never bad-mouthed that racetrack. It was a difficult racetrack, but I went there so far and ran twice and made big money both times. Use your head, that's what you've got it for. Use your head, get your car fixed, get it right. You can drive it. . . . Racing is an obstacle, and you have to overcome it. That's always been my philosophy, at any racetrack we've ever gone to.

MARK MARTIN

■ *Mark Martin has had more than his share of great runs on the NASCAR circuit, but he's made his mark on history in the International Race of Champions, which he's won four times. Martin also chose the inaugural victory at Las Vegas last year as his other greatest day, in part because of the historical significance of the first win at a new track, but also because he had just made the move to a new racing team.*

Well, you know I'm not the kind of guy that is a real good interview in that category, because I'm not too big on reliving those kind of things—I'm more interested in making history than enjoying it. And that's where I keep my focus, but the best wins or the biggest wins for me would probably be in Las Vegas or the IROC win at Indy this year that sewed up the fourth IROC championship, which was a history-making thing.

Of course, three is history-making the year before, but you know that meant an awful lot to me. How colorful that was, I don't know, or how colorful a story I could tell about that IROC thing, I'm not really that sure. . . . . everyone has their limitations—one of mine is being able to colorfully describe to you how that race went, other than we started last, like always.

In IROC, you know, the points leader always starts last, and we got off to a reasonable start and got past a number of cars, a good number of cars on the first lap. And then they had a big wreck right behind me, which was sort of key in that whole deal because I got past the wreck instead of in it. And then, incredibly, somehow I managed to pass when nobody else was doing any passing, one by one by one, and crawl my way to the win.

I don't know how in the heck I did it, I never dreamed I would be able to pass there. . . . I just absolutely can't explain the success I've had in IROC, I don't know. I've been real fortunate in that series, and that is a very big deal, I mean to me.

The highlights of my career today probably rests on top of those four IROC championships, separated by one second-place run—four over five years with a second in there—racing against NASCAR's best, and everyone else, too.

What you do is, you take advantage of every opportunity that you're presented with, if you can. I just was on the gas, and when I saw an opportunity I took it, and the opportunities were there and open for me in such a way that—*bang, bang*—I just got through there. There's not any particular thing [I did], and I can't say, "Well, I planned it that way," I just passed everybody that I could and the opportunities seemed to present themselves real quick several different times in the first lap or two.

The IROC cars are just . . . as even as they can make 'em. I had a good car that day, and it seemed like the longer we ran, the better we did. I found just a little niche of how to get more out of it through the corners, in terms of getting the car to get through the corner fast and not have any front-end push. They started off a little loose, but then they tightened up.

And then the racetrack in Indy is far from my favorite, because it's a rectangle—flat, square corners, 90-degree corners—my favorites are sweeping banked turns where you could run two and three abreast and race. That doesn't keep you from doing good . . . [but] it's a very difficult racetrack. My favorite racetrack in Michigan, because you can run bottom, middle, high, or anywhere in between, you can race three cars side by side through those turns and not even crowd one another.

But you've gotta race it wherever the race is. They have a huge race there at Indy that pays a ton of money and garners a lot of attention, and I hope to win a Winston Cup race there soon.

You just drive the car—with the IROC cars you don't get to make any adjustments, you just drive it as fast as you can. Basically, all you do is sit down behind the wheel and you go around the track as fast as you can go—to me that should go even unmentioned, because a driver is someone who gets behind the wheel and goes fast. Just ask me how you go so fast on road courses, I say, "It's just like driving back home where I learned how to drive on country roads"—all you do is drive the car as fast as you can and stay out of a ditch.

That's all road racing is. . . . it's nothing. Racing is driving a car and staying out of a ditch. You know, I'm pretty bad to oversimplify, but . . . that doesn't always make for great writing but it's the honest thing. You just get behind the wheel and you go around the track and you say, "How can I go faster and not hit that wall?" or, "How can I go faster and not slide off the edge of the track?" or whatever it is, you know?

You tweak it and work it and you flirt with that ragged edge—you flirt with that edge and you find the things that you could do to just push it, you know?

It was really neat, because Arlene and Matt were there [Martin's wife and son], and at Indy they put the car on a platform and they raise it up way up in the air—that was just really cool, it was really neat.

It was neat because my Winston Cup race team shares in half of the winnings, so they all make money. I enjoyed sharing with them, I shared well over a half a million dollars over the past five years with 'em, with the guys that work on the race team, and around my program. Not just the guys that work on the number 6 car, but all the stuff that we do in racing—sharing that, it's real exciting for me to win that money because I know I'm giving a huge portion, half of it, to those people. And so they pull real hard for me. . . .

The first one was different, because I didn't have time to celebrate. I had another appearance in Arkansas in just about three hours, so I had to hurry up, and I was there by myself—me and my pilot were all that was there. And I had to hurry up, get the hat trick done; and get the trip presentation done; quick, run into the press room and answer their questions as quick as I could; run to the car; run to the airport as fast as we could; get on the airplane and fly to Arkansas to my appearance and sign autographs.

You know, it was quite different, that was a very strange experience. My pilot and I just rode down the road toward the airport with our chests puffed out a little bit, you know. We were on the run . . . and something's kind of fun when you are on the run like that, one thing to the next—it was a proud time.

. . . The history part of it hasn't played out much. There was a real neat trophy that we got with it that I see in my house once in a while, and that's cool because it's different, and it says "Brickyard"—"Inaugural Brickyard IROC Race"—and that's a neat deal. And the only other part of the history part of it is telling you right now. That's the next time I thought about it. Someday when I'm in my rocking chair that'll be a fun thing to talk about.

Vegas is awesome—beautiful racetrack, great to drive on, we had a brand-new team in 1998, all new members. I'd walked away from a championship team the year before, to a new deal and a brand-new Taurus that was unknown—we didn't know for sure how good was gonna be—and we won the third race out of the box, which was Vegas.

Paid a lot of money, had a big trophy, and it was an inaugural race, and they tell me that makes a lot more history and that should mean something. So someday . . . I guess I'll be able to kick back and say, "Yeah, I won that inaugural race at Las Vegas." But it was a real special win, for the reasons of the risk that I had taken by changing racing teams.

The car was good, and the cars had fared real well at Rockingham the week before, so it was proving out real well. But going out into the season we didn't know for sure what we had. I'm not too big into confidence, I don't do the confidence thing much, because confidence just doesn't win races. Performances do, and you got to put out a great performance to be a contender to win, so that's really where I focus on.

It went well—I think we led the most laps. We were very strong throughout the day. We had some problems with pit stops, but we managed to crawl our way back to the lead each time, so we had a very strong car. [The pit problem was] just a new team, a brand-new team.

We led a long time at the end—I don't even remember passing for the lead, because when we passed for the lead, we didn't know it was for the win 'cause it was a long way to go. Jeff Burton ran second, he was a good ways back, we were in comfortable shape, and the time just sort of ran down.

The celebration . . . it was pretty neat; you know we had a couple of showgirls there, we had Wayne Newton there, the race team that was ecstatic, Jack Roush . . . The family wasn't there, but it was a wonderful win, a very, very, very special win. I haven't even thought about it [this year]. We'll go there and do the same thing we did last time, give our very best performance and see what we turn up with.

[I pick] the IROC thing because of where it was and what it was—fourth championship, three in a row to set the mark out there, where not many people are going to have the opportunity to reach as far as history goes and what that means.

And then at Vegas, it's just the relief of knowing that maybe we had done the right thing, changing the team, and a sense of accomplishment for a new group of people that had been thrown together just two months ago. [Making a major transition after all the success we'd had]—that's exactly right. And to have that . . . You know, nobody wants to be pointed out and said that "I told you so" or "You shouldn't have done that . . . you really messed up"—nobody likes that. I didn't want to have to deal with that.

■ *After making a name for himself as the ARCA Rookie of the Year in 1993, Jeremy Mayfield began the process of moving up the ranks in Winston Cup to post a banner year last year that included a career-high number of top-ten and top-five finishes that allowed him to place seventh in the points standings. But Mayfield's biggest achievement was his first Winston Cup victory at Pocono, a rain-shortened affair in which he bested the likes of Darrell Waltrip, Jeff Gordon, and Dale Jarrett.*

I'll have to say Pocono—you know, my win at Pocono, first Winston Cup win, was probably the highlight of my career.

At the end of the season, it was probably the best year I ever had starting out. I had really run good in several places, you know, felt like we were in position to win, had several top fives under us. Led a lot of laps going into that race at different places, went into Pocono with a lot of confidence. It's one of my favorite racetracks, it's a place I always seem to run good at—I'm not sure why, it seems like I adapted well to that place.

I got a really good setup for it, and got a good feel for it. We had just come off two or three top-five finishes, and it was going in there, I felt really good about it, my confidence was up, and I had a great deal. I qualified third, my race setup was real good, I led a bunch of laps and thought, Man, this could be the day.

It rained on us, we had a rain delay, and I was still wondering what was gonna happen, and still didn't know how it was all gonna turn out. So it was a day that was kind of up and down.

Gordon and I were running first and second, and we came into the pits, and both of us got a 15-second penalty, and I thought that was gonna cost us the race. Speeding down pit road, they got both of us.

We went back out and made that back up, and then, you know, it rained again. And I thought, Man, what's going on here? . . . ended up winning the race. Passed Darrell Waltrip—he was leading the race when I was running second, and I passed him for the win.

When I passed him and took the lead, I led from then on out, and to do that was definitely a memorable moment. I mean, he was one of my heroes, a guy I always looked up to, from Owensboro, Kentucky, for a lot of reasons. To pass him for the win was pretty amazing.

I felt good about the car, we had a good race car. I had always run good there, but I never really qualified well, and to qualify third there, for me, was really good. I'd always qualified in the back, but I always raced good. But man, starting up front, got a good pit spot, and I just felt good about it from then on.

Qualifying is so important, I think it's everything. To start up front, you get a better pit spot, you don't have to start in the back and pass all the cars and burn your tires up. You get to stay up front, pit up front—if you're in the back, you always pit behind everybody else, so it's hard to gain spots in the pits. So just qualifying up front, that set the tone for the whole weekend.

The pitting strategy didn't really [get] affected by the rain delay. Some places it does, but it didn't that particular day. It was just a sit- uation where, when the rain came, it was a mental distraction, but other than that it was pretty good. I think it [the rain] helped us; the track didn't change, it stayed about the same as it was at the begin- ning of the race. So that probably helped us, a little rain coming, you know. We were concerned about that, what it was gonna do to the track conditions. It didn't really seem to affect our car, which I think really played a part into us winning.

I think to win my first race . . . and you know, the second-place guy was Jeff Gordon, and the third-place guy was Dale Jarrett. When you do that—man, that's tough company, and it makes you feel like you earned it, it makes you feel like you didn't luck into it. It wasn't a fluke, I flat-out . . . We won the race, and that's a good feeling.

It was the greatest moment of my life—that was my whole dream. Not all my dreams, but that was one of the biggest dreams I ever had, to win the Winston Cup series. When you get here, it's so tough, as a rookie, especially. You know, four or five years ago when I started, it seems like the win was . . . I wasn't even close to winning.

That whole year, beginning of last year, I feel like I was getting closer and closer and closer, and when you finally get in victory lane, you feel like . . . It's just a relief. It's more of a relief than anything, the feeling accomplishing that in your life is totally undescribable. It was awesome. That's one of the good things about my career, I've gradually gotten better and better, and my team's gotten better and better, and I've been able to deal with the media a little bit at a time in different steps. That was just another part . . . .

. . . We stayed after tech [inspection] and stuff, I blew home, I had a bunch of my friends waiting at my house that night. Monday night we had a big party at the shop, and the Mobil One people came in, Roger and Walt, everybody involved . . . we had a victory party at our race shop. We did some celebrating. . . . It was something I'll never forget, the feeling of that, and that's what makes me want even more and more to win more races now.

That's kind of the way it was for us—after Monday night, I was like . . . "Okay, now we've gotta go on." At the end of the year you look back—Yeah, we won, but that's not where we want to be. And the first one was great as our first one, but it doesn't take long to get over that where you want to win more races, and win on a weekly basis.

I learned a lot . . . my confidence was definitely up, but we went through an up-and-down–type season. We won, and then we came back and ran good in a lot of those places, but we had a streak of bad luck hit us, and it put us back into reality.

And I think it's made us a better race team, you know, it gave us a little taste last year, and this year we came back and we've gotta really buckle down and go here, because it's a tough series. If you sit still, or think because you're winning, you just sit there and don't change anything, you're not gonna win for very long. . . . We learned that.

The next race, the next one that I win, I think that will be right there at the tops. Right now, I feel better about my team, my chances, myself, my experience, as I ever did. I feel like right now, this is the best situation I've ever been in. So I'm thinking the next race we win will be right there at the top, and every win after that.

That's just my first one . . . that was my first win, but it doesn't last long. You've gotta keep going, and why I chose that one is just, it was an up-and-down day for me, it was a career highlight.

It seems like I learn so much every week, it's hard to pinpoint one thing. But I learned a lot, I learned how to win a Winston Cup race, so I know what it takes now, and . . . it's tough. Probably the experience factor more than anything, what it is as a driver, how to win. You see, some drivers run pretty good every once in a while, and this, that, and the other, and to win a Winston Cup race, you've gotta be good, and be the best car and the best driver all day long—five hundred miles.

There's not really one key, it's everybody doing their part—the best pit stops, the best cars, the best engine, having the best of everything, and everybody pulling their weight.

RALPH MOODY

■ *Mention chassis design and great ownership teams to anyone who knows a bit about racing history, and they'll instantly know that you're talking about Holman-Moody. Born and raised in Massachusetts, Ralph Moody Jr. was a superstar in the New England midget and spring circuit before World War Two, and he went on to drive in both the NASCAR modified circuit as well as the Grand National circuit in the 1950s. He had his greatest success when he teamed up with John Holman to form one of sport's most dominant ownership teams, with a list of drivers that includes Fireball Roberts, Fred Lorenzen, Cale Yarborough, and David Pearson (he's commonly credited with teaching Dan Gurney how to handle a stock car).*

Moody never did quite get around to naming his greatest day, but in this interview he takes readers on a rambling tour through racing history, discussing chassis design, a memorable Lorenzen victory at Darlington, Holman-Moody's partnership with Ford, and Mario Andretti's victory at Daytona, all the while offering some intriguing thoughts on modern racing and some of today's drivers.

I've had a few of them. . . . We had a lot of different things. One big thing we had, was Daytona, winning the race, because we had a lot of Fords in there. We said, To hell with any more positions, we ought to win more of 'em. I thought it would be a bigger thing to have more than just a winner, to try to get 'em all going.

They said, Ah they didn't care. And we got going about that stuff, and they said, "Well, we'll give you ten grand for every one you have on the road."

We went around and around about that thing. There were Ford people, you told 'em you could help 'em, and what we did was a lot of times you'd be working with people on other teams that didn't want to listen to what was going on. We wound up with five [winners] in a row, and I'm still looking for the ten thousand dollars.

There were things like that where it didn't make any difference whether you got paid or whatever happened. But we had things like Lorenzen at Darlington, and he was kind of fresh at it—a lot of times he was racing with people he didn't know what kind of tactics they'd pull on him and all. Curtis Turner was pretty rough about what he done to people; he ran for us, too.

And I told Freddy, "It looks like you're gonna be up there with Turner at the end of the race," and I told him what to do about getting by him, because Turner, if he's leading the race at the end of the race, he ain't gonna let you by him. He'd stick you into the wall, or knock you into the racetrack before he'd let anybody by him—this was in 1963, somewhere along there.

I kept repeating it, and he said, "Aw, you keep telling me," and I said, "Yeah, but you've gotta listen. If you listen long enough, you'll do what your supposed to; if you don't, you ain't gonna do it." He'd get mad at me about something, and say, "You keep telling me," and I said, "Yeah, one day you'll remember."

It came to the end of the race, with about fifteen laps to go, Freddy tries to get by him, going into number one on the outside. Turner run him up high, almost drove him into the fence. So then you had to wait, you couldn't say much of anything to him, so I said, Well, I preached enough to him, he oughta be able to do what the hell we're talking about.

I had told him that, when he tried doing that, Turner'll think he's just a young kid, didn't know what the hell was going on, and I said, "The thing to do is do the same thing, over and over again." And he did it for about fifteen laps, he'd go to the outside, and Turner would push him up into the wall. And he'd try it again and he'd push him against the wall, and I said, "Keep doing it until the next-to-the-last lap. When they get the white flag, do it again but duck to the inside, he'll never expect you're gonna do it."

That's what happened—he won the race. That's when Freddy got in front of him and moved out a little ways ahead of him, and after you got the flag and went down the backstretch, Turner went down in and ran into him.

And the next morning Turner came over to our shop, he had a big old black Cadillac at the time, a new one, and he drove it right through the damn rolled-down doors. He was some kind of hot about that.

But different things like that happened, you can think of a lot of things that happened like that. It was just outstanding, what you had somebody do, the things you could tell somebody and get 'em to do these things.

I first started out racing like everybody else, you didn't know what the hell you were doing anyway. I ran for a man that had a million dollars, but it wasn't much of anything, then I got a hold of [a car] of my own and that wasn't much of anything. We didn't run much for a couple of years, we didn't know what we were doing, to have money or anything else to run with, just off and on we'd run.

And I got with a guy that had a pretty nice midget. The problem back then, people put those things together and they knew about as much about chassis setup as a man on the moon. Everybody had [the attitude] . . . you know, it just had four wheels on it, and you drive the hell out of it.

So I got with this guy, and . . . we got home one day, and I told him the next day, "You know, this thing would run better if we just, instead of going to every race, if we just stay home and figure out what's going on." We sat down and talked about what we had to do, and we did some different things, and that was back in 1936 or 1937.

And we had a little Ford 60, a little V-8, and we figured out what you need to do with this thing to make it work, because at different places, different tracks, if you hit some bank or a flat track it was a lot different, so right there that was one of the first times that we put screw jacks on all four corners of the car.

Of course, you had 'em in those cars like that, and you couldn't see 'em under the covers, because of the grille covers and all that kind of stuff in the back. We started adjusting that thing differently to see what we could make it do—we made it turn upside-down the first time.

But after a little bit we practiced with that kind of thing to make it work. . . . The first thing you do is stay home and start figuring out what the hell you're doing wrong and try to fix it. We did that when we first started racing, and from then on every once in a while you just sit around and talk with your people and get everybody's ideas and do something different. If you're in the racing business, any kind of racing, any day, tomorrow or next year, somebody'll be sitting down and thinking what they're doing. If they don't, you're not gonna be running up front.

In 1957 I got started in that thing—Pete Powell was the man, we were doing business down here [in North Carolina], but we weren't doing much anywhere else with any other clubs, IROC or USAC or anything. And I was driving home once, and I said, "I'm gonna get this Ford together and take it up to Milwaukee."

He said, "That's USAC, they're all Indy car drivers." I said, "Well, they've all got two legs and two hands like we do, so let's go up there and see if we can win something up there and we'll get some business." And if you're in the performance business, if you've got something that works, people will want to buy it.

So we went up there the first race, and those guys, they've got nice tow rigs, nice trailers and stuff, carriers, and we had a 1957 Ford tow bar—we were towing it on the ground, a station wagon pulling it, engine in the back with a toolbox. And I had two guys with me, and my wife went along with it, and when we got there we hired another couple of guys, we went around racing a little bit, and when they seen us pull in there they all came around and looked at that thing, and it didn't look too good, because we were running a lot of dirt [tracks] down around here.

Of course, their cars were all pretty and everything, everybody kind of smiled at me. So we run three or four practice laps, and it was getting near the end of qualifying, and the guy said, "Hey, you'd better get out there and see if you can qualify." So we went out there and set a new track record and sat on the pole and won the race, and then we hooked up and left.

And USAC, [they said] they'll send you your money. And nobody knew who we were, the only thing we had on that thing was a rebel flag. And we went to the second one and did the same thing, and the third one done the same thing, and the fourth one sat on the pole and it rained it out by the time it started. So nobody knew who the hell we are and what happened or who we were or anything else, so we put ads in the paper, who it was and why we were there.

We started doing business at that circuit. So that was quite an accomplishment, to go out and do something like that.

All the guys we had who were drivers for us were good at what they did, and they paid attention to what the hell you talked to 'em about. Guys like Lorenzen and David Pearson, Bobby Allison, Donnie Allison, Curtis Turner, Joe Weatherly—those guys were race drivers. You just can't pick one you say that's better than the other—any one of 'em can win races any day that's going on, given the right circumstance.

All of those guys . . . David was just a hell of a nice guy. He was one of those guys that was like Bobby and the rest of 'em, nothing upset 'em, very seldom you'd see 'em get mad about anything. They really got after the job all the time, they just got the job done. Nobody can sit there and pick somebody—you might think you're picking somebody, but if you start putting two and two together, there's no way. They all compare.

There's so many things . . . you get into that stuff, and it's either win or lose, and you lose a hell of a lot more than you win. David won a lot of stuff for us, two championships, but I took Bobby and put him in a Ford at Rockingham—he hadn't been in one of those things—he wins the race, and he won three out of five there.

If you're in the business yourself and you race yourself, you can see who's the driver, who's the people you want. And there's always a lot of 'em out there, under the right circumstances, guys out there today that's not winning, but under the right circumstances with the right bunch of people around him, he'll win.

Jeremy Mayfield is one of those examples—he was down there with Cale and they didn't do nothing, and everybody says, "Aw, he ain't any good." He does pretty good all of a sudden; he learned how to drive when he changed and went somewhere else. And that's just the way it is.

I'm the one that built the first square-tube chassis for Ford, I built a lot about that. You can't keep going like we were going, with a Pontiac and a Chevrolet and a Ford, and all of 'em with different chassis and all of 'em with different running gear. And to make the thing like it is today, you had to have one kind of setup, completely, because that was the way things got to go in other kinds of racing, you make a kind of car, or maybe two kinds, some of the circuits would have, but you get one kind of car, and you go out there today and you take the skin off it and they're all the same.

This is what I was trying to tell 'em, to have a circuit and be able to run it, you need to have each and every one of those things doing the same thing. There's a lot of reasons why. One of the big reasons is, you can police it, what the hell they're doing with it. The other reason is, if you go to a racetrack, and somebody needs something, everybody's got the same damn thing. And if everybody's got something different, you've got five or six different kinds of chassis set up, you've got a hell of a mess.

The aftermarket is gonna be the ones that pay the dealer what you buy, and if you've got this thing like it is today, everybody builds the same kinds of things to put on those race cars. You can find more parts for those damn things than you can buy.

The safety things, we argued. We took two 1958 Thunderbirds at Darlington, with side bars, door bars in the car, and they made us take 'em out. So that was the rules, you couldn't do that; so if somebody gets hurt, safety got hurt.

That was kind of the way it went for us. . . . Bill [France Jr.] was hot, he wanted to drive stock cars, you know? But he would come around and say, "Yup, hell, we've gotta keep from hurtin' somebody," and different things like that went along with it. And our place was the one that came up with the things, and Bill said, "Well, do it, fix that."

The first car we ran with a square-tube frame, we took it to Bristol, Tennessee. And it ran so quick that, Christ, it was going home, so we had it out there not even running. It was the first square-tube frame, and when you look at what's happened with that, it's still the same thing today, that's what they still use.

And now there's a little more safety bars in 'em, but back then they wouldn't let us put 'em in, they didn't want any more. They wouldn't let you do that.

The thing is, the thing that makes it work, it's like . . . Jeff Gordon. Jeff Gordon is lucky as hell he got out of Ford and into where he's at. If he'd've stayed where he was . . . I don't say Ford hasn't got something good, that was not the problem. The problem was, he got with a team that's doing what it's doing, and I don't think he'd have gotten with a team like that if he'd stayed where he was. And he's just lucky as hell . . . and he's a hell of a race driver, but you gotta have the people around you to do like they do at that place. Dedicated people. . . . His crew chief is really smart, he was a race driver before, and he knows what they're talking about. I don't think Jeff would ever get that where he was, right now, if he'd stayed somewhere else.

There's some people that are the same way. Like I said, there's people out there that can run up front all the time. It's the team that just doesn't seem to be able to get over the top, although there's quite a few people today that's really good at chassis setup and overseeing the people.

You go around to the shops and talk to the people and see what's going on—there's a lot of friction going on, the guy's a crew chief, and somebody's better than he is, and they don't get along or they half-assed get along. And there's little friction around all those teams. . . . Look at Earnhardt's team, it all fell apart because it got that way. If he got back now with the right kind of people, I think he'd be running up front again.

It's a complicated thing. . . . I'm training a guy that was with the Lajoie outfit, but the trouble was that the guy that was running that thing won't let him crew-chief a car, he won't let him do the setups. And this guy, I did it with him driving cars, and he learned his stuff, and he's studied stuff, he knows how to work it, and he knows why he works it. But the problem is to get that guy where he can do his thing, and I think he's gonna be in another place pretty soon.

But you just have to find some guy that's dedicated enough to study the whole situation. He spends hours going through chassis setups, to see what it comes out with on scales and all that stuff. He gets the background so he knows what's going on—but it's hard to find those people, they don't want to spend that much time on it. They make a lot of money, they don't have to do nothing. You know, I don't think there's anybody that works in those shops that's worth anything at all that doesn't make a thousand dollars a week.

So they should worry? [Laughs.] Just go to work and do what the man says, and the hell with anything else. There's new people that don't do that, they want to do something productive and learn something, but there are only a few of 'em.

A lot of things have taken place. . . . I've won races at times when you think, Boy, that was a heck of a deal—you was in a position where you didn't think it would happen and you wound up getting it done. But at other times you wonder why you didn't do it. . . . It's hard to think about some of those things that happened. When they happen it's a pretty great thing, but it gets lost, you forget a lot of stuff about that thing, too.

In February 1967 we went to the beach [Daytona] with Mario Andretti. It was at Riverside out there, and they were talking about putting him into a race car. And they said, "Hell, he's too little, he can't drive one of those things." So I got in on the thing and they said, "Just have him come, and we'll have a race car for him, we'll see if he's too little."

So that's what happened, it took us fourteen days to build a car, and took it down there. And he had a lot of practice, I drove the car and got it working, and there was some hesitation for him, because he'd never been in one in any place like that. Tried it at Riverside and other places and just never did anything.

When race time came, we had him up front and Freddy up front, with stock outfits. I had to run any car that ran out of our shop, and I had to be named as the owner, insurance-wise, and all that. But my partner, he thought, "Well, here, this is going on, now I've got Andretti;" he went to NASCAR and had Freddy change to his name instead of mine, because he figured, well, Freddy won the race.

Freddy ran second. It caused a big stink. Everybody said, "Well, there's no way you're gonna win when you get down there, you don't know where the hell he's going, he's gonna go off and hit everybody." He gets behind, he runs out of gas, he couldn't find where the pits were, he had a bad time. But boy, he'd run up front, he'd go back up front again, and hell, that car, there were all kind of write-ups in the paper about it. That was quite a big thing back then.

■ *In 1947, Bud Moore began his career as a driver along with Joe Eubanks, running a 1937 Ford flathead V-8. Initially Moore found his calling as a crew chief, and then as a car owner, dominating the modified circuit in the late 1940s and then transferring that success to the Grand National Circuit in the 1950s. By his own reckoning, Moore won a total of sixty-three races in his illustrious career, and the list of drivers who drove for him includes the likes of Speedy Thompson, Joe Weatherly, Buck and Buddy Baker, Bobby and Donny Allison, Benny Parsons, Dale Earnhardt, and Ricky Rudd. For his greatest day, Moore chose his victory at the 1978 Daytona 500, as Bobby Allison took the car to victory lane.*

Hell, they've been all great, every one of 'em's been great to me. Well, you know, winning Talladega three or four times in a row with Buddy Baker was one thing, then winning the Daytona 500 with Bobby Allison in 1978 was another thing, and I guess having Dale Earnhardt in the two years he drove for me was very exciting.

Had a lot of good times when Rick Rudd drove for us, won a lot of races, and going back into the early 1960s, when we won the championship with Joe Weatherly in 1962 and 1963. And one of my other thrills was winning the Southern 500 in . . . I believe it was

1956 and 1957, with Speedy Thompson and Buck Baker—we had both of those cars and both of those drivers, winning the championship then in 1957.

Baker, you know, he was running Chevrolets back then. I was the chief mechanic and stuff—however you want to call it, crew chief, whatever it was back then—on them two cars. . . .

We just won a lot of races back then. I think we must have run about forty-five or fifty races at that point, during that time, running 100-mile races here and there and all over the Southeast. It was a good deal, and getting on up to the 1960s, 1961. When Joe Weatherly started driving for me in 1961, I think we won twelve or fourteen races with him in 1961, and then in 1962, I don't remember how many we won, you can probably check the records somewhere.

And then winning the championship in 1962, and then turning around and coming right back and winning it in 1963. That was with Pontiac. We switched to Mercurys in the fall of 1963, and the first race we ran with a Mercury was in Darlington. I've been with Ford Motor Company ever since.

And going on up the ladder, we got into the 1970s, and we were the first to run a small-block engine, 350-cubic-inch engine, back in the early 1970s. And finally NASCAR done away with all the big engines, and went to the small-block engines back in . . . 1973 or 1974.

We went to Talladega—I had Buddy Baker start driving for me in 1974—we won three or four races back-to-back and ran second in the other two in Talladega with Baker. We won some other races during that year, that period of time. When Baker left me in 1977, we hired Bobby Allison in 1978, and we went to our first race at Daytona with him and won the Daytona 500, and that was a big thrill in my career.

We also left Daytona and went to Rockingham, and had Rockingham won, and Bobby had got hurt in a modified car about three or four months earlier, up in Minnesota. So we got to about fifty laps to go, and he had to have a relief driver, so we put his brother Donny in the car, and we ran second. The old silver fox, David Pearson, beat us, with about two laps to go. I don't remember how many races we won in 1978, but we won quite a few in 1979 and 1980 with Bobby Allison.

We had Benny Parsons in 1981, and we won the last race that NASCAR ran at College Station Texas down there in 1981 with Benny Parsons. And then . . . we had Dale Earnhardt for 1982 and 1983, and we won quite a few races with him, won Darlington and a few other races—you know, big races during that period of time.

I know this: that we led about every race we ever started in with Dale, and if we'd've had just a little bit better valve spring in that area, with just a little bit more knowledge of what we're doing right now with valve springs, we'd have probably won the championship with Earnhardt in 1982 and 1983, and probably [would have] won half the races we were in.

We had Rick Budd in 1984, and 1985 and 1986—we had him about four years I think. And we won races with him every year. I really enjoyed working with Ricky, he was a fine person and a heck of a good race driver. As you know, he just signed a deal to drive for Robert Yates, so I think that's gonna be a big change in his career— I'm anxious to see just what's gonna happen. Ricky can do the job, he's a heck of a good race driver, he knows how to win races, and he's won so many races, I'd just like to see him win a championship before he retires.

You have to go back in the sixty-three races I've won in my career, and hope to add some more. . . . I think you're gonna have to say [the greatest day] was the 1978 Daytona 500 with Bobby Allison, because the Daytona 500's the granddaddy of 'em all, even right now, you know, it's still rated the most, with Indianapolis. It's just the first race of the season, it's the biggest race that we ran, all the way up through the area, since NASCAR started. It's just one of the prestige races to have run, and to win the Daytona 500—that always gave you a heck of a good send-off, first of the year.

We had to outrun the Pettys. You know, Richard Petty was always strong there, and David Pearson; in fact, Buddy Baker ran good there—I'd say Baker and Petty and Pearson was our biggest competition. It was a thrill, you know, just to win that race. You can go back most of the time, if you look back over the charts and everything, you could name 'em on your hand, there was about five of us that won most of the races—not all of 'em—but I'm gonna say that we won ninety percent of 'em.

And I could always go to the racetrack, and once we practiced and qualified, I could about tell you who was gonna win the race. I could always, out of that five back then, I knew if he didn't have any wrecks or any problems, I knew who was gonna win the race. I could always tell how good his car was, one particular day, and how good he was getting around the racetrack, and this kind of stuff. You always knew for that day, where you [were]. . . . Myself, the Wood brothers, the Pettys, Junior Johnson, all of us, we sorta halfway knew before the race started who had the best car for that race for that day—you know what I'm talking about?

I think the biggest change that's come along with NASCAR was when we went to the small block engine, 357 cubic inches . . . 358, I believe it is. We started out when we ran the small block, with 530, 535, 540 horsepower. And now, who could ever believe that in that length of time now we're up to 750 with the same amount of cubic inches?

But the biggest thing that's happened, you know—back then we were turning the engines at around 7000, 7200, we got to turn them 7500, and then we got to turn them 7800. Now we're turning them 9000, so . . . it's hard to say. You couldn't have made me believe back in the 1970s or even in the 1980s that we would have had 750 horsepower out of those same engines today.

Because of the fact, you know, you say, "358 inches, that's all that's there," you know? And when we got up to 650 horsepower, I said, "Jesus Christ, it's gonna bottom out here." But it never did, it kept going, and all of a sudden we were running 700, and then the next thing you know it's 720, and now all of a sudden it slowed down, it didn't jump quite as fast, it went to 730 and then 735 and

740, and now it's up to 750. It's amazing, as far as the engines are concerned.

Chassiswise, the chassis's been about the same, because NASCAR's got a rule on the chassis itself and the roll-bar configuration and all this stuff. There hasn't been a whole lot of changes in the chassis itself, it's basically the same chassis we've been running for the last ten or twelve years. The biggest change has been the shock absorbers, the springs, and the tires. Right now, the technology is all in the shock absorbers and the swaybar and the springs and the tires.

Everybody's got the same chassis, as far as the steering geometry and all this kind of stuff, and about the best car you can buy on the market, if you go have one built, is the Hopkins. With all the engineering that's been put into that car, in that chassis, there ain't much changing you're gonna do unless NASCAR changes things around a little bit, if you're gonna do anything on that car.

But all the technology now is in the shocks, the springs, and the tires, so I don't know how far this technology's gonna go. I know you hear 'em talking about dropping the air pressure a pound, a half a pound, this kind of stuff—it affects the car quite a bit. This is true with the radial tire, it's the way the shocks are being done now, and all the engineers are working together now to get this; just exactly how they can do all this and keep the footprint of that tire on the pavement and get more grip, with the air pressure, the shocks, and the softer springs and the bigger swaybars.

I don't know how far this technology's gonna go, but everybody's really gonna have to get on the stick and go to work, because this is the way it's going. Some of the teams are really ahead of some of the others on it, some teams have got a lot of catching up to do. We've got some catching up to do right now, and we're getting people in the place now where we think we can get on the right road with the shock absorbers.

All the drivers were great that I had drive for me, I liked every one of 'em. We got along real good, all the ones that came along and drove for me over the years. I'm just thrilled to know that I had the acquaintance and the privilege to have these drivers drive for me. I liked every one of 'em, and they all done a heck of a good job, and I felt like we won races with those boys, and we won championships, every one was great.

I know we had a little better luck with some that we did the others. I'm just proud to know that I was associated with all these drivers that we did have, and we really had some really good relationships. They all were great, I loved working with Bobby Allison, I loved working with Ricky Rudd—the biggest thrill I had was working with Dale Earnhardt, trying to keep him calmed down.

I think there's a couple of things that need to be addressed that probably would help things a little bit better. I think that too much effort's being put on the qualifying part of the situation; this is making it very hard on everybody. I think that they should do away with the qualifying engines, [so that] you've gotta race the engine you qualify with.

And number two, I think that everybody should have to qualify with a full load of fuel just like they race, not qualifying with two gallons of fuel in the car and putting all that lead up in front of the car. The driver goes out and he spends the whole day on Friday trying to get things qualified. You go test and that's what everybody is doing is they're running qualifying setups; you don't run no race setup, everybody's running qualifying.

So if they made everybody qualify with a full load of fuel, that's the way you race, and then you would be more toward a race setup in the car than you would be qualifying setup. It would help everybody, and you wouldn't use up so many tires, it would cut a lot expense on that part. There's a couple or three things that I think, in my opinion now, that would help the situation, and I think it would help everybody a little bit better.

And that's one thing where you've got the multiple-car teams—single-car teams have only got so many tests, that's where the multiple-car teams are gaining on a lot of the guys. They have won by going to run the qualifying setups and this kind of stuff; they don't go run race setups, they go run qualifying setups.

You go test everybody just like we test over in Charlotte. We tested over there a few weeks ago, and when we got through, we hadn't run a total of about twelve or twenty-four laps on that car. Now, on the other car, we ran it the next day, and we probably ran it about fifteen or twenty laps. So all this was being done with no fuel, just two gallons, three gallons of fuel in it.

Now, if we'd have had a full load of fuel in there, the springs would have been different, the swaybar would have been different, the shocks would have been different, everything would have been similar to a race setup instead of a qualifying setup. When you do this, too, a couple of times we didn't get to qualify until on Saturday, and everybody's sitting there, no time to run race setups. . . . My idea of the whole thing is not qualifying, you go there to run a race.

I never dreamed [racing] would ever . . . I knew it was gonna get big, don't misunderstand me on that; I didn't think it was ever gonna reach the height that it's reached today. I do know that when we ran at Daytona in 1979, the first time it was worldwide-televised, the Daytona 500, and that deal with Cale Yarborough and Donny Allison wrecking and gettin' out fighting and all this stuff, that was the first worldwide coverage on TV. To me that's the first thing that really started things to rolling.

With the TV coming on board, and all the sponsorships and all the big money coming in, that's what made NASCAR what it is today. It's made a hell of a spectator sport out of it. . . . I mean, heckfire, when you sit down [in front of] your TV on Sunday and sit there for three hours on the edge of your seat watching a race, that's one of the biggest thrills going.

I tried to race back in 1947 when we first started—the biggest thing, my problem was, I took down too much fence. [Laughs.] I don't know what was wrong, I just did not have the driver talent to drive a race car, and with me and Joe Eubanks, me and him had the car together, so he started driving and doing real well, and I felt right then that the best thing for me to do is just build these cars and let somebody else do the driving.

I won some amateur races, quite a few of them back then, but still . . . I got a better kick out of, and I still do right today—instead of driving, my biggest thrill was to be the car owner. And I always felt like when I got to the racetrack, we lined up the cars out there, and they all lined up two abreast and got through playing the national anthem, they said, "Gentlemen, start your engines" . . . my biggest thrill came to me right then, to try to outrun all them other guys.

TED MUSGRAVE

■ *Ever wonder what goes through a driver's mind when he gets a truly big lead? A veteran of the Winston Cup circuit for the last decade, Ted Musgrave's greatest victory took him back to his ASA days when he posted a most memorable margin while winning an ASA race in Winchester, Indiana. Musgrave's other greatest day was an equally memorable Midwest victory in which he won an historic memorial day dedicated to the great Tony Bettenhausen.*

Well, actually, my greatest day in auto racing hasn't happened yet—let's put it that way, I know something's coming up here sooner or later.

All kidding aside, there's two that kind of stick out in my mind that. . . . It goes back a few years, too. You're sure that every day is one of your greatest days . . . like, "Wow, we ran really good and this and that," but if I really remember back growing up and going through the ASA ranks, a lot of Winston Cup drivers ran that series— Mark Martin has, Rusty Wallace, Dick Trickle, myself, Alan Kulwicki—a lot of 'em have gone through the ASA series.

I ran a race, it was in Winchester, Indiana, it was a very, very high bank, half-mile race track, which I believe they still race on occasionally, I believe it's called *Saturday Night Thunder,* or *Thursday Night Thunder,* something like that, where the USAC midgets and stuff run there.

If you watch it on TV you can understand what I was talking about—it's a very demanding race track, high speed, high banks . . . and then the ASA series, at the end of the season . . . I think when I won it they called it the Winchester 400. It was a very prestigious-type race, just due to the fact that it was very, very hard on the driver and very, very hard on the equipment.

And if you finished that . . . It was a feat to finish the race—if you finished on the lead lap, that was really, really great . . . I forget what year it was, too. I'm trying to remember it as I talk, but I can't right now, the years go by so fast. [*It was 1986.—Ed.*]

I actually qualified very well, I think I was either in the front row or the second row of the race, and in the course of the race my car was just working flawlessly—for some reason everything clicked, and I was able to lap the field *twice*. [Guys say], well, I won by a half a car-length, or I won by this or that . . . I'm talking two laps on the field.

Now, I'm running around there like you're saying, and you're thinking, "Oh my goodness, I'm leading this thing, I'm leading this thing," and you keep going, and you think something's gonna happen, your luck is gonna run out sooner or later. But as it wound down to even the last ten laps of the race . . . I mean, you're listening to every little thing in the car, thinking, "Oh, boy, something's gonna happen." You hear noises and things, and you're feeling things that you probably never felt before.

It's really something to win this thing, and here you get a chance, and not just by trying to chase somebody down or fend somebody off—here I am leading this thing by a couple laps.

And I even . . . Just to break the monotony, of the tenseness—I think it was with ten laps to go—I asked the guys if I could come in and get a hot dog. You're so keyed-up, so I pushed the button and talked to the crew, and radioed and said, "Hey guys, I know I've got two laps. . . . I'm hungry, could I get a hot dog?"

It was one of those deals where you just give a sigh of relief after you say that, just to kind of get if off your chest. It was kind of funny, and sure enough, I do believe . . . I think we did back off our pace, and I think I may have lost one lap back to the second-place guy and won by one lap on the overall. Because they did say, "Okay, we've got the thing in the bag, don't push it." At one time I'd say we were two laps up, and I think we won the race by a lap over the field.

Oh, you had your ASA regulars, your Butch Millers, Mike Eddy— if you look back through the years, we had very, very stiff competition there. Maybe Dick Trickle might have been there. Mark Martin was not there, I know that for sure, because he would have won that thing by two laps. You have your Bob Sennekers, your . . . Gosh, there was a group of people.

But at that particular time, like I say, I had a very good race car that day, and the crew was great. I mean, you could not have picked a day where everything went right, that one just . . . everything went perfectly right.

That was a big key to winning that race, was having a car that was flawless, where it would do everything you wanted it to do. . . . It was like, everything was in your command. Anything it wanted it to do. I mean, if you dreamed up a perfect situation handling the car, and this good—because at this particular racetrack, you're kind of on the edge, it's almost like running the Bristol, Tennessee, of NASCAR.

You could change your line and still have the car work good, you could pass the guys on the high side, you could pass 'em on the low side, you could do just about anything you wanted to do, within reason. It would work, it's like, "Boy, I can't believe this thing's working so good, we come off the corner nice and straight and fast," and when you get something like that, you can do more things than anybody else can in the race, because you can pass anybody at any time, where some guys would have to wait until a certain corner, where they're a little bit better than their competition.

Ours was better everywhere on the racetrack.

It's kind of unusual, but not really, because if you go back through the history, its a very demanding race, and if you go back through . . . I think nowadays that you won't see this, because the competition is so much better, equipment is so much better. But as you back up through the years, you see that winners, maybe only three cars finished in the lead lap, or two, and then maybe eighth place could be even six laps down or eight laps down. So there was a pretty good spread in there.

The series actually is a pretty good traveling series that goes on anywhere from the Midwest, sometimes up into the Canada area. And it was very highly regarded as a good training ground . . . people from there would get into a higher level of racing, go into the Winston Cup or the Busch Grand National or anything like that. It was like the premier traveling series without having the top level.

It's a series also that, not only did you have experience at longer races, there were pit stops involved, because of the long duration—every race was anywhere from two hundred to three hundred to four hundred laps. That kind of keyed a guy on making your decisions in the pits as far as tire adjustments, or tire-pressure adjustments—having a very good pit crew to keep you on the lead lap during those times, and a crew chief that would calculate a lot of things out on this deal, too. It wasn't just . . . you jump in the car and you were a one-man band—it took everybody to make it right, kind of like it is right now in Winston Cup.

Well, actually, victory lane, it was kind of unique, because it was set up right on the front stretch, right under the flag stand, we'd start the car there. And then, I believe at this particular time they still weren't on the national TV, live deal, but they had a lot of radio, a lot of press. It was kind of neat because lot of the drivers and drivers that had driven in that race that were retired, more or less, they all came out and shook your hands.

And man, that was a great showing, to see something like that. You're getting bombarded from a lot of people, a lot of pictures, a lot of things—it's kind of everything everybody dreamed of having, on a lower scale. Naturally, if you get in your uniform and win your Winston Cup and stuff like that, there's so much more hype. . . . You're talking as big as you can get without having live TV on you right there.

It's something to remember—you go back with some pictures, of that particular race, and you're showing . . . there's twenty people, your crew, and everybody all kneeling by the tire. And you've got the trophy queen, you had the track promoter shaking your hand, just a bunch of stuff like that going on.

And it was in the fall time of the year, too, it was toward the end of the racing season. And to finish up the year with that, you know, on a high note, was kind of a lot of momentum for the whole winter and the upcoming year. Sure, it might happen, you have it happen early in the year, and things don't go very good at the end of the year, it kind of sours that—what do you want to call it—that memory, that pride of what you've accomplished. But having it at the end of the year, that kind of lingers in your mine . . . all through the winter, it just sticks with you, so that was really good.

Nope, nope . . . I didn't get the hot dog. It was kind of funny, like I say, it was just because you could tell through the voice of the crew chief, about what was going on, okay—you know, lap times, where the second-place [car] was, and the laps counting down. You could tell the tension and the anxiety in his voice, because it would actually be possible that we were gonna do this, pull this off. It was a nail-biter, and I just had to do that, to kind of breathe a little bit, to feel a little better.

The other one was actually in Cherieville, Indiana, a place called Iliana Motor Speedway. It was another deal at the end of the year, it was the Tony Bettenhausen Memorial.

Now, this is a half-mile racetrack, flat, and this racetrack has been there for . . . I think this year may be its last year in existence, because of the growth around that area, the Gary, Indiana, area. But the race-track has so much history, and even my father, when he raced, raced there. And I imagine this racetrack probably . . . in the late 1950s was in existence.

In this particular race, it was the crown jewel of the racetrack, the end of the year. The very last race was a thing called the Bettenhausen Memorial. Oh, my goodness. Through the years, all the people that race anywhere in the Midwest, always came to that race to try and win the field. Even my dad tried, my brother had raced, he tried, a lot of different big-name race-car drivers probably went through if you look at the history, who won this deal—it's very unique to win this race.

I had the fortune of winning this race back in . . . I think it was either the year before or the year after I won the Winchester race. The same group of people, same crew, same owner, all that. And that was really memorable, because my dad was there, my sisters were there, and I know my dad, he's raced in that race, I don't know how many times, and came close to winning but never got the chance to win it.

And I did. And he was in there, we took pictures in victory lane, he was with me and all that kind of stuff, so that one really kind of sticks out in my mind, too.

That one wasn't nearly as easy as the other one was. But there again, with this car and this crew that I had, we were really on the cutting edge of being the really top dog everywhere we went. The car was very, very good, it was maintained well, and the race kind of played out that way, too.

We were probably, if I remember it, were not the fastest car in the qualifying, but we had a very good-handling and consistent car, which you needed at this type of racetrack. It was only a 100-lap feature, and I do believe there may not have been any pit stops. I think it was a straight-through 100-lap race.

It was a racetrack, too, where you just had to more or less pace yourself to the end, and save yourself—don't beat the car up, don't wear the tires out. And . . . I'm trying to remember, because this was so long ago, I think we just kind of worked our way up silently, just kind of easily creeping our way up toward the front of the race.

I don't think we really led that thing until the very end of the race, of it may have been with twenty laps to go, or something like that, to take the lead out and just kind of run away from 'em, because everybody just kind of ran so hard in the beginning of the race, to take the rabbit too fast. They wore themselves down, where I just kind of was the tortoise, where I just kind of hanged on and at the end stepped on it, and got the win.

It's so hard to remember. If you're looking at the race twenty-four years now, every race in my life, every year for twenty-four years, I try to pick one out, how it played out—it's pretty tough. Don't get me wrong, I do see highlights every now and then. I know the car, what it looked like, and the number, and things like that. But how the race played out was pretty tough to remember. I do remember it just faintly, that that's the way it went out.

Butch Miller finished second to me in the Winchester race, I remember that. Butch Miller now is in the NASCAR truck series. The one that happened at Iliana, I do not remember that one. Just about every hot dog that was in the Midwest—Wisconsin, Illinois, Indiana, Ohio, Michigan—it was a regional deal.

The track itself, they were both half-mile racetracks, but they were completely different as far as the banking, and how you had to attack the racetrack. See, Winchester, that racetrack, you had to attack it, but you had to respect it a little bit, like they do at Darlington, where if you're not on the ball and you're not thinking every inch of the way, you can run into the wall, because at Winchester you run right along the top of the wall in three and four, I mean just inches away.

At Iliana Motor Speedway, it's just the opposite, it's a flat racetrack, it's kind of like . . . Oh, I'm trying to compare it to a modern racetrack that we run on. You know, you run on the bottom of the groove, right along the white line in the corners, it's flat. . . . The asphalt, I don't think it's ever been repaved, so it chewed up the tires real good. So you had to more or less not attack that racetrack, because that's what a lot of people did, they just went out and attacked the racetrack.

My theory was, okay, you just kind of think about the race car, you conserve the race car to the end. So, yeah, both racetracks had similar characteristics, but you had to drive them differently, and you kind of had to pace yourself differently between the two.

The Bettenhausen race at Iliana also had a trophy more or less like they have at the Indianapolis Motor Speedway, where your name was engraved on part of the plaque, they had squares on the trophy. And your name went on there, and it was like a traveling trophy. You actually didn't get that trophy, it stayed with the racetrack and on display at the racetrack, and your name was on there with all the win-ners from all the previous years, dating back to . . . oh, man, it must have been the mid-1950s or something like that, early 1960s.

We're talking, I think this was . . . I want to say somewhere around 1986. There was a lot of names on that trophy. If you go back, you know, born and raised in that area, and going to that race-track for many years, even when my dad started racing and raced there, I'd be in the grandstands, and I'd hear all these names of drivers, all rattled off through the PA system. And then winning that race and looking back through that trophy, on the names, I can re-member some of those names going back to when my dad raced. But even still, at that particular time, there was a lot of names on that tro-phy where it's a regional type, where you may have seen a Tom Rapp or a Dick Trickle, or . . . Joey Fair from Michigan, that was always a threat over in that area.

Their names were on that trophy also, all your champions from all around the Midwest that come to this race every year. Only one's gonna win, and their name's gonna be on that trophy. And so it goes back, there's plenty of real good race-car drivers that ran that race, but never got their name on the trophy.

Well . . . [both of those races] meant a lot, like I say, going back to the Winchester race. I've won some ASA races, but those were okay, and I beat 'em by three seconds, or whichever, and it was kind of just a ho-hum deal. Where the Winchester was kind of a . . . well, that was like a crown jewel also, that was a very demanding race, very tough—very few have repeated wins there. And to win by such a margin, to have a flawless day like that, that kind of stood out, the circumstances of how we won it. And then the other one, the Iliana racetrack, that was just something, the win itself, to me . . . Deep down, okay, I know my dad's tried to win this race, my brother's tried to win this race, a lot of my friends have tried to win this race.

And I've had the fortune of succeeding and winning it, and actu-ally, I can say it was a racetrack my dad ran weekly throughout the years. And I'd be at the racetrack before I even started racing, helping him on his car at these races.

Well, it turns around where I'm the one racing and he's in the pits, and I won the race. So that was very memorable. I don't think he said a whole lot, he was smiling so much, because a lot of his friends that he raced against were there, too, with their sons and stuff, and he was just getting congratulated by his friends and people, his competition that he ran against.

It was kind of like the end of the year, it was almost like a family reunion of race-car drivers. He had a proud moment himself, even though he didn't get a chance to win it, he was there when his son won it, and had all his friends there, too, watching—that kind of thing.

It's about the career, you know, even though I'm in Winston Cup here and we're doing a lot of stuff, those still really rank right up to the top of anything I've done, just because, more or less what I said, the Iliana, what happened is because my dad raced on the racetrack. My dad has not raced on a Pocono, Pennsylvania, or a Michigan, or places like that.

Here it was winning a race on stomping grounds where your dad competed in, your brother competed in, that's kind of what really sets it on top. I could probably win a race in the Winston Cup series, and—don't get me wrong, it's gonna be very, very memorable—but at the same token, I believe it has more family value inside in the heart to win that particular race than it would right now to win a race where, maybe a racetrack that my dad has never even seen before, or anything like that.

It just goes back to a former feeling. . . . It had a lot more value to it back then than it does now.

■ *Back in the early 1980s, Gary Nelson was crew chief for Bobby Allison when Allison won his first Winston Cup championship, outdueling Darrell Waltrip during a grueling season in which the drive for the title finally came down to the last race at Nelson's "hometown" track in Riverside, California. But Nelson's greatest accomplishment in racing occurred a decade later, after he became a NASCAR official, when the man known as NASCAR's "traffic cop" helped design and implement a life-saving technical innovation that finally ended a long-standing safety problem that had claimed the lives of many drivers over the years.*

Probably the day that we tied up the Winston Cup championship in 1983. It really . . . was the end of a long year, so it's part of the greatest year that I had.

But the day—it was a real close points race between Bobby Allison and Darrell Waltrip in the 1983 season, and as the season wore on we traded the points lead back and forth, and both teams were very competitive and very strong. There was quite a rivalry between Junior Johnson's team with Darrell Waltrip driving, and our team with Bobby Allison driving.

Everybody, it seemed like—media, fans—had chosen sides, and it was pretty well split, kind of like the Hatfields and McCoys almost, sometimes. But as we went through the season it went back and forth, and finally we had a couple strong runs in the fall that put us a little bit ahead, you know, the last few races.

We got to Riverside, which was the last race of the season in those days. And the day of the race, we felt pretty comfortable, the car was running fast, and the crew was on top of their game, and Bobby Allison was known for being a road-race driver. Everything was going in our favor, the oddsmakers were kind of betting on us, and the first lap of the race we get a flat tire.

And we come in the pits, and change the tire, and we don't lose a lap, but we're dead last. And so everybody, all the mathematicians, everybody took out their calculators, and said, Well, if Darrell Waltrip finishes where he is, and Bobby Allison finishes where he is, the championship goes to Darrell. I don't remember where we qualified, you could look it up, and I don't remember where Darrell qualified, either. But I do remember . . . our plan was to protect our points lead, not try to win the race. So we stayed with our strategy, and the yellow flag came out, and we were able to at least close up to the back of the pack even though we were still pretty much running last.

And so I thought, Well, we'll just take our time and move through traffic, and everything will sort out. We had to finish within a couple or a few positions of Darrell, even if he won the race, we had to be, you know, I think in the top five. He was up running pretty competitively, and we were back in the pack some, so there was way too many positions between us and him for us to win the championship.

And so we started slowly moving up, and next thing you know, Darrell and Tim Richmond get tangled up coming off the last turn, and spin off the track, I'd say, in the first third of the race. So all of a sudden our emotions are just the other way—Hey, we're doing fine, Darrell's the one that's having the trouble now.

But he got going—he was behind us, but he got going again, and there was a yellow flag, and he really didn't have any damage, he was just behind us. And we weren't really all that far up in the pack, but we were in pretty good shape, so we started feeling pretty good again.

And then we had another flat tire to put us behind again. So now Darrell's up ahead of us, and we're back down in the dumps, we're down in the hole again, it's probably near the halfway point or so, not quite halfway yet. [It was] just punctures, it's abnormal to have two in one race, but it is normal to have flat tires. We were wondering if it was meant to be or not.

Then, as we were gaining on Darrell again to catch him, the engine started to miss, and as we went father into the race, the engine missed more and more. And then clouds came in and it started to rain, they stopped the race under a red flag, and here we are with an engine that, we don't know what's wrong with it, but it's not running right, and Darrell is ahead of us.

So we're in trouble, we're gonna lose the championship. But then it stopped raining, and the race restarted, and we were able . . . The car would smooth out enough that it was able to move back up through the back, and we got ahead of Darrell. And we started feeling pretty good again, and then it started to rain again.

So the race kept dragging under caution. It wasn't a hard rain, it was just a light rain, but enough to where they put out the caution. Finally, we were riding under caution thinking, "Man, if this race restarts, we've still got an engine that's not running right, and Darrell's still got a great chance of beating us."

And then all of a sudden NASCAR put out the checkered flag and called it a day for rain, so we became the champions right then.

That was quite an emotional roller coaster, but it was my greatest day. A little bit of everything—you're vying at the end of a year of intense competition and now it's the last race, in that intense of an environment. My mind ran the gamut from, "I wonder if there's a sharpshooter going after our tires" . . . I mean it, it just went everywhere. I just couldn't figure . . . "Okay, everything's all right, we're back on top," and something else would happen.

It was such a roller coaster of emotions—more, "Okay, there's no way we can have any more problems, we've had more than three or four races' worth of problems in a half of a race, so it's gotta end." And then all of a sudden something else would happen.

I guess if I were to describe what was going through my mind, [it] was . . . victory, defeat, victory, defeat—you know? Which is a long way apart from running midpack and just being there. We were really working hard for that championship, and to see it go away and then come back and then go away and come back, and then finally come back, and have the weather, which we thought was gonna put us into the loser category—all of a sudden the weather came back and caused the race to end early, which put us in the win category. So we were cursing the rain at one moment, and all excited that it was raining later.

The season in 1983 was race-to-race for our team. We wanted to win every race that we could and we raced hard, right up until that last race, when we finally got a little bit of a points lead, [when] all we have to do is protect our lead.

In doing that, that strategy change may have been part of what threw our rhythm off, or whatever you may call it, where we were so well-focused on winning and each race all season, and doing whatever it took to get that car up front. All of a sudden we're racing a conservative strategy, which we had never done.

And that conservative strategy may have been part of our problem, you know, with the engine miss. . . . Maybe Bobby had been [taking] more conservative lines through the turns and picked up debris in the tires, whatever it might have been. As we analyzed it later, we thought if we ever had the opportunity to do that again, we would not go to the conservative strategy, we would just race like we knew how to race, what got us to that point.

It went through our minds, and I think Bobby kind of picked up the pace after the second flat tire, and drove more aggressively. But from a crew-chief standpoint, I never gave the orders, or I never changed the agreed-upon strategy that we had done as a team before the race.

I knew Bobby well enough to know that he had a little bit left in him, and he was reaching down deep to make up the ground from the flat tires, and I didn't say anything about, "Hey, you need to slow down," or anything like that, I just pretended like, "Okay, we're all sticking to our strategy."

Well, the champion, in those days, if you didn't win the race, just went to the garage. And so we drove the car into the garage, and . . . one thing I remembered about it was it was Bill Elliott's first Winston Cup win, he won the race. And there were a lot of Bill Elliott fans that were very excited that he had just won the race, and most of them were Bobby Allison fans that were very excited that he had just won the championship.

So we were getting surrounded in the garage by well-wishers and congratulations from all over, and then the people would run up to the winner's circle, which was about two hundred yards away, and do the same for Bill Elliott. So media, fans, everybody, were really making that trip back and forth quite often, I remember the crowd staying for hours after the race.

One of the reasons, maybe, was that we were underneath the roof of the garage, and it was still raining. But I've got pictures of that celebration, and every time I see 'em, I remember all of the individuals, and all the efforts, and how proud I was of the whole team. And in my mind, Riverside, California, was my home track. I grew up just a few miles from there, and began my racing career by sneaking over the fence to watch stock-car races when I was very young. And all my friends and relatives were in attendance, where any other race they couldn't come to, in the South or in the East.

We went to the track a week early, and we practiced at the track, and I remember we had two cars, and we tried both cars to see which one was the most consistent. Not so much the fastest, but the most consistent. As we were preparing—this is a week before the race, there was a weekend off on the schedule—we were having a hard time trying to determine which car we were gonna race, in the final race, they were both so equal.

And I said, "Let me help you, Bobby." And I got in one car, and Bobby got in the other car, and we held a drag race down the back straightaway, which was about a mile long, to see which car . . . You know, rather than Bobby drive one car, get out and drive the other car, just to see which car had the best acceleration, at least that might be the tiebreaker.

And so, Robert Yates was the engine builder, and several other guys got up on the bridge that was about three-quarters of the way down the back straightaway. And they would watch as Bobby and I came around the last turn side by side, and we would both hit the throttles the same time and come up through the gears and see which car was ahead when we got to the end of the straightaway.

Well, the car I was in was faster, I beat Bobby to the end of the straightaway. And we . . . did it several times, and each time the car I was in was quicker. And we came back to the garage, and Robert Yates said, "Now I've built both these engines, and I know that other engine's better."

And Bobby said, "Well, let's switch cars." So we switched cars, and I was driving the other one, and we did the same thing, and I beat him again.

We got back to the garage, and everybody was scratching their heads, and finally Bobby Allison said . . . "Gary, what rpm are you shifting at?" And I said, "About 8200." And Robert Yates just about had a heart attack, because he had given instructions to Bobby to shift at 7900. But I hadn't heard that—I was shifting at 8200, and the engines weren't designed to go above 8000.

So Robert thought both of his engines now had been overrevved, but it turned out to be okay. I was revving it a little higher before I would shift each time, not knowing—I thought the engines would stand that rpm. But Robert had gone with a conservative engine in both cars, and everybody was kind of befuddled as to how I could beat Bobby Allison in his own car and then switch cars and then beat him again.

Well, we had lost the championship the year before, to Darrell Waltrip and Junior Johnson, and they were pretty confident going into the 1983 season that they could beat us again. And so we were a little pissed off that we'd got beat the year before, we looked at what we did wrong, and we had tried to address that in the off-season without losing the strengths that we had.

. . . It was a close race, championship race, in 1982, but we ended up on the short side of it. And in that last race, our car wasn't very competitive, what it needed to be, because we went into the race behind in the points. We needed to have a strategy where we would win the race or run as well as possible, to get as many positions ahead to make up that deficit.

Well, that may have been a little bit of what caused us to drop out in 1982. And so that really played on our minds in 1983, and gave us that strategy to be conservative. I think the thing, if you asked me what really sticks out through the season, was the intense competition between myself and Junior Johnson, as really the focal point—or the managers of the two teams, the leaders actually of the two teams going flat-out for the championship.

Junior seemed to have unlimited resources at that time, and we didn't have the money or the support—at least we didn't feel like we did—that Junior had. But we were still able to hang in there. And we had a bunch of guys that we felt like had one thing that they didn't have, and that was the determination, especially in Bobby Allison, who had never won a championship in all his years of racing.

And that turned out, after he's retired now, to be his only championship, after having such a great career. And Bobby Allison had actually driven for Junior Johnson at one time, and came up short on a championship.

It wasn't . . . We never had any wrestling matches, but we certainly didn't invite each other to dinner, either. There was a few bumps and bangs on the racetrack, and a few pit-stop strategies that were less than, uh, sportsmanlike, where a tire maybe leapt in front of the car from the other team or something, that would cause a delay in the pit stop. There was a lot of very intense competition among some very intense competitors who knew everything in the book. There was not an idea that wasn't tired, I don't think.

The hard part was trying not to get caught up in the emotions of it, and sticking to the performance on the racetrack, and let that speak. But as everybody knows, Darrell Waltrip is very good at the psychological part of the sport, and definitely, he was at the peak of his game in those days.

So we would constantly be getting barbs, or shots, through the media, or whatever. And because of his wit, and his ability to make those kind of comments or remarks, the media would flock to Darrell, get his comments, and then rush over to us and ask for a response.

And it's very hard, especially for me, I was just . . . I was pretty young, I didn't have much maturity in those days, and, "Hey, he said this about you, what do you say?" It was very difficult not to get involved in that.

We couldn't compete with that psychological game—I mean, our answers would come out sounding dumb. . . . "Well, we'd say, sticks and stones can break our bones . . ." But obviously he would get to us here and there, and kind of angered us sometimes. But in retrospect, you look back and say, Well, that was part of the strategy, you know? And he was very good at it.

Since I've been with NASCAR, the day that I witnessed the roof flaps work, to me, gave me the biggest sense of accomplishment of anything that we've done. We worked very hard to try to make the cars, at the top speeds, when they would spin, to stay, to keep all four tires on the ground. And we weren't getting very far, we were trying every idea we could think of. . . . Monday, Tuesday, Wednesday, we would be off testing anything anybody could think of, to try to solve this problem.

And we came up with the idea for what is now known as the roof flaps late in the fall, and I don't remember the year exactly, but I think it was 1993, late in the fall of 1993, to make these roof flaps. And we made a decision, really in December, to make every change that was gonna compete at Daytona the next February, which was two months away; to have these roof flaps on the car.

And a lot of guys called us up and said, "Are you crazy? This is a lot of work, and a lot of trouble, and you don't even know if they work." And obviously we couldn't ask somebody to drive their car 200 mph to spin out just so we could see if the roof flaps worked.

So we weren't sure. . . . We thought so, but we weren't sure. And, you know, every team had to buy three or four sets of these roof flaps, put 'em in their car, and come to Daytona. Well, the roof flaps cost about $1,100 a set, and times—you know, in the Winston Cup and the Busch series—a hundred and twenty-five teams, each of them buying three sets or so. . . . There was a lot of other people's money spent.

And I was getting a lot of heat from these guys that were spending this money for an unknown commodity, you know? "Will it work? Well, I'll spend this money, but will it work?"

"We don't know."

And so we're sitting there, or at least me, completely nervous. . . . I mean, I was really concerned that the first guy spins out and his car is airborne, that they're gonna lynch me on the nearest tree.

We got into the 125s that year at Daytona, and Richie Petty, who is Kyle Petty's cousin, was the first one to spin exactly in a spot, and at the speeds where in the past he would have tumbled. It turns out, his wheels, his back wheels, got airborne, the roof flaps popped open, and his back wheels went back down on the track.

And me watching that, and seeing it happen, and knowing that the roof flaps did their job, gave me the biggest sense of accomplishment and pride and, you know, just a good feeling, that, hey, they're not gonna lynch me, number one, and number two, it really did work and it may do a lot to change the sport. You don't know what would be different, but we do know that it wouldn't be as good as it is now.

Our answer to all of the people that really lodged or logged a complaint, or even a concern—"Hey, we're spending this money, we're doing all this work on our cars, is this thing gonna work?" Our answer was, from the beginning, "We don't know."

So everybody knew what our position was—"We think it'll work, we've done a lot of testing, a lot of drawings and engineers, and everything we can get our hands on tells us it'll work, except for, the real test has not been done."

[Richie Petty's] mother gave me a big hug—I'll always remember that. [There were] comments and articles and stories . . . news stories, that kind of thing. "This is a neat thing, how come nobody thought of it sooner?"

At the end of the year that year we got recognized. . . . I don't remember what the name of the award was, but they give you a trophy, and Jack Roush [got] a trophy. I've never been big on trophies, so I accepted it, thanked everybody, and put it in the attic. We just went about our business of trying to make the sport better. I've kept 'em, but I don't know what to do with 'em—pass 'em down to the grand-kids, or whatever.

■ *After starting his career as a motocross driver, Joe Nemechek switched over to the stocks in the late 1980s, making his way up the ranks before winning a Busch Grand National championship in 1992 with his own team and making his Winston Cup debut the following year. Nemechek won a pair of particularly memorable races that year: the first, a show-down with Dale Earnhardt at what was then NASCAR's newest venue in Miami, Florida; the second, a particularly eventful final race in which he finished sixth and picked up enough points to edge Bobby Labonte and win the championship. Nemechek won his first Winston Cup race at Loudon in 1999.*

Greatest day in auto racing. . . . Hmmm . . . tough one. Well, I guess the year would be 1992. We were racing at Homestead, and . . . we qualified really good, and then at the start of the race, we had a miss in the motor. Evidently they broke a spark plug when they put 'em in, before we rolled it out on the line.

They started the race, and the thing was missing—bad missing—and we got a lap down, and they got it fixed. Well, we made up our lap, it was toward the beginning of the race, they went a long-enough time where we got lapped. Made up our lap, came just about all the way back around and got up in the top ten under green. . . . The car was awesome.

And went through pit stops, took the lead of the race. And we led the last portion of the race, and toward the end, that's when Dale Earnhardt was still running Busch, it got down to him and I had a two- or three-lap shoot-out.

We bumped, and banged, and the last couple laps . . . I knew where he needed to run to go fast, and he kind of knew where I needed to run to go fast, so neither of us was giving. And we rubbed each other hard. . . . One thing I remember was coming off the corner, my corner was full of smoke from rubbing tires with him, and I looked over at him coming off the corner, and I think he was looking at me—he was just smiling.

And we raced down the back straightaway, I got ahead of him, and he gave me a pretty good tap on the rear end and turned me sideways. And it's the last corner, last lap, he turned me sideways, and I just stood on the gas, wide open, and it slid sideways all the way around the corner, and I beat him by a fender.

I knew where he needed to be to run good, and I wasn't gonna let him run there, because I could run a couple different lines, so I was making him run a line that his car wouldn't work in. Dale and I were good friends, and he had helped me out a number of times—sponsored me the year before; he's one of the greatest people that I know, I mean he really helped me and my family get going in racing.

I'm trying to remember what he told me after the race. I felt I had a better car, and I wasn't gonna give an inch. I mean . . . just like he would do to me, he made me earn it. And I think that's what he told me after the race in victory lane—he came up, and he was all smiles, and he says, "Made you earn that one."

Yes, he did.

That was back in 1992, and we could run two-wide. Since then, the groove hasn't been too wide. . . . I mean, the track was real raceable, and it was one of the closest races they ever had there.

That track has always been one for me that I've always really enjoyed and really ran fast at, and run good. The years prior to that— we went there in 1991, I think, and we had run extremely fast every time we'd ever been there.

Well, I was really excited, really excited. . . . And to beat the man, you know? He was the man back then, and to race with him side by side and beat him—it was pretty neat.

That was a long time ago. . . . I've won some races since then. What'd we do to celebrate? I think we went out to eat that night—we went out and ate lobster. Our sponsor was Texas Pete Hot Sauces, and the lady that runs it, Kathryn Garner, she took us out to this big seafood joint, and everybody had lobsters.

It was a big year for us, we were having our best year ever. We won two races, and sat on the pole a few times, ended up coming down to the last race to decide who was gonna get the championship, either myself or Bobby Labonte.

And the last race was at Hickory Motor Speedway, and we had to finish at least sixth or better, and Bobby had to win. And Bobby was having an awesome day; he was leading, and actually he got me a lap down, or it was almost a lap down, at one point in time. And somebody wrecked, and we managed to stay on the lead lap.

For myself . . . I mean, we got spun-out like six times that day, people were running into us, and it was the most unbelievable day I've ever had at the racetrack, as far as getting wrecked. And, yeah, here it was the race that would determine the championship, and for some reason everybody, you know, I felt it was like everybody ganged up on me. We actually hit the wall, and the car was all tore to pieces after the race.

But we ended up finishing sixth. I just had to regroup. I knew what my goal was, and that was to win the championship. We weren't running real good, we were running okay, but not real good, but our car was working good enough where we could get by a lot of guys. It seemed like we'd always be at the back end of the field, and they'd restart the race, we'd have to work our we up, but we always seemed to do it.

It was awesome—we knew what we had to do, and when that race was over, it was just a big relief. We were so excited, and, I mean, we had worked so hard all year, and [had] limited funds, as far as sponsorhip money. And the years before that, we were really struggling, as far as financially, with no sponsor and stuff, and then to win . . . It was awesome.

I had a lot of confidence before that race, because we had outrun him at a lot of other tracks before that. We won at Indy, and we should have won a few other races that year and gave 'em away. My confidence was high, and our team was awesome.

We had a couple things happen, a really disappointing race at Bristol. . . . We qualified decent, and the first lap, when they dropped the green flag, it broke an A-frame. And we lost like sixty laps changing the A-frame at Bristol.

I mean, every one of 'em is special, that's why it's so hard, but that's one that's most memorable in my head. Just being out there, and coming from behind, being a lap down, and making that up and coming back to the front and racing with the best there is in the business, and beating him. That happened on another occasion, at Richmond, you know, we were a lap down, and came back and won the race, too.

There's been a lot of things that have happened. . . . It's just gaining more knowledge each year. It's figuring out what you need to do with the race cars to make 'em better, I mean, there's so many variables that go into a race team. And I'm learning something new every time I go out.

Greatest day on the Winston Cup circuit . . . See, there's so many of 'em. Probably one of the greatest ones was, we sat on the pole twice in one year—one of 'em at the inaugural race out in California, and one at Pocono. All that stuff happened close to the time my son was born. . . . I mean, we've had some great runs in the Winston Cup car.

They're all exciting—sitting on the pole at California was a pretty awesome deal. I'd have to say that race would be number one, and winning the championship would be number two. . . . I mean, I overcame a lot of odds in both of 'em, but just being out there racing with Dale Earnhardt and Mark Martin and all the rest of 'em that were there—it was a neat day. I've had a number of poles in the Busch car and the Cup car—to get a pole in a Winston Cup car is pretty tough to do, and I've been fortunate enough to get two of 'em.

And we've led a lot of races, and we just can't capitalize on that first win. Hopefully that'll come soon. Just trying to be more consistent, trying to get better every week, but be consistent and finish races. [I've] just been involved in a lot of accidents and had a lot of dumb things go wrong, and you can't have that happen.

COTTON OWENS

■ *Cotton Owens won a total of fifty-four races in NASCAR's modified division in 1950 and 1951, including an almost unfathomable twenty-four in a row. He won the modified championship in 1953 and 1954, then switched over to become a mechanic in 1959 when the Daytona International Speedway opened, running part-time and sharing his car with a stable of great Dodge drivers, starting in 1963. Owens chose a series of Daytona moments at his greatest days, starting with winning the pole at the first televised Daytona 500 in 1960, along with some of his great runs at the old beach course in the mid- and late 1950s.*

I guess going to Daytona in 1960 and winning the first live-television race for the pole position—we had a race there for the pole, it was televised live. I guess I'd say that was one of the greatest.

. . . Mostly Pontiacs were the fastest cars then; I guess we had about six Pontiacs. As well as I remember, we ran pretty near side by side the whole race, the four cars, and I was fortunate enough to win it; it was Fireball [Roberts], Jack Smith, and, I believe, it was Joe Weatherly. I won it, I think Jack was second, I don't remember the other positions. I broke the rear axle in the race itself—it happened fairly early, I'm not too sure, I think I was either leading it or running second when I broke the axle.

I thought it was CBS that televised the race at the time, I'm not sure. Ingemar Johansson, champion of the world, was there at that time. As I remember, it was live, I might have spoken him while I was in the car, that was about it.

I won the race in 1957 and set a track record for the mileage that still stands. They didn't break the record in 1958, and that was the last race on the beach. So I won that race; also, I won two modified races in 1953 and 1954, so I loved that beach.

The beach was over four miles long, and we ran up the beach, we ran from south to north, and then we came down the pavement on the back straightaway, which was a narrow two-lane road. Then you had really gear down and brake to get in the south turn, because you ran a whole lot faster, I think, down the pavement than you did on the beach, because the sand let you slip so much.

It was just a racing tire we ran on, that I believe Firestone came out with, I don't even think Goodyear was in it at that time. They'd been running at different places—I didn't even use any brakes going into the north turn—we put it into a long, broad slide which automatically slowed you down so that you could gear the rest of the way.

The south turn you strictly had to use the gear on the engine through the transmission to get slow enough to get into the south turn, because you didn't have enough brakes on the car back then—we ran stock brakes. It's really hard to say the speeds we hit because of the slippage; the rpm would be up more on the beach than it would be on the back straightaway, but yet the speeds were greater on the back straightaway than they were on the beach, because of the slippage on the sand.

You knew you were running . . . even on the sand, because it would start skating on you. I think we qualified at about 140-something in the measured mile, ran approximately about 140 or 145 up the beach, because my car was a whole lot faster when we qualified. Down that back straightaway, I'd say we hit about 160.

As I remember, we had all the big boys there at the end, which was Curtis Turner, Jack Smith, Joe Weatherly, the Flock boys . . . we had 'em all. I bet you there was fifty, sixty cars started that race, and I started third and took the lead on the very first lap. My engine wasn't putting out exactly right when we were qualifying, so I qualified third; we straightened it out later.

We made a pit stop. I lost the lead, due to the pit stop, to Paul Goldsmith. I was running him down, and his engine came apart, I'd say, with about ten or twelve laps to go. We pitted right there in the sand, we never changed tires—all you had to do was clean the windshield and fuel. You did not have any extra amount of windshield-washer fluid, you had to use a stock jug, and that didn't last very long, so I found out how to clean the windshield by catching the spray off of another car for a moment and then diving out behind it; I'd clean the windshield and turn the wipers off.

We were a long ways out in front. I forgot who actually ran second to me in that race, but I was a good ways in front of him. My brakes were gone, I was having a problem getting stopped down on the south turn. I was strictly using all the pumping I could do, plus gearing it down all the way down to first gear. I used the clutch to keep from overrevving the engine—I never would let it turn over 6000 while I was shifting gears. If it went over that, I'd feed the clutch in and drop the rpm, just ease it out and keep doing that.

It was a great feeling to know that . . . you know, I didn't run Grand National regular, that I could come out of the modified division and beat those guys at their own game, because they'd been running Grand National all along and did not run modified. Curtis Turner and Weatherly jumped back and forth there some, but they were about the only ones. In the modified division we used a lot of rear ends and quick changes, and in the Grand National they wouldn't let you use anything but an open rear end, which would let one wheel spin if you didn't work it just exactly right. You had to drive the race car different.

You actually had to see the race to believe how close we ran to the people. . . . Back then it was absolutely the most dangerous race track that's ever been run. In 1958 the tide came in a little early, and we actually ran within three or four feet of the people going up the beach. They had a grandstand in the north turn, and I think they had a small one down in the south turn.

They lined the whole racetrack, the back straightaway and the beach; there was a part right on the beach where they could sit on the hoods of their cars. It was exciting—it was also one of the most dangerous things, because if two cars had tangled, there ain't no telling how many people or cars they would wipe out. I don't think they ever did have any spectator get hurt, though.

Victory lane was right there on the north turn, sort of like a judges' stand that we were up on. I didn't scratch the car, the car was always sandblasted from the sand. Hardy Earl presented the trophy that NASCAR has got on display there now.

We don't really know how many people came out on the beach. I'd say more like ten thousand, maybe twelve, on the north turn and down the back straightaway.

Winning the modified [at Daytona] was in 1953. I believe we had a hundred and some-odd cars start that race. And I developed a slight miss in the engine, so I ran second for the biggest portion of the day, until with about ten, twelve laps to go, it cleared up, and I went by the lead car and won it. I rode through it. It wasn't really the speed that much, it was hurting, of course; I don't know how much it was hurting the speed because I wasn't leading. As soon as it cleared up, it didn't take me but a lap to go back into the lead.

I believe Herb Thomas actually ran second to me that day, but you had the Weatherlys and the Turners and the Flocks—they all were there. Winning that one was great, because it was one of the biggest races I had won. You know, there was so many people there, and you outrun 'em all, that it gives you a great feeling.

I guess I pick those because it was some of the first; I would say those are the ones I'd want to be remembered for most. I really loved the beach, because it was a great challenge—you had acceleration, you had breaking, you had it all—you had speed, you had it all there. It was just about like what you'd have with a road course, really. You had to go through the gears and the brakes and acceleration and try to stop the thing.

I think everybody during the winter wanted to go racing there—and as far as the field goes, doing the Daytona then was just as big as it is now.

BENNY PARSONS

■ *Racing fans across the country know simply him as "B.P.," the analyst who takes them behind the wheel and under the hood of each NASCAR race every weekend. But early in 1975 he was a driver who got a little help from a friend to win the Super Bowl of stock-car racing, when a driver who normally never got into trouble suddenly spun out. Benny Parsons won twenty other races in his NASCAR career, but none was more memorable than his Daytona 500 victory when none other than Richard Petty offered to take him along for a ride.*

February of 1975. Well, I don't remember too much about it, to tell you the truth. I just know that at the end . . . there was a caution flag with thirty laps to go. And Davey Pearson was leading the race, and I was running second.

Richard Petty had the fastest car that day. He split a radiator seam, so the car would only run about ten or twelve laps and it would lose water, overheat, and he had to come back in and put more water in the car.

So they restarted the race with, I guess, thirty laps to go or whatever. And the next fifteen laps or so, David Pearson had pulled out to about a five-second lead on me, and I had no one to draft with. Richard Petty made a pit stop to put water in for the last time, and he came back on the racetrack on lap 188.

And he came on the racetrack in front of me. And he pulled up and waved an arm, which—I knew exactly what he was talking about—said, "If you want to go catch this guy, hang on, and we'll go for a ride." And we did, we went for a ride.

We closed within about . . . again, I'll say about a second and a half. It's been twenty-four years, so my recollection is dim. We closed probably within a second and a half or so, and we were getting closer and closer. We came out to the start/finish line to complete lap 197, and coming off the second corner . . . I see smoke and dust, and a car has spun. And I go by, and I see the car spinning, and it quick comes out of the dust, and I see it's Pearson.

And my first thought was, "Man oh man, the number 21 car has spun out," and you never saw the number 21 car in any kind of trouble. It was shocking. "The number 21 car has spun out! I mean, what in the world . . . The number 21 car has spun out!"

I'm thinking all the way down the backstretch. About the time I go into turn three it dawned on me. . . . I just won the Daytona 500!

So the next three laps were . . . quite something. Because, again, we had a tremendous lead on whoever was third. . . . [*Editor's note:* Bobby Allison finished second, Cale Yarborough finished third, and David Pearson finished fourth.]

. . . When Earnhardt won in 1990 and everyone came on pit road and gave Earnhardt skin, they high-fived and what-have-you as he came down pit road. . . . [But] those gestures did not go on in 1975. As I did come down pit road, the crews came out on pit road exactly like Earnhardt's situation, and clapped as I drove down pit road. And that was really, really awesome. It was pretty numbing, to tell you the truth.

I talked to Richard in Richmond about it the next week. I would guess that, at that point, Petty and Pearson had a tremendous rivalry going. . . . It was just phenomenal. And maybe Richard just wanted somebody else to beat David—I don't know. . . . When I was a kid I heard a statement that's very true: Don't look a gift horse in the mouth.

[The car] was a Chevrolet Laguna. . . . I don't remember exactly what broke, but something broke in the qualifying race, I think maybe the gear did or something. So we had to start thirty-first. At that point in time, that was the farthest back anyone had ever started to win the Daytona 500 on the two-and-a-half-mile race. Since then, Bobby Allison won starting back in thirty-third or something.

We just ran—we raced, and we just raced and raced and they threw a checkered flag and we went home. It wasn't . . . Auto racing just certainly was not anything as big, not nearly as big, as it is today.

As a broadcaster, it would have to be 1992—Atlanta, Hooters 500, whenever that race was. Four or five cars went to Atlanta with the chance to be the champion. I think Davey Allison was leading the race, leading the points championship by 35 or something; he had to finish sixth or better.

He was running pretty good, but he crashed coming off turn four. And then it basically shook down between Alan Kulwicki and Bill Elliott. And the punch line, the end result, the driver who led the most laps was gonna be the champion, because those two cars were better than any other cars; it looked like they were gonna run one-two.

And so the driver that led the most laps was gonna be the champion. And Kulwicki led one more lap than Elliott did to win the championship by 10 points. It was the most dramatic . . . I mean, the racing was terrific, the racing all day was terrific.

The race for the win down to the very end to the checkered flag was not that exciting. But the drama that played out that day was unbelievable. They knew [about the points situation] early enough that Kulwicki . . . went to the last gas stop, because he knew that he had torn out first gear earlier. It was gonna be a green-flag pit stop, and he knew that he was not gonna be able to get out of the pits.

Bill Elliott was gonna win the race, and he was gonna lead the most laps. He was gonna lead all the laps from that point until the end of the race. So Kulwicki had to run to the point that he led one more lap than Elliott, being that Elliott was gonna lead the rest of the laps.

The reason I pick Atlanta was because the drama that played out that day was unbelievable. . . . You didn't know what was going to happen, you had no idea. They had to run to the checkered flag, because if Kulwicki had fallen out, if he didn't make it back to the line and two more cars beat him, Elliott becomes the championship.

And then Kulwicki pulled off that Polish . . . you know, did the Polish victory lap and what have you. . . . Kulwicki had taken the *T* off the nose of his car—the *Th*—it said *"underbird"* on it. And he was the ultimate small-time guy, he was the owner/driver beating Junior Johnson's operation.

I picked Allison, I think he was running up front, and just got collected to a crash. . . . Pearson was lapping a car, Cale Yarborough, and they somehow made contact.

All of these drivers are so good—and Jeff Gordon is, and Earnhardt is, and Jarrett is, and Mark Martin is. Equipment means so much. . . . You know, Jeff Gordon, if he were to get in Bobby Labonte's car, would he do the same, better, or worse? I don't know the answer to that question. To try to rate drivers is just very, very hard and it's really unfair, because equipment does mean a great deal.

The best I saw was probably Petty. On certain things Richard Petty was unbeatable, on other things there was David Pearson, and then Darrell Waltrip came along, and Cale Yarborough—they all had certain attributes, or whatever the word is I'm looking for, that made them a winner. They had strengths in certain areas.

If it turned out to be that you had to hunt for a groove, and search for a groove, Richard Petty was gonna be the toughest guy around. If you took care of the equipment and what-have-you, David Pearson was gonna win. If you just had to run five hundred laps as hard as you go against adverse conditions, Cale Yarborough was gonna win. They all had certain strengths that made them what they were.

Winning Daytona was a very humbling affair. . . . It was a big thrill, but it was also very, very humbling, because I started racing just outside Detroit on a quarter-mile dirt track in a car that a guy bought for me and gave to me and paid $50 for.

You know, it's probably twelve or thirteen hundred miles from Detroit to Daytona Beach. But trust me, it's a lot farther than that from a quarter-mile dirt track to winning the Daytona 500. You know, along the way there were probably two hundred, three hundred, four hundred people that had a direct impact on helping me get to that point.

And here I am in victory lane with twelve or fourteen people.

. . . You just want everyone that you've been connected with to share that moment with you, every guy that helped you out, so you could say, "Thanks, man, what you did paid off." It's so humbling to do something like that and be the only one and get all the attention, when you know that there were so many people that helped get you to that point.

PHIL PARSONS

■ *Following in the footsteps of his older brother Benny, Phil Parsons achieved his dream of winning a Winston Cup race in the late 1980s in a head-to-head shoot-out with Geoff Bodine at Talladega. But Parsons' other greatest day came in 1994 at Charlotte when he realized his other racing dream after becoming an independent owner/operator in the Busch Grand National series.*

I'd probably pick a couple. Probably the Winston Cup race I won at Talladega in 1988 was certainly a highlight. We knew we had a real good car, we qualified third for the race, led quite a bit of the early going.

They had a caution flag, I'm not sure what lap, after twenty laps or something like that. . . . We elected to stay out where most of the people pitted. It was just borderline, I think we were leading the race at the time, so basically we had no one else to gauge off of, but we decided to stay out and most everyone else came in.

We stayed out and led some more of the race, then it got time that we needed gas, so we had to pit under green. So now everyone else has this number-of-laps cushion on us because they pitted under a caution flag. We had to pit under green and came out on the racetrack just in front of the leaders, so we were racing around there to try to stay in the lead lap and catch Ken Schrader, who was leading the race at the time.

He was trying to pass me to put me back a lap down, and spun out. He didn't hit anything, and he came back to finish, I think, in the top five, but that brought out the caution flag, him spinning out, so that allowed me to come on back around and stay in the lead lap, which was really key. Now, maybe we could have got our lap back later—but obviously if we don't get that lap back, we don't win the race—at some point throughout the day.

We had an awesome-good car—it was an Oldsmobile, Crown Skoal Oldsmobile. So then it was a matter of just systematically working our way toward the front. We got up into the top ten fairly quickly after the caution flag—I don't remember what lap it was—then worked out way back into the top five.

The race kind of shook out. Geoff Bodine and I kind of ran off from the field, so we were pretty much gonna decide it among ourselves. We talked about it on the radio; we wanted to move with ten or fifteen laps to go, to try to get around him; just in case something happened, we didn't want to wait until the last lap and then have something happen.

With ten, fifteen laps to go I was able to get by him—I was leading, we had an 11-second lead on the third-place car. I think Ricky Rudd blew an engine with about ten laps to go, so that bunched the field up, obviously. We were leading on the restart. They had a restart with, I don't know, four, five, six laps to go, and Bobby Allison ended up getting by Geoff coming out from the white flag. So obviously I'm trying to keep Geoff behind me prior to that, and then it was a matter of trying to keep Bobby Allison behind me for another full lap. He had another pretty good run at me, but we were able to kind of zig where he zigged, and zag where he zagged, down the backstretch, and kept him behind me and brought it back around.

We somewhat shot ourselves in the foot by staying out there when everyone else came in, but then we got a real good break by being able to get our lap back. It was just a matter of staying out of trouble, because we had such a good car, staying out of trouble and trying to do the right things in the draft to try and get the lead. And then once we got the lead it was a matter of trying to keep him behind me.

Geoff Bodine and I drafted for a long, long time, and we were able to pull out to an 11- or 12-second lead, and then when that caution came out there at the end—then myself and Geoff ran one-two, there were about five or six cars in the pack back then. Again, Bobby Allison was able to get by Geoff for a second, and that was how we finished.

Those things happen. . . . Five laps earlier maybe everybody would have stayed out; it was one of those decisions you make. If the caution would have come out five laps before we needed to pit for fuel, then we would have looked like heroes. It was just one of those things that happen during the race.

It was really just a big, big moment, something I worked my whole life for. What a thrill it was to be in victory lane with all my crew, and my wife and daughter, who was at that time about a little over five months old.

So it was a big thrill, and then I know, on the way home—we were there late, obviously, and we went up in the press box—and afterwards we were late, and we stopped to eat in Aniston on the way home, and lo and behold, Geoff was in there eating with his brother Brett, who . . . Brett and I are really good friends. We ended up picking up their checks, that was a good time.

We're talking about ten o'clock at night or so, by the time we ate—I'm guessing roughly nine or ten o'clock—the adrenaline was flowing, we were just gonna drive to Atlanta or get a motel room because it was so late. But the adrenaline was working so we just drove all the way home, and got home two or three o'clock in the morning.

That's my first and only Winston Cup win. . . . I also had a race in North Wolfesboro that I finished second in, so that was a whole lot of fun, too, and a big moment, but that wouldn't surpass the win at Talladega.

In 1994 we won a Busch Grand National race at Charlotte, and that was probably the other big moment, a favorite moment, of my career. That was with our own race team, for one thing, which really made it special. We did it on a very limited budget, I had one full-time employee—you know, racing against the Mark Martins, the people that typically run the Busch series, the Terry Labontes and the Bobby Labontes and people like that.

Stellar field of cars for a Busch race, and again, we had a real, real good car that day. I think we started about ninth or twelfth, I don't remember exactly, got up in the top five pretty quick, stayed in the top five the whole first half. And at that time at Charlotte they ran the race in two segments; you would run halfway and then they'd have a fifteen-minute break, and then you would run the other half.

I think we ended up finishing third in that first segment, maybe to Mark Martin and Michael Waltrip. And then the second segment we made some adjustments during the halftime break, or whatever you call it. The car was pretty good anyway, so I'm sure we didn't do much.

We ended up taking the lead somewhere during the second segment of the race, and then there was a caution flag for our final pit stop. We all came in the pits, and we had a lug-nut jam in an air wrench, and that put us back to fourth or fifth on the restart without a whole lot of time left—maybe thirty or forty laps to go.

Again, we just systematically worked our way up to the front, we were able to get past Michael Waltrip for second, and then ended up passing Mark for the lead, and were never headed from that point on. The split really didn't have any bearing on the race, other than they just split; they don't even do that anymore, they did it for a number of years there.

All the guys that had helped me, all of 'em had full-time jobs—except again, I had one full-time person, and for them to be able to come to victory lane like that, and for us to share that, was really, really special. Not that the one at Talladega wasn't special, but for all of these guys that had done it for nothing, it was kind of a reward for their hard work without getting paid for it. That was really a big thrill.

Afterwards, my daughter had a dance recital, and we went to my daughter's dance recital. One of the guys ended up having everybody over to his house later that night for kind of a celebration, and after the dance recital we went over there.

Sometimes I wonder if the Charlotte race wasn't a little more special than the Talladega race, and then at other times I think conversely, the other way. It's just hard to compare the two.

I guess being at Winston Cup is the ultimate, and it's something I always wanted to do, and I was able to do that for a number of years, and then I found myself without a ride. So then my wife and I got together and said, "Hey, what are we gonna do?" and it was really her idea. . . . It was my idea to get a Busch team going, and I really couldn't find a sponsor for it—we're going back to 1991. And she said, "Why don't we just get a car and run when we can, run when we have sponsorship and when we can afford to run?"

So that's what we did—we started off very small, we ran six races the first year. Then I think we ran seven races the next year, and maybe ended up running nine races the year after that, then eleven races the year after that—1994—but again, only when we had sponsorship and were able to afford to do it.

And at that time we were racing against a whole lot of people— we picked and choosed our races, so all the races we ran would have a full complement of Winston Cup drivers and highly financed teams. So it wasn't like we picked on the little races where none of the Winston Cup people showed up—we picked on the high-profile and more competitive races. We were always very competitive.

Then I ended up with some rule changes after that season of 1994, and I ended up going to drive for somebody else for a year, because I didn't have any sponsorship lined up and it was going to be an extremely expensive year, transition-wise, because of the rule changes.

We were changing engines, going from V-6s to V-8s, so I decided to drive for somebody else, but in doing that I just sorely missed being somewhat in control of our own destiny, and the fact that if there's something that you wanted to try, something that you thought would make you go faster, not having the authority or any say-so to do it was hard to deal with.

So we decided in the winter of 1995 . . . to go back on our own to get sponsorship to do the deal and try to do it right. And we were fortunate enough to get a sponsor, and here we are.

. . . Obviously it takes a whole lot of time, and that's basically work every day, but we've got some real good people now, and some real good funding from Alltel Communications—by far the best we've ever had—so we have more people than we've ever had. That's freed me up a whole lot to not have to be here every minute.

We had twins back in June, so I need every minute I can spare, so I appreciate it.

■ *If Richard Petty was The King, David Pearson's status in the hierarchy of NASCAR royalty was as The Man Who Ran with the King, and in fact bested him on more than one occasion. The greatest day of the driver who eventually became known as the Silver Fox took him back to his first victory at Charlotte in the early 1960s, as he discussed his memorable victories at his hometown track of Darlington and his many runs with Richard Petty.*

My greatest days. . . . Lord, I don't have no idea which one to pick, they were all good to me. I can't complain about one thing in racing.

Well, I guess the best thing would probably be when I won the first race, the Charlotte 600, in 1961, because I was just a hill boy, just had my own car, and stuff like that, and I just picked out, bought a Jack Smith used car. And anyway, Ray Forrest went to Charlotte, and didn't have a driver, and, of course, some of the guys—Cotton Owens had always told me he would give me a chance, which, he never had heard of me or anybody else, 'cause all I'd done was run short tracks.

So they called me and asked me if I wanted to go try it, and I ended up winning the race. And I went on to Daytona, July 4, won that one, and then I won Atlanta the same year. And at that time no driver had ever won three big races in one year, and me being a rookie, too, starting out like that, that was . . . that fixed me right up, put me right on top.

Actually, when they called me, I went up and tried the car out, and he asked me how did it feel, and I said, "I'll tell you the truth, I don't know how it's supposed to feel, I've never run this fast before." I don't know exactly how fast I was running, but I led for about three-quarters of the race.

And I just know that we were running awful good, but I had a lot of flat, bad tires. . . . I was just lucky we were on the straightaway when I had 'em. And I think I won the race on a flat tire. I didn't know it at the time, but I was about six or seven laps ahead when I came off the fourth turn. Well, I blew a tire coming out of the back-stretch, and when I came off the fourth turn, I seen 'em waving—they had the white flag out, getting ready to wave it.

So when they brought it out there, I said, Well, I'm still going into a pit stop. I only had one lap to go, I knew I was leading the race, but I didn't know I was that far ahead. And of course, Fireball [Roberts] let me, three or four times, because it was the right rear, and we didn't have ratchets back then, and I couldn't even mash the gas—it would spin, especially on a flat tire.

When I came off [turn] four, he was still waving the white flag, and I knew then that I was still leading, if I could just make it to the flag. I don't have any idea how many tires I blew that day, but I know it was quite a few—everybody was blowing tires. It was just the race itself, and tires back then, they didn't have the inner liners that they have now. You could tell when one would blow, you could hear it. Back then I was lucky, I was going up a straightaway every time I blew one.

I was just tickled to death to get to go run, because I knew that was a good car, a 1961 Pontiac. So when they called me and asked me if I wanted to go run, I threw everything I had down. I was trying to get ready to go, myself, and I said, "Lord, yeah, it would just tickle me to death to get a chance to go up there and run a car like that. For a little hill boy like me to go up there and run that good . . ."

I was working with a guy, John Sewell, helping him put on roofs, and he said, "What if you go up there and win that race?" I said, "I'll come back here Monday morning and tell [you you] can take this job and shove it." And that's exactly what I done. . . . Of course, he knew I was kidding when I done it, but . . . [Laughs.]

After the race was over, they was interviewing me and all, and they wanted to know if I wanted to thank the guys that were helping me, and I didn't even know their names. I didn't know—I said, "I'd like to, but I don't even know their names." The only one I knew was Ray, and I really didn't know him, I hadn't met him until they called me and I went up there to drive his car. He just asked me if I wanted to drive it again, I do remember that, and I said, "Well, sure."

So he said the next race he'd run would be Daytona, so I went down there and run that one, and won that. Daytona was different, but Daytona wasn't so big back then, and you could see the asphalt was kind of new in 1961. I think the first race down there was in 1959, or something like that. So the car stuck tight there, you could just tell that you were running a lot faster.

But when you run fast, it don't matter if you're running on a mile-and-a-half track, or two-and-a-half miles—to get the car to run fast, you've gotta loosen it up to where it will run free into the corners and run fast, to where 175 [mph] feels like just like, if you didn't run no faster than that, it would feel about like it would if you were running 200. You still have to have the car right on the ragged edge anyways.

Of course, it tickled me to death, being young, and the speeds . . . If you wanted to race, you wanted to race, so it didn't matter how fast you were running.

Fireball finished second, and I think Fred Lorenzen finished second at Daytona. Understand, of course, I was drafting Fireball. Fireball had had problems and had to pit or something. And when he come back out of the pits, he had put his tires on; he came up and passed me, and they told me just to hang on to him. I drafted him, and we went on up together, and I passed Freddy Lorenzen, and, of course, I ran first and Fred ran second. I think it was Fred, I'm pretty sure it was.

Daytona was about like it was at Charlotte—I couldn't believe it myself. . . . I knew everybody a little bit better, but not much, because that was just my second race as far as running that car. Of course, more people knew me then—nobody knew me to start with; they started noticing me a little bit more, because I did win at Charlotte— especially after I won Daytona, it really helped.

At Atlanta, it was just like they are today, there are four or five cars that run up front. Well, that's the way it was back then. Of course, Ray Forrest had one of them that ran up front, and I just happened to be in that car. I ran up front all day—I'd say in the top five all the time, anyway.

I thought I was a big wheel by then. I remembered running with Fireball, Joe Weatherly, things like that. When I went to Charlotte, I remember thinking, Here I am running with Fireball and all these guys I've heard of before. I just always felt like, if anybody could do it, then I could do it too. I said, "This car don't know who's driving it, whether it's Fireball driving it or I'm driving it—if it'll run up front, it's gonna run up front." I just always felt like I could do anything anybody else could do.

I didn't know that nobody had ever done it, winning all three, until I done it. And they told me, they talked about it, newspeople and everybody else: nobody had ever done that, won all three in one year, three big races in one year at that time. It was a good deal for me, it really was.

They picked me. . . . Of course, I had my own car, and I was just working every day and spending what money I could get, to put it on the car, and I had to do the work myself, and all that stuff, I was just learning. I didn't know what to do to cars, and stuff like that. It's like the people that are running today, like Dave Marcis, he does his own work and stuff like that, and that's about the way I was back then. I didn't have the money, and the backing—well, I didn't have no backing. I done it all myself.

Like I said, it just happened that he didn't have a driver, and he called me, and then I drove for him. And it just so happened that I won that one, I guess. Then, later . . . let's see, 1962, I ran a few races for 'em. He tried to run Bristol and places like that, which was short-tracking racing. He didn't know anything about setting cars up for short-track racing. We went up there, and of course we didn't do no good, and of course, he quit. He finally quit racing.

And I went with Cotton Owens after that, then I won a championship—that was in 1966. Then I went with Ford Motor Company, Holman-Moody. In 1967 I won a championship, and then in 1968 and 1969, with them. I actually didn't run for it but three times, and I won it all three times I ran for it. That makes you feel good, you know, to do that.

The best race I ever ran was probably . . . I guess . . . I don't know, I sure don't. Because I felt like I run good in all of 'em, I really do. Especially the Wood Brothers car, when I went with them, that was another car that was a real good, strong car. I know when I was with Ford, Holman and Moody, we was at Daytona, I think it was 1969 or something—I forgot who was driving their car, I think it was Cale [Yarborough] or somebody, he asked me to take his car and try it out for him and test something—and I went out there and drove their car, and it really drove good.

I kept staying out there and running pretty good for a while, just trying to figure out what all they had done and mine wouldn't, because theirs handled so much better than mine did. I know Dick Hutcherson was crew chief for me at the same time, and he said, "Hey, I can't believe you went out and stayed out there that long. You ain't been runnin' that long when you went out there"—not that I had a car that would drive as good, and I made that comment about them.

It was a good, successful time when I was with them—in fact, everybody I've ever been with was a good time. I got along good for everybody I drove for; of course, I didn't drive for that many. But the ones I did, I got on good with 'em.

Winning the championships, of course, means a lot, and I would have to say, as far as the next race goes, after I won my first one, is probably Darlington. Everybody always talks about how tough Darlington is, and I always seemed to do real good at Darlington. But I always liked it, because it was more . . . You have to keep your mind on what you were doing sometimes there.

There were just certain places you could pass back then, and now you can pass about anywhere, they've got the track fixed now where you can run two abreast, or three or four, or one or two now. But before, you couldn't do that, it had to be single-file going through there. And you had to judge a car to make sure you would catch 'em coming off the corners, going into corners, because you could take a slow car down there, and if you didn't drive it just right, the fast car could never get around you.

I always felt like Darlington would have been my home track, you know, because it's South Carolina, and I always wanted to do good there, with everybody talking about how tough it was to win there. I remember when I was working on old short-track cars, my cars I was running short tracks with, half-mile tracks and stuff like that. I'd listen to the race [on the radio], they'd talk about the orange [car] rubbing the guardrail, running 130, 140 miles an hour, and I'd say, "Those people are crazy, going up against the guardrail that fast." But that was the fastest way around it, really, and I learned to do that.

I always liked it, who I ran against was about the same ones everywhere you went, the same guys. I guess day in and day out, as long as I was in my whole career, I enjoyed running against Richard Petty more than anybody, I really did.

We ran together so much. . . . I remember up in Maryville, Tennessee, one time, we used to run, and I'd lead awhile, and I'd back off and let him go in front. Of course, back then you didn't get points for leading the most laps or anything like that, and we just put on a show, really. I know up in Maryville one time it was hot, and he was pushing me pretty hard, and I said, "Well, there ain't no sense in getting my tires hot and stuff like that," so I'd just back off my car and let him go. I'd let him go, and then when it came down to the end, I caught him, but I just couldn't get by him, he just hung right on inside, and there was no way I could get by him, and he won the race, and I was second. We've talked about that, Dale Evan, his crew chief, every once in a while, how hot it was and about the way that happened.

We ran one and two I forgot how many times—I think it was

sixty-some times, that might be it. I think I beat him thirty-four times, and he beat me thirty, something like that. It was good on the track and off the track; we would rub each other, and if we could get our front end under each other, we would push 'em sideways and stuff like that, to get around. But we never knocked each other out from meanness—you know, you can move people over without spinning 'em out.

Nowadays it seems like a lot of 'em they just go ahead and spin 'em out. And I can see it, and the people driving can see it, but the people in the stands don't see that thing. A lot of times they don't do it, but they can keep from doing it, and don't.

I expect the money's had a lot to do with it—I expect it has. A lot of it's jealousy, and it's just like, a lot of 'em get more money now just to start the races than we got running all year—people getting half a million dollars to run a race car, and they haven't even won a race.

That's ridiculous—I would never pay it. I'd make 'em earn it some way or another, some way. But now, if you can get out and talk, you really don't have to drive, I don't think. I understand that the cars are so much better now, they've got wind-tunnel tests and stuff like that, got so much down-pressure that the cars don't ever move in a lot of places, like Daytona, now.

It ain't like it used to be. It used to be you used to have to hold your breath when you went into that corner, and you didn't get it back until you went out the other side. Used to be you could wait and draft and stuff and pass a guy coming off turn four, draft by him, and win the race. But now, the way they've got these restrictor plates, everybody running about the same speed, you have to do it way back off of two to get your start and try to get by 'em. It's quite a bit different now than what it used to be.

KYLE PETTY

■ *As the middleman in the racing history of the Petty family, Kyle Petty's list of greatest days ran the gamut, from his first day in 1979 as a fabricator for his father Richard in one of NASCAR's most memorable Daytona 500s, to his first race with his own team at Daytona in 1997, to this year's Daytona 500, when he watched his son Adam make his successful run as a Busch Grand National driver. As one might expect, the one constant connecting Kyle's experiences was the importance of family, both from a personal perspective and in the historical context of the Pettys as NASCAR's first family.*

God, I probably . . . Man, I've had too many great days. I think that's the problem. I could tell you, the way I look at it, I've had . . . if I look back, I've had three days, three things kind of stand out in my mind.

And the first one is, when my father won the Daytona 500 in 1979, the same year I won the ARCA race there. But what was special about that year was that we were working here at Petty Enterprises. I was eighteen, we were working at Petty Enterprises, and we were a little shorthanded. So there were only like three of us that worked on the Daytona 500 car, as far as hanging the body, fabricating the car.

To go to Daytona, and to win the race, for him to win the race, and me to have been a big part of helping build that car, it was a huge day for me. I always wanted to be a fabricator, I think being a fabricator in a race car is like the coolest thing.

Second-biggest day for me would have been two years ago at Daytona in the 125-mile race. We ended up fourteenth, but that was the first year that I had my own team—PE2—and we made the race just by the skinny, skin, skin. . . . I mean, that was just like . . . there it is. We were just there, you know what I mean?

But that was a huge day for me personally—as a driver, as a team owner, and as a company, that was a huge day for us.

And then I'd just go to this year, into the Saturday before the 500, when Adam ran his first race at Daytona and ended up finishing fifth, sixth, seventh, wherever—I think he finished sixth. That was a huge day, I think, for me as a father, to stand back and look at it . . . you couldn't be any more prouder.

So I think . . . it's not the success part of a racetrack maybe, sometimes. Like I said, for my father it was being the son that worked on his car—and to just be proud of the fact that I helped build a car that my father won a race with. For me, it was to build my own team and be a driver, and to do that, and then for Adam, it was to be his father.

I don't think there was a highlight in 1979, because if you go back to . . . And let me say this, because you gotta remember, that's the year of the wreck, on the backstretch where Bobby and Donnie got in a fight. We were gonna run third that day, which was still a great day, and to run third was gonna be phenomenal.

But then with, what, three-quarters of a mile to go, you end up winning the Daytona 500. So I don't think there was a highlight to that day—it had been a highlight of the week for us. I had won the ARCA race, my father had run decent all week long, STP was beginning to pull back some of their money, so we were looking for sponsors, so we wanted to run good. And then he ends up winning the race. So I think for me, just going through that week, there weren't a lot of highlights.

Now, going back to Daytona, you know, we go to Daytona, qualify incredibly badly with my own team. We were really slow, we struggled, we worked—there's still pictures around of me cutting up the car in my driver's uniform, trying to get more speed out of it. And when you start having to cut up a car at Daytona, when you're down there at a race, you're in trouble.

. . . For me, that was just four or five days of just pure torture. And then all of a sudden, ecstasy—just for the fact that you'd made the race, you didn't care about the 500 at that point in time. I could have give a flip less about the 500; it was just that we had survived the race, and we had made it and we were competing on the same level with the Hendricks and the Roushes and the guys that have been around for twenty years.

So there wasn't really a highlight for that, there was just the act itself that made it a highlight.

And I think leading up to Adam's stuff was the same way. You take an eighteen-year-old at Daytona with a brand-new Busch team—he tested well, nothing special. We went back, he qualified well, nothing special, but just to step back and look at the overall picture and say, "God, he's the first fourth-generation athlete in America, he's a fourth-generation Petty, there's always been a Petty running in this sport." And then he comes to Daytona and has a very respectable, very, very solid sixth-place run in his very first race.

As a father, that was just a big day for me. But it was nothing phenomenal, nothing special leading up to it, it was just there.

I mean, you can prepare. . . . You know, I think it's not what you say, it's what you *don't say* in a lot of cases, you know what I mean? I think my father just told me the same stuff—where the bad places on the racetrack were, where the bumps are, don't get caught on the outside of somebody right here, make sure you protect yourself here. Just little basic things, and use common sense.

And that's basically the same thing [I told] Adam, was, "Go out and do it." And I think you're afraid to say too much, because you're afraid you'll hurt him, because they're gonna do better than what you anticipate they're gonna do, and that's kind of the way I am with

Adam. I'm afraid to give him any advice, because he does so well without me.

That's why I say, it's not really what you say, it's what you don't say. It's what you learn—what I learned from being around racing for twenty years before I started driving; it's what Adam learned from being around racing all his life before he started driving. You already know so much, just through osmosis, just from being around, hearing conversations.

You know the lingo, you know the talk, you understand what the good times are, you understand what the bad times are, so that there's not really a lot that you can say. It's just, go out and physically do the job, and this is a sport where you can't talk somebody through it.

When I look at it, and I say, "What were my three greatest days?"—these were three great days that really had nothing to do with what we were doing on the racetrack. For me, I look at 'em, and those are races that stand out in my mind because we were so successful at Daytona that entire week, with my car, with my father's car . . . my grandfather won the Daytona 500 golf tournament that week, so it was just an incredible week for the Pettys, you know what I mean?

And really, I had nothing to do with the cars, other than the fact that I helped build my father's car, and I was proud of that. That was big, then Adam, then when I started something, it was building the team and putting together a group of guys that showed that they could go to Daytona and be competitive with anybody. And the same deal with Adam, it was saying, You know, this kid's lived in my house for eighteen years, and he comes out here and runs with Mark Martin and Jeff Burton and the Winston Cup guys. He knows what it takes to race.

And I think that's what made 'em great days—not so much the cars, because I don't think the cars stood out; I think they were almost secondary in some aspects.

You know, we don't celebrate much. I'll say this about the Petty clan here—you know, you're only as good as what you do today. And as soon as that day is over with, you're looking for bigger and better things. When it's all said and done, we all go back to the motor home, or we go back to the hotel, and everybody tells everybody they did a great job, and everybody hugs or kisses and then you go back to work by seven o'clock the next morning to get ready for the next race. And that's kind of the way we approach it. So . . . you internalize your celebration, and it's not a big party or anything like that, you just go on and race again.

I think they hit you when they're happening, you know what I mean? I really think you know it's a special day, or you know it's a special time, but even at that, no longer it goes the more special it gets. I think the 1979 race and that race a couple of years ago, 1997 at Daytona—when I look back on 'em they're more special to me now, just being a part of that.

And the people that were a part of it, I look at 'em and they've gone on to other teams and done other things, but still, to me, they're part of my team because of that. So I don't think there's any one thing that makes 'em stand out, you just kind of look at it over time, and I don't think they get any more . . . They do get more special, but they're just special from the very beginning.

I think that's the one thing—there is no change to the way we approach it. The way we approach it is, you go out and you give 100 percent, and you do the best you can every day, and if you get beat, you get beat. But you don't beat yourself.

We try to leave the race shop with the best people working on the cars, and the best-prepared cars we can, and you don't beat yourself. You try to be innovative, you try to be leaders, and you try to go on down that road, but you can't allow yourself mentally or physically to get beat from internally, and that's what we try to do. And I think that's why this place has been so successful, is because all those years, the DNFs and the failures we had were not because of something that happened here, it was because of something that happened somewhere else.

I wouldn't even venture to guess what [my dad's best day] is . . . because I know a lot of times I heard him talk—that some of the races that he ran, he won his two hundredth race in 1984, and then he didn't win for a while—but some of the best times he had in a race car happened after 1984, because he still loved to drive a race car. Even though he wasn't being as successful as he had been, he still just loved to drive a race car.

I think that's what it's all about, is to love the sport.

■ *As we move into a new century, the notion that there are records in sports that will never be broken has been sorely tested in the last few years. But if there is a record in the world of motor sports that is truly unassailable, it would have to be Richard Petty's career mark of two hundred NASCAR victories. In this interview, the man who became known as "The King" offered up this account of his greatest day—the July Fourth last-lap shoot-out at Daytona that he won in 1984, with then-president Ronald Reagan in the stands. Petty also talked briefly about his greatest days with the other three generations of Petty drivers: father Lee, son Kyle, and grandson Adam.*

I guess when you really get through the whole shaking and stuff, I was real fortunate to have a whole bunch of great days, all the things that we were able to accomplish.

But probably the best one, or whatever, the one that was the biggest, was the 200th one, in 1984 at Daytona, because we wound up having the president of the United States start the race. He showed up, and then we won the race on the last green-flag lap, running side by side with Cale Yarborough. And then when that was over with, we—all the crews and the wives and everybody, the NASCAR people—got to go down and have a picnic with the president of the United States, and that was pretty awesome, you know what I mean?

And then it was the 200th win—all that stuff added up, it was sort of a Hollywood deal that nobody would have believed if you put it in a movie.

We'd won the 199th one at Dover, probably four or five races before that. We'd been to Charlotte and some other races, and we were really anticipating the win any week, you know what I mean? It was a big hullaballo, press deal, all this stuff, and then when we got to Daytona, we were pretty good.

And it wound up that Cale and myself were just superior to all the rest of the people; it was just a two-car race, really. We were able to run, and we raced with each other back and forth—he led, I led, I don't know if anybody else ever led the race or not. I don't remember about the first [part] there, but through the middle and the latter part, it was just strictly a Cale Yarborough–Richard Petty show.

The cars were all but equal. Basically, there was a lot of hullaballoo around it, but we didn't pay no attention to it, because we were trying to win the race. When it came down to the end of the race, I was leading the race with like three laps to go or something, and Cale was right on my bumper, and I knew that he was gonna do the slingshot deal the last lap. But I didn't know when he was gonna do it, where, or what I was gonna do, because I didn't know what he was gonna do.

Just as we came down to the start/finish line, both of us saw somebody wrecking going in [turn] one, they was down in the infield coming off the racetrack. So then we both did our last-lap deal two laps early, and I think that if either of us had anything figured out, it went out the window, because we had to do it real quick, it was just a reaction deal.

And so we went in the first corner, Cale went real high and got a good run and started at me on the backstretch, passing me going in the corner. And when he did, then he went in a little bit faster than what we'd been running, because he had a good draft, and he went high on the racetrack.

I was able to still stay wide-open and cut down beside him, and I had done the same thing in 1976 with David Pearson—the only thing was, I never cleared David; I thought I cleared him, and we got in a wreck coming off of [turn] four, I pushed him up against the wall, we got in a big crash. So I'd been in that situation before, and I knew I couldn't do what I'd done before, and I didn't get as good a running start on him as Pearson, so all I could do was get up beside him.

We just ran side by side, and then we sort of leaned on each other a couple of times. He was trying to get me down, I was trying to get him up, and we were smokin' everything comin' down the front stretch. We were running up on some lap traffic, and we were running a little bit higher than what we usually ran, but I was trying to keep him from getting a running start.

Anyhow, we beat and bashed, and I beat him by about three car-lengths. And then, when we came back around the next time, he stopped; he came down pit road because in his mind, that was the last lap, even though it was a caution lap. And as he came down pit road and his crew got to screaming at him, he went back out, still running second, he ran third, because I think Harry Gant went by him while he was going down pit road. It was just an action-reaction deal. . . . We got lucky, it was meant for us to win the race, and we did.

I knew he was gonna go low on me, that's the natural place to go. I knew he had a quick-enough car that he could just zip on past me. I was worried about being in the last lap, that I didn't get a chance to do the same thing to him. It kind of surprised me when he passed me and he couldn't stay in the groove that he wanted to stay in. When he moved up a little bit, I just stayed in my groove and I was able to cut down under—that really surprised me, it kind of caught me off-guard.

That was my only chance—if he'd went on and stayed down in his regular groove, I wouldn't have been able to do nothing. He got such a momentum going down the backstretch, when he turned the car, it just didn't go where he wanted it to go.

. . . Even though this wasn't the last lap, it was the last green-flag lap—it was a typical Daytona deal, where the first-place guy sort of hung out, okay? And I had slowed down a little bit before that. With maybe ten laps to go, I started slowing down a little bit, hoping he'd go ahead and go on. But I knew better—you know what I mean?—and he knew better.

So it was just a typical deal that I got caught out there leading the race with ten laps to go, and there wasn't nothing I could do about it. I couldn't even pull over and let him go, you know what I mean? He wasn't going to go nowhere; if I would have come down pit road he probably would have followed me. [Laughs.] In his mind, he knew that he had a 90 percent chance of winning the race if we made it to the last lap. So, again, it wound up being a typical Daytona deal, especially then, because the cars had a lot more "go," they wasn't restricted as much as . . . they are now, so they had a lot more throttle response.

Most of the time, if you had a dominant car, you didn't have nobody behind you when you came to the end. It came down to a shoot-out, like 1976, you know, Pearson had dominated the race, and we'd gone two or three other years that I was a dominant-enough car, me and somebody, to be able to sort of get off on your own. There wasn't ever a three- or four-car operation, it was always a two-car shoot-out. That made it a lot easier, because then you just had to figure on one guy, you didn't have to figure on what two of 'em were gonna have to gang up on you, or whatever, whether you was gonna gang up on them.

I guess it was a relief as much as anything, because it was the 200th. We weren't setting any records or anything, but in our own minds, we'd set 200 as our goal. And the way it worked out, we never won anything after that. [Laughs.]

But the deal was that when the race was over, we weren't thinking about, "Hey, the president of the United States is here, we've gotta go up in the booth and talk to him," or any of that stuff.

What happened, they had told us before the race, they said, whoever wins the race, not to go to the winner's circle—to stop out on the racetrack at the start/finish line, get out of the car, and go up into the announcers' booth, and talk to the president . . . you know, get some pictures, the big PR deal.

I pulled around and stopped out on the racetrack, and by then part of the crew was out there, all this stuff. So when we got out of the car and walked up through the grandstand, a bunch of hullaballoo and stuff, and then the boys took the car over to the winner's circle. And we went up into the press booth and talked to the president, and he was awed by the whole deal, that we were running 200 miles an hour and beating each other . . . there was smoke flying off of the tires, all this stuff.

His eyes were as big as silver dollars, he got excited about that part of it, because he'd never been to a race, didn't know what was going on—all of a sudden they have one of the better races, it's coming down to the end of the race, and they're beating and bashing each other without knocking each other out of the way. So he was awed by those things.

Anyhow, we stayed up there for about ten minutes, done a little chitchatting, just all about nothing, and took some pictures and stuff. Then we went on back down to the winner's circle, and they took all the winner's-circle pictures, and then after that all of us went back and cleaned up and got all fixed up in an hour, hour and a half or something, and then we went down to the picnic deal.

Me and Bobby Allison got to sit with the president, that was great. . . . When we went on down to the picnic deal and stuff, we got to talking about kids, and just a bunch of chitchat—nothing serious, you know what I mean, we didn't get into any politics or any of that kind of stuff.

It was fireworks for us, and then it was Fourth of July, the whole deal, it was a fantastic day.

I don't ever remember talking to Cale about the race. We probably did, sometime. . . . The race was over, he ran third and got beat, so to him, he was looking for next week, and I was, too.

I think it was a slow impact—the 200th win was a big deal that day, and then the next day we were looking for 201, and we did for five or six more years, we never got anything. But I think as time goes on, the 200 gets bigger than it was then, because you see the boys coming along now, and they win races and stuff, they've won forty or fifty or sixty races, you know what I mean?

Earnhardt's won seventy-four races or something; he ain't gonna be here long enough to overcome that. And even the young boys, like [Jeff] Gordon, he's won forty-some races now . . . but you figure, to win 200 races, you've gotta win ten for twenty years, and nobody's gonna do that, you know what I mean? I think as we look forward into the future, that a lot of these boys are not gonna run, their careers aren't gonna be as long. I think the trend is getting to be the younger people, the way it's been the last five or six years, people are looking to bring new people in and get ten or fifteen years out of them and then go get somebody else.

The key, to me, was family, being in a family operation, a family business, and knowing that no matter how bad I done, I wasn't gonna lose my ride. Then we came along and we were lucky enough to get hung in with STP, and that was a lifetime contract—as long as I drove a race car, they were gonna back me. So we didn't have to go out every year and have to worry about having a sponsorship and all this kind of stuff. The deal was, we were family with them, they were family with us, I had my brother working here, and cousins, you know what I mean?

And the same basic crowd stayed together for fifteen to twenty years—they knew they weren't gonna lose their job if we didn't win a race, I knew I wasn't gonna lose mine. So when things went wrong, we just got our heads together and said, "Okay, what can we do to make it better?" That was what made my longevity so much . . . I was in one place, I had to work with the same people, and they worked with one person also, so it just made a heck of a combination.

When things went bad, then everybody got their heads together and didn't blame anybody. Everybody sat down and said, "Okay, what are we doing wrong?" A lot of times when you're a driver for somebody else, then the driver is the first one that gets the blame, even if the tire blows out, it's his fault, the motor blows up, it's the driver's fault.

That was one of the keys, was that if the motor did blow up, I didn't blame my brother [Maurice], I talked to him, and said, "Okay, we don't want this happening again." He knew it more than I did, he didn't want it to happen. . . . Or, if we made a bad pit stop . . . the pit crew came together and said, "Okay, we ain't gonna let that happen again." It was just a deal that was coming back to the fact that it was just one big family—all of the names might not have been Petty, but it was still the Petty family.

So everybody knew that if you had a bad day, everybody knew that you weren't gonna let that happen again, and we worked together to do it. Nobody pointed fingers, everybody took the blame; if somebody made a mistake, you didn't have to get on to 'em, they knew it before you did. All that stuff just made for a good, close-knit operation.

We've had a couple of good deals with the family as far as greatest days and that deal goes—the first race that Kyle run in 1979 at Daytona, an ARCA 200-mile race, he won the race. And I mean, that was just unbelievable; the deal was that my dad was there. . . . Of course, Adam wasn't born then, so he wasn't there, but we were all there in the winner's circle, we couldn't believe it, either. We were just kind of pinching ourselves; here's a kid who comes out and he's eighteen years old, he's never run a race in his life, and he got lucky enough to win a race. So that was a big, big operation for us.

Then we took Adam this past year; last year, he'd been running ASA and he'd won a race in it, sat on the pole a couple of times. Anyhow, came to Charlotte, and they had an ARCA race in Charlotte, and this was the first time he'd been in a high-powered car, a big car on a big track. And he goes out and wins the ARCA race at Charlotte. I was there—my dad wasn't there, but Kyle was there; I was there, naturally Adam was there, all the mothers were there . . . it's an awesome, awesome feeling when something like that happens.

Kyle's been doing it long enough so that watching it is part of the show. When you've got a grandkid coming along, it's sort of like starting all over again. Not only for Adam, being he's just starting, but it's like me starting all over again. I'm trying to put myself in Adam's deal, because I can't drive, and I'd like him to express himself like what I'd do if I was there.

So it's sort of like a second coming, or a third coming, you know what I mean? You would look at it and say, "If I could just help him a little bit, get him a better car, a better crew, and talk to him about things that I would like to see him do, that I think he needs to do." And then you talk to him about running a different groove, or handling the car different, and then you see him do it, and it really makes you feel good.

That's one of them really awesome feelings, when in Richard Petty's mind, he's probably sitting there thinking, "This is me at another age." Even though I don't like him, or he doesn't think like me, I still think he thinks like me. What I usually do when I do talk to him is I say, "Look, I'm just gonna tell you these things, I'm not getting onto you, I'm not telling you what to do, I'm just giving you some experience and stuff that I've had. You take it and use it like you want to use it. . . . If you want to use it, fine; if you want to do something different, that's fine, too."

You sort of lay a groundwork out there, and if he uses it and needs to use it, that's fine. But if he's smarter than I am on some of the stuff now, because things have changed so much that he can't do what I say—or if he does what I say he'd get in a lot more trouble—the deal is he has to balance with what I tell him, with what Kyle tells him, and what he sees and then what he does. He's gotta balance all that up, he's got a pretty big résumé behind him, but he can't use it all at one time—he has to make the decision on what he's gonna do.

My greatest day as an owner . . . probably would be, we had a pretty good weekend at Martinsville this year. Jimmy Hensley won the truck race for us on Saturday, and then John [Andretti] comes back and wins the Martinsville race on Sunday; with two laps to go or a lap to go, he passes the leader and wins the race. That was an awesome deal, too.

Golly, man, I've had a bunch of them with my dad, too. Probably the greatest day, even though it didn't wind up that way later on, was when he won the first Daytona 500 [1959]. We thought he won, and then it was three days before he got the race—they gave it to somebody else, you know what I mean?

That was an awesome, awesome deal, because it was the biggest racetrack at the time; it wasn't the biggest race at the time, but we knew it was gonna be the biggest race, and that was an awesome deal for him, for us, and for Petty Enterprises.

I started the race and blew up after seven or eight laps, so I was in the pits all day, trying to get him to go back straight. [Laughs.] I was twenty-one years old, I was still a kid—twenty-one-year-old people now are a bit older than twenty-one-year-old people when I came along, because the work has opened up so much. So I was awed by the whole deal, not only me being on the racetrack, but then watching my dad win the race.

The biggest thing that he taught me was being patient with what I needed to do. Racing with people wasn't what paid the money, it was winning the races was what paid off. I used that philosophy throughout my career; it's [not] a big deal to go out and lead races and set records and stuff, you've got to be there when the race is over in order to win the thing.

So I think he taught me that, hey, you've gotta take care of the equipment, you've gotta be close enough to strike if you're ready to do it. Just the idea of winning the race more than running the race. He taught me, he wound up where his philosophy was to win. He always said, "Win as slow as you can, because they don't pay nothing extra to run fast."

I think, if you put it to him, that was the biggest win of his career. He wound up winning three championships, and fifty-four, fifty-five races, at that time. . . . when he quit; then he won more races than anybody, more championships, and more money. He was the top dog; even though these other guys were more flamboyant, he did it low-key, from a family standpoint, and he just went out and done the job.

I just sort of look at it that we came along—my father ran the first Winston Cup race that they had—and we came along and grew up as NASCAR grew up, so we were just a part of the growth. . . . Some people look at it as being a bigger part, we look at it as just being a part; because if we hadn't've been there, maybe somebody else would have been there, but we happened to be there.

And then we needed, NASCAR needed, everybody else that was

there in order to make it work. In other words, it wasn't a one-man show, or a one-team show, it took all the teams that came along, all the building years, it takes everybody to put the show on and make it interesting enough that more people come back the next race.

Again, as NASCAR grew, and the France family grew, then the Petty family grew along with 'em.

You look back through history, there was always somebody that come along and done their thing when they needed it. We go back, and, you know, say, Arnold Palmer came along when golf needed a kick in the pants, you know what I mean? Michael Jordan sort of came along when basketball needed something. . . . Babe Ruth came along when baseball needed something. I hope that the Pettys sort of fit into that category—that when racing needed something, we were able to come along and contribute a little bit to help it go to the next level.

■ *Most of the drivers in this book chose great victories as their greatest day . . . but Hut Stricklin chose a pair of great memories that perhaps capture the essence of racing just as well. One was an outstanding run at a tough track; the other, a run against a good friend that became even more memorable in light of a later tragedy.*

My greatest day in auto racing. . . . I'd like to think it hasn't come yet. [Laughs.] . . . Actually, I've been pretty fortunate to date, I've had two greatest days . . . in auto racing. Of course, the first one happened in 1991, at Michigan, when I finished second there to the late Davey Allison. [*Allison died in a helicopter crash on July 13, 1993.*] He and I battled all day long, back and forth, first and second all day long, and really had the time of our life. Then we got to fly home together in his plane after the race, and rerun the race all over again, back and forth to ourselves. That was probably one of my biggest days, certainly one of the most memorable, at least.

And then, probably the other one was the time at Darlington, in 1996, I think it was, the Southern 500. I thought we qualified tenth or something that day, and we had just an awesome car. It was just . . . a deal where everything we did that day, it was the right move—whether it was things I was doing in the car, to things the crew chief was making, to things the pit crew was doing. Everybody did their job to the utmost best, without any kind of flaw whatsoever.

We led the most laps that day, and ended up finishing second to Jeff Gordon—he passed us with around seventeen or eighteen laps to go. But that was pretty much a miracle day for us, because we led so many laps and came so close to winning—to have it taken away there at the end, we had some overheating problems, things like that, that kind of cost us a lot of our chances to win.

Still, it was a good day, a good finish for us, but it was somewhat disappointing, too, to be so dumb and have to give it up like that at the end.

I think we qualified something like tenth, we got the green flag—they dropped the green flag—we went and kind of held our position there all day for . . . probably until about the first pit stop. Really didn't pass anybody, or maybe not many, and, I want to say, maybe a hundred miles into the race it seemed like our car just became so dominant.

It was like the first hundred miles it was just decent, and we really didn't make any kind of adjustment, I remember plain as day, just like it was yesterday. We had talked on the radio—Felipe Lopez, my crew chief at the time, and myself—we talked about it, and he asked me what kind of adjustments did I want or anything. I really didn't know what to tell him it needed, because the car felt so good I really didn't want to do anything at the time.

When we made our first stop, four-tire stop under green, and we came back out of the pits . . . the car from that moment on was so dominant, we ended up going from tenth to first right after that stop, and personally had the entire field about a lap down. . . . I think there was about three cars there that wasn't a lap down, and I think one of 'em was Jeff Gordon and the other was Mark Martin. Everybody else I think we had pretty much lapped the whole field.

It was really the most awesome feeling, especially when I look back on that race. . . . You don't really get to capture, when you're in the car, you don't really feel the emotions like you do after a race when you step back from a race and think, Wow—what you just did. To be so dominant and so good that day at Darlington, which is the toughest track on the circuit, it was pretty awesome.

Darlington was actually the first superspeedway race I had ever run. The first time there was in 1982, at that time it was the Darlington NASCAR they called 'em, those little four-cylinder cars. And I thought all superspeedways was like Darlington, never knowing . . . the other ones was gonna be different. . . . I think the next one I went to was Atlanta, and I was like . . . pleasantly surprised.

Darlington always reminded me of a racetrack there in Birmingham. I know Davey Allison and myself used to talk about that racetrack, actually both racetracks. It was actually a thinking man's racetrack. . . . It wasn't so much who had the fastest car or who could run the fastest lap, it was a racetrack that you, like everybody says, you've always gotta race the track, and you've got to continually think—you can never put your brain in neutral there.

Always, every time I ran Darlington, I always had a clear head going into the race, knowing what I had to do, and pretty much . . . I don't want to say *forgetting* about the competition, but you pretty much just about have to really concentrate, to think all day long. You plan for the last fifty or one hundred miles of the race, and do the first, at that time, four hundred, staying out of [trouble].

. . . It's really kind of disappointing when you're out there running, because nobody is on the radio telling you, "Hey, you've got a lap on the field," or "You've just about lapped everybody." Nobody's telling you that on the radio, and I think, especially at Darlington, you're so intrigued in what you're doing, and so caught up in what you're doing, that you really don't think about what you're doing, almost, as far as . . . you're thinking about driving, you're not thinking, "Hey, I'm leading this race," or "I'm running wherever I'm running."

I've said, I get more excited now when I talk about it, or when I look back at that race, different things, than probably when I did then.

It's so hard—racing at the Winston Cup level is so hard and so tough to get—to have a good run, or to be successful, and especially to beat guys like Gordon and Martin. They've got exceptional talent, and they've also got a lot of money behind 'em, and just an awful lot of things that really make them dominant.

And to be a class ahead of them, on that given day, is just overwhelming, to imagine that you could actually get one up on them, especially with the team that we had then. Not that we didn't have a good team, because we did, but the group of guys there that we had was hard workers and great personalities and everybody got along great and all that stuff, but . . . we weren't the team that had the ten engineers behind it—all that stuff that all the top-notch teams have now.

I think it's a combination of a lot of things. I think the crew chief I had back then, just like now, he's an exceptional guy, he's very smart, very methodical, he gives the car what it wants rather than trying to say, "Here, we're gonna put this under." He reads the car well, and I think that was a big key.

I don't want to say that I did anything different, because I don't really think I did. . . . I always go to bed early before a race, and try to eat right, and do all the right stuff, and I didn't do anything different that weekend than I ever had.

It was pretty much just a combination of things. We had good engine people that really worked hard, spent a lot of late hours and long hours on the engines and stuff that gave us good power then. They didn't really . . . they couldn't make power [out of] money, because we didn't necessarily have [money] then, but they could stay up later than other people, if that makes sense—and they did make it up in that aspect of it.

What happened there . . . Michigan was always a good track for me, it's really not my favorite. I don't know that I really have a favorite on the circuit, but it's really not even one of my favorite tracks. We finished fourth there in my rookie year one time, and it's just been a racetrack that seems to have been good to me over the years.

This particular time I was driving for Davey's dad, Bobby, and we had been having a pretty exceptional year that year. There again, we had a lot of good guys on that time; one of the best crew chiefs in Jimmy Finney, he was crew chief then. We started this race, in practice we'd been fighting a problem with the car. For some reason or other we couldn't seem to get the car to start right in the center of the corners.

I guess Davey had come over there and talked to Bobby, and he was having somewhat of a similar problem, he and I both kind of shared information all the time back and forth, told each other what the other one had, different things like that. He and I both kind of hit on something, the thing that you see now, like Martin and Burton and different ones sharing information, he and I did that quite a bit.

And I think, when I look back on that, that was always a big help to me as well as him, too. But that day, we didn't qualify well, it was like seventeenth or eighteenth, which is not that bad, but anyway, at the drop of the green flag our car was pretty good. I think Davey started somewhere way up ahead of us. It just seemed like the longer we ran, there again, our car was just really good.

The car had been really loose all day, and I had come on the radio several times and told the guys how loose the car was, but I said, "It sure is loose, but it sure is fast, and I don't want to do nothing about it." So we worked our way to the front, and seesawed with Davey all day. I'll never forget, it seemed like he led awhile, I led awhile—I'm gonna say about halfway, we were pretty much gone. I think Martin made a charge at us there at the end, but he didn't get to us.

It was just finally the last pit stop of the day. We came in for whatever reason, I really don't even know what happened. But they beat us out of the pits on a pit stop, and he [Davey Allison] never relinquished the lead for the rest of the day; I finished second to him. At that time it was pretty exciting.

You know, what was odd about that day, and about that weekend as a matter of fact—two guys from Alabama finished one-two on Sunday, and then on Saturday two guys from Alabama finished one-two in the ARCA race. That was very odd. If you wanted to do good at Michigan that weekend, you had to be from Alabama.

As a person, there was probably nobody in the sport that has done more for me that has done more for me to help me get to where I need to be at, than him [Allison]. He tooted my horn so many times when I couldn't, and opened doors for me when I couldn't, and just did an awful lot for me to get where I'm at. Probably besides him, the only other one would be Donny and Bobby Allison that done as much.

As a race driver . . . I don't want this to come out wrong—but I never really thought Davey was . . . I never really thought he had the natural ability that say, a Dale Earnhardt's got, or something like that. But Davey had an ability to teach himself what he needed to learn to be successful and to do good at it, and to drive.

You know, it seemed like he had such a knack at it that was like you, you could see him, from the time he started until his last race he ran, the guy just continually got better and better and better and better. I think it's probably a combination of, one, what he was learning about the cars, and I think another was the feel that he had, that he could relay back to whoever his crew chief was at the time, Larry McReynolds, or Joey Knuckles or whoever it was. He just had such a great feel.

I don't really feel like he had the Dale Earnhardt natural ability, but he had such a self-taught ability. And really . . . I don't know that many people would ever notice that about him . . . just from being around him. Because I was around him before he ever started driving . . . because he and I kind of grew up together, running around Birmingham, chasing each other around the grandstands.

It's pretty unbelievable—that family was so famous and so on top of the world at one time . . . to have things happen to them and be so out of it now, it's just unreal.

He's a pretty neat guy, I tell you . . . I miss him a lot.

HERB THOMAS

■ *From 1949 to 1956, Herb Thomas had a relatively brief but memorable NASCAR career, winning a pair of Grand National Championships in 1951 and 1953, and winning nine races in 1952 while finishing second to Tim Flock in the points battle. Thomas's greatest day, though, came after he teamed up with Smokey Yunick, when he won the last in a series of three memorable victories in the Southern 500 at Darlington.*

I don't know what that would be, there've been so many of them. Winning Darlington the third time, I guess, would be a good one.

It's been so long ago, I don't know where to start. I had forty-eight wins, I won the Grand National, I had three Southern 500s that I won, 1951, 1954, and 1955. I was driving a 1955 Chevrolet in that third one, Chevrolet had just come out, and Smokey Yunick built his own car. We won without changing tires—that car was just built for racing. There wasn't anything that compared to the Hudson, until that Chevrolet came out, it was more like a Hudson.

I know I wasn't far back, I don't remember my pole position, I was pretty close to being up front. I just got out there and went. I didn't want to run too hard, I was just trying to take care of the car.

I was the first one to do that, to win three Southern 500s. I guess that would have to be it, or being the first one to win two championships. I didn't get to run too long before I got hurt in 1956, just from 1949 to 1956.

The car was running pretty smooth, I was running along, just conserving my tires. When the others started blowing tires, I just kept going along, and I went along and won the race. I can't remember the mileage per hour that day, it was pretty good for a small-block Chevy.

I think Joe Weatherly was leading the race, and he blew a tire pretty close to the end, but they were pretty close together, he was driving a Ford. A lot of people blew tires that day, they were just wearing, they didn't have 'em set up right, I guess, or something, and of course the Chevy was light, and I was preserving it.

I believe it was a Firestone tire, if I remember. I've got some pictures of it, and it shows that it had some tread on it, even after the five hundred miles. I had a pretty good average that year, speedwise. Bud Baker won that race in 1953 at 92 mph, so I would have an idea it was in that range. Of course, it's according to how many wrecks they had, to the miles per hour. I just had a smooth race and stayed out of trouble.

In the other two I was running against Chryslers and Oldsmobiles, and this was the small-block Chevy. I had been running in a Hudson, until they went out in 1954. The Hudson was a heavier car, but it was faster, but the Chevy didn't lose any ground, either. Smokey Yunick set it up with Maury Rose—he was working with Chevrolet then— that USAC driver. He was there; I remember a lot about that, it was a pretty big win for Chevrolet. It was the first win for a small-block Chevy on a superspeedway. They had won some hundred-milers, but it was the first major win. I won with it on the short track in March— not that car, but another one that I just bought out of the showroom. I liked the car, and they came out with that in time for September, for the Labor Day race.

It was pretty well toward the end when I passed Weatherly. The first Southern 500 was in the Hudson in 1951, and I had been running my old Plymouth. Marshall Teague had two Hudsons, he got me to drive one. It's hard to say, but I guess that third one would be more of a record, it was more of a win for the small-block Chevy back when they came out with it. That's the same thing, they're still running that today.

I had a third and a fifth in those other two races. One time I was leading in 1952 with maybe eight or nine laps to go, and I broke a crankshaft. I lost that one at Darlington, but I had a real good finish there—that was one of my favorite tracks, I entered that race six times. I didn't get to run there in 1950, I qualified a Plymouth, then I came home and bought a new one I was gonna run it in place of it, and they wouldn't let me run, so I didn't get to run in 1950. I think the insurance company called in or something and said, "Hey, you can't race that car. . . . Johnny Manse won it on a Plymouth."

■ *In 1989, at the age of forty-eight, Dick Trickle was the Winston Cup Rookie of the Year. But for over thirty years before that, Trickle had been a short-track legend in the Midwest, with over twelve hundred wins, who helped define the local circuit, barnstorming around the country to race wherever there was a potential victory and a purse to win, and running occasionally in the Busch Grand National and then Winston Cup as time and schedule allowed. Dick Trickle's trip back in the time capsule took him through his early days to his greatest victory at the Milwaukee Mile, encompassing a lifetime of racing memories that hearken back to a bygone era.*

My greatest day in auto racing. . . . The problem is you have over forty years, and naturally, in forty years I've had great days and bad days. You know, of course, you win some and you lose some, and it's just hard to pick one out.

. . . See, I'm originally from Wisconsin, and Wisconsin is a great short-trace state; as is the Midwest for late-model stock cars. When I started racing it was just stock-car racing—you know, Saturday nights or Sundays, whatever. . . . Then it got to be a circle where you could run as much as six times a week within a hundred-mile radius.

Of course, the granddaddy of them all is the Milwaukee Mile. I won many races in central Wisconsin or Midwest . . . or the short track, whether it was at the Dells or the Conner or the Golden Sands—you know, the nightly races, all the way from Wednesday to Sunday. But, the Milwaukee Mile was kind of like . . . you know, in just our little state there, would have been the Daytona of the state of Wisconsin.

And I had gone down there and hadn't won—had the opportunity to win the Milwaukee race, had run USAC back in 1968, 1970, 1971 right there. And then ASA went on in there and ran some in the early 1980s, whatever. All my efforts—I hadn't won at Milwaukee, back when ASA started running there in the 1980s—I finally won Milwaukee. Of course, I've won a lot since.

. . . It was kind of like *the* track in Wisconsin. Back when I won the first race at Milwaukee—because of the "almost dids" and the engine failures when I was leading, and the blown engine in front of me that got in the way one time when I was gonna win . . . [It seemed like I was] always gonna win but not take home the checkered flag. So I always remember winning my first Milwaukee race as kind of a stepping stone.

But then you get up into 1983, down in Jefferson, Georgia, which was Jefferson Speedway back then, but now it's Peach State Speedway. And I believe it was in 1983, they build a World Crown 300, which was well-advertised that all the best short-trackers in the country should come, because whoever wins this race will be the king of short tracks.

In fact, the trophy was the cape and crown and scepter—and, of course, if you won the race, who wants to wear that? But if you won this particular race, it paid $50,000 to win in 1983, and some of the greats from the West, Midwest, Southeast, whatever—whoever was somebody—went to that particular race because it paid $50,000 to win, and a big purse in those days was $10,000 and maybe they had about two or three races over a five-year period that paid maybe $20K, but eight to ten thousand dollars was considered a big purse.

This one paid $50K, and I put my whole fall into it, because it was a late-fall race in 1983, and I put a lot of effort in, completely built my car up from bottom to top, end to end. Every bearing, every piece of that car, was redone and polished, buffed, shined—because if you could win $50,000, it would make a whole difference in your annual, almost your decade, you know?

And I did go home winning that race, with my largest short-track purse . . . plus you got to wear the crown and the cape (laughs), which you wouldn't do if you didn't win. And of course, they told me it got put in a glass case, and you could use it for a trophy later on. That one stuck out, naturally.

Of course, then you go on to about 1990, and I won the Winston Open down here at Charlotte in my first full year of racing Winston Cup, realizing I'd run my rookie year, almost a full year prior to that, won Rookie of the Year in 1989. And then Cale Yarborough hired me to run the Phillips 66 car, won the Winston Open, and came in the first half of the Winston from the back, up to sixth.

We had bias tires back then, and I was moving on to where I might have been able to win, but at the midbreak, we all put on a set of tires, and that particular set of tires, the stagger closed up on and I got a push the last half of Winston. I might have won the Winston the way I was running the first half. It was only the tire-stagger problem that took it away from me, perhaps.

That was kind of a big race for me, winning the Winston Open, and getting a good run in the Winston.

The first time I raced out of the state of Wisconsin was 1966. I went down to Rockford, Illinois, which is on the edge of Wisconsin, but it was still the first National 200 in the fall, the first one they had—they've still got it today. And I went down there in a whole new arena, whole new era, had to change my car because of the specific rules. It was a fall race, car season was done. My cars . . . At that time I raced five nights a week, and they weren't handsome to look at and they weren't pretty, but they were fast.

The locals there, the racers, I was a little behind the times, I had a two-barrel carburetor, where you could run a four-barrel down there, so I took one from a wrecking yard. But I couldn't get it to run, and they snickered a little bit at me. My car didn't look like it was gonna be a competitive car. But by the time the day was over, I'd won the race by . . . I lapped the field and won my first out-of-state race in 1966, the Rockford Nationals—short-track nationals, they called 'em.

And then, the following year I thought, Well, how good am I? You know, you run against your locals, you win more than your share, but you don't know what you are when you get out. It's like a college player or high-school player thinks he's great until he gets to college or pros. You don't know—you're good at what you do for where you're at, but how fast is my car and my team?

The following year, I went down to I-70—Odessa, Missouri, near Kansas City there. They had a 300-lap race, and I won that, and that kind of gave me momentum, to not just stay in central Wisconsin where they had three- or four-hundred-dollar feature races on Friday night, Saturday and Sunday, Thursday night, Wednesday, which . . . Over the week you'd do good, because you ran five times and, you run in the top five, you'd probably make a couple thousand dollars.

And in the early stage we could build a car in the wrecking yard, realizing, as time went on, pretty soon you designed and built your own chassis, and you bought parts; it got to be quite technical over the years, you had pretty technical and well-rounded race cars. And the tire bills went up and up. We started out on street tires, then we went to slicks, and better slicks, and wider slicks, and more and more money was spent, and the pay scale never seemed like it went more and more, you know?

So I had to start reaching out and running special events, from Canada to Florida. Of course, my stepping stone was winning at Rockford in 1966 and then the following year, in 1967, going down and winning in Odessa, Missouri, the 300-lapper, which told me, Okay I am competitive, I can afford to put gas in the truck and take my three or four guys with me and we can run to Cayuga, Canada, or to Cincinnati, or to Mobile, Alabama, or wherever it might be.

So although I ran locally there, on maybe Tuesday-Wednesday-Thursday, and maybe even Friday night, we'd jump in the truck and maybe haul to another state and run a major event that would pay eight to twelve thousand dollars, and were able to make a living doing that. Some of the races are special because they were stepping stones to another thing, some are special because of the monetary pay on 'em.

And then you get back to other specials—like in the last two to four years of racing I lost some very close friends and competitors, Kyle Mabrebelt, who races in Wisconsin, Larry Dietches, who is from Wausau, Wisconsin, who kind of ran from California to Florida, and all back then, too. I lost some really good friends to incidents or accidents and injuries. And then, of course, years after that they would have a memorial. Once a year at Wausau Speedway they have a memorial for Larry Dietches, who is quite infamous, and a dear friend of mine. I've won his memorial many times, because I really put a lot of effort in, because it's like Larry's watching me.

Of course, at the Wisconsin Dells where Lyle Mazlow got killed, a close friend of mine and a fellow racer, I won a lot of his memorials. Now, they were always special because they were his races, memorials for him. I put as much effort into a race that probably paid just a fair market pay, which wasn't much up there, but it was close to the heart that I race for those.

So there's monetary reasons that you win, there's infamous reasons you win, there's personal reasons you win. Of course, all this while I've gotta put food on the table, because racing was my life and my career and supported the family. So it was pretty important that I get consistent finishes to maintain a racing career, to maintain a house and food for the family.

I'm sure General Electric or Motorola or Intel or Microsoft, they all started in a basement someplace, or a hobby in the garage, or whatever. In my career . . . I started racing out of high school just because I wanted to race when I was nine years old, and just fell in love with it, and all I wanted to do from that point on was drive a race car. Built me a junker when I was fourteen, fifteen, sixteen years old, and just went to a Saturday-night car place outside of this town or that town. Knew nothing . . . had no family of racers or nothing, had to learn from the ground-level up. Built my own cars and engines for the first twenty-five years of my career, with some support of buddies and guys that would help me. I mean, I would do major work, but you always need someone to hold the other end of the rotor, or clean parts, or something. I got some support from some of my friends; I was just glad for the help in the early years. As the years went on, I was able to hire people to make my team better and more secure.

I love racing because we know the height of racing today, which is tenfold from what I ever would have expected to be in my first five, ten years of racing. For me to be in at the professional level is another thing, but I guess I really appreciate the fact that racing has gone all the way from white car to blue to you-name-it. It's everywhere, it's not just Southeast support anymore, or Midwest. . . . I remember when you were looked down upon if you raced. Now they look up at you, it's a complete 180.

When I started racing, the motorcyclists and racers were just like scum of the earth. Now it's almost the opposite, at every level . . . because it's the top shelf, naturally. But I really appreciate it personally, because I love racing to the point where even if it wasn't at this level . . . if it was still kind of where we were looked down at, I would be doing it, because I just enjoy the competition, the mechanics, the technology. I come from a blacksmith-born, engineering-type background, although I never schooled beyond high school, but you learn a lot on the job.

I think racing is tenfold [beyond] where I ever thought it would be, which I'm very proud of, because it was my game anyhow. And I have the question asked of me, Is racing going in the right direction?

For some that's been in it for forty years, or some that's been in it for twenty-five years, or raced in the late 1970s or early 1980s—maybe not. Or for fans. But we are getting ready for the new fans and for the new drivers. You can't make racing today for the twenty-five-year fans, the thirty-year fans and racers. I'm not saying it's wrong—it ain't the way that we did it.

But don't you think in ten years from now it ain't gonna be the way we did it ten years ago? We are setting the stage for a new group of fans, a new group of drivers, a whole new millennium. So, yeah, it is going in the right direction, but not for a guy who used to sit at a dirt track in the front row and get full of dirt. He'll say no.

Ask a sixteen-year-old that's going into the new era of motor sports, he'll say yeah. If you use the broad spectrum, I think racing's going in the right direction. Of course, NASCAR's taken it to great heights, as have individual owners and promoters. You take the speedway corporation today, with Bruton Smith—he sets the stage, he's made show palaces out of racetracks, and complete racing facilities for the fans, the racer, the TV, the media, whatever. It isn't done single-handedly by a driver, by an owner, by NASCAR, by a track or a car owner. It's kind of a unanimous ball, you know?

The deal right now—$35 million for ten years to put a name on the Charlotte Motor Speedway. Who would have thought of that ten years ago? Now the racing facility is getting paid just to carry the Lowes' name . . . I mean, where does it stop? I don't see it stopping. It's gonna go for ten more years, and then the worse that's gonna happen is it's gonna level off.

It's a great sport. I've had my opportunity to go to baseball or football games, it made me appreciate race fans. I think the race fans are the best fans—they're hard, they're true. I believe our fans buy more stuff because of our sponsors, than any other fan. If Phillips 66 sponsors me, there's gonna be a lot of fans that get a Phillips 66 credit card. When Phillips 66 goes out of the racing business, there's gonna be a lot of people that cut up the cards. It's now genderized, 42 percent female, which brings the families and the children into effect. It's probably at the kitchen table in New York City, whereas before it was just in North Wilkesboro.

It's making things happen that ain't natural . . . our schedules get so busy. You've got four fans want your autograph, they don't realize that you've got to be from A to B in seven minutes, and you could sign those four, but by the time you sign those four there's gonna be twenty fans, and then you've gotta say no to twenty. And they say you wouldn't come home to sign autographs—well, they don't know what's going on on the other end of it, and this is gonna happen more and more.

It's quite a game, the schedule's getting bigger and bigger and bigger. Las Vegas, we're going there this week . . . I don't want to say it's a hustle now, it's terrific.

There's a twofold story here: Teams win races, not drivers. . . .
Now, Jeff Gordon does a great job in the race car, he's very professional, and he does a great job. And you can't take anything away
from . . . you know, they all have their eras—Dale Earnhardt; Bill Elliott, a couple of years earlier he was the man to beat. It goes in eras,
and it's a team effort. I don't think Bill Elliott's any worse a racer today than he was when he won those races, but he doesn't have the
team that's clicking to today's rhythm, if you follow me.

The number 24 team, with Ray Evernham involved and all the
sponsors—it's the team to beat today. If you put another driver in, it
would still be the team to beat, although I don't think another driver
would do it better. Don't get me wrong, I'm not taking away Jeff's
professionalism and the experience that he's got. You can't wager
that—it's kind of like taking your high-school team over to play football against the Green Bay Packers. It's a deal where you know where
you're at with your team. I feel I'm a top-five driver, but I haven't had
a consistent top-five team. Of course, any driver that didn't think
that, he'd have to get out of the business.

I like real racers . . . but then you go back to, "Is racing going in
the right direction?" Where I came from, it was man and machine,
and you built it, you worked on it, you changed the tires, you welded
on it, and you beat on it, you did the bodywork, you painted it. So I
kind of like that kind of racer, naturally, who's really involved with all
those things. Although with today's sport, that's not the way it is, because that driver is not an all-around anymore; he's busy doing the
media and taking care of his sponsors and the charity, whatever—all
he can do is coordinate with the team, have meetings, and get feed-
back to the crew chief.

In order to get bigger and bigger, it can't be man and machine anymore. It's gonna be team, and sponsor, and driver and media person-
nel, PR people . . . it's gonna be politics, it's gonna be money, as
with any major sport, it just gets bigger and bigger. As part of the
driving, I would enjoy to go and drive some little half-mile track, couple hundred–lapper . . . but you can't go backwards.

There's two things I like—there's real racers, because I come from there, and there's some of them out around the country, whether it's a Mike Eddy or a Mike Miller or a Bob Senneker. These guys are just as good racers as the Earnhardts and the Elliotts and the Wallaces. . . . Of course, I know all the Midwest stars that are great today, from Kulwicki to Mark Martin to Rusty—they were all my juniors, I taught most of 'em for the first third of their career or whatever, and they're all friends of mine. Ken Schrader, you know, he's a racer. You can't help but like the guy, he's a racer through and through.

. . . Of course, we've all had to step in line to what the beat of the drum is today.

But if one sticks out that's done as much for racing—has been probably the best ambassador through the era—you'd have to say Richard Petty. Because he is today, and has been, the best ambassador; I'm talking off the track, as much or more so than on the track. There's nobody gonna ever do for racing, from a personal standpoint, as much as Richard Petty has.

You can take the Earnhardts and Gordons and all of 'em, but there's nobody that will fill his shoes completely, although they will all do the best they can. And I'm not saying they won't do a good job, but he has maintained it. I mean, today, he's still a super ambassador for us as an owner and whatever.

My first experience with him was a bad one. I raced him since about 1970, I raced him Grand National—Winston Cup, today they call it—just a couple races a year here and there, maybe a Daytona, maybe a Charlotte, maybe a Rockingham. Like in the early spring before our main season got going up in the snow country.

I never raced seriously, because I held my rookie status until 1989, when I won Rookie of the Year. But I raced for different teams, just individual teams that didn't race all year. In the late 1970s, or maybe early 1980s, I went to Rockingham, and I was running around, I made the race, and I was probably gonna get twentieth or something, maybe fifteenth, but Richard came underneath me off of [turn] two and went right into the side of me and knocked me into the wall.

Evidently his car pushed or he lost control—I'm sure he didn't do it on purpose. But it hurt me because it was one of my single little efforts that I made to run Winston Cup, and somebody told me, "Well, maybe you're not supposed to pass Richard Petty"—it was just a joke, naturally.

When I ran against Richard was when his team had gone over the hill a little bit, and he wasn't as competitive. I didn't race against him during his prime years, because I was racing the short tracks in the Midwest and he was racing the Grand National down here. So when I started running and Richard was still driving, he was at the end of his career.

Back a couple years ago, many a time people have come to me, business owners, sponsors, they said, "If you'd have been down here twenty or twenty-five years ago, you'd be an Earnhardt or Waltrip, one of the kingpins." But I said, "I have a better life and have had a better life than any of them. I would not give up my last twenty-five years."

And the dual side of that is, if I would have been down here twenty-five years before, it would be getting to be old stuff to me. Now it's only nine, ten years that I'm in it, so the newness is still fun, I enjoy it, it's a new challenge. But do you think the ones that have been running Winston Cup for thirty years are having as much fun as I am the last ten?

So I still enjoy it. I'm around the race track, I don't go hide out and go to my motel, I come around the pits, and you'll see me involved with the car, coordinating, running back and forth between the Busch and the Cup and doing this and that. There's so many that I would go back and relive; in fact, I would go back and relive the last twenty-five years and not change a thing.

You go down and you remember the personal gratitude, your friends, fans, family that you race for, sponsors. . . . You remember that first win in Milwaukee. I remember that win at Jefferson, Georgia, there, I remember the Winston Open, I remember the highs. . . . You could jump over the moon at that time, you're wide open. But the next day you have to get ready for the next race, you have to be able to celebrate in a hurry, because you haven't won the next one yet and you haven't competed.

So, win or lose, you have to get rid of that in less than twenty-four hours and go on, just as you did before you won. I think through the years, although there's a lot of personal value, a lot of personal joy, I maintained a level, win or lose. I was the same on Monday. That's something you almost have to teach yourself to do, because there's many Mondays that are gonna come, and you want to be the same man Monday as you were last year, next year, and five years from now I'll be the same person when it comes Monday, whether I won or whether I lost.

That's something I think a true sportsman type has to learn and work on. He can't get overjoyed when you win and you can't get the opposite when you lose. What is losing? Today a fourth-place finish isn't a loss, realizing you always have that number one position, but back in '92 I didn't have a ride . . . I'd driven in '89, '90 and '91 in Winston Cup and I didn't come up with a sponsor and a ride come '92, so the Raymont team with Butch and Bob Hilley didn't have a sponsor either, so they called me just to go run Daytona.

They didn't have the money to run the year, and we took a non-sponsor's car there, and it was kind of an individual-type effort, and I got fifth at Daytona in '92. Well, that's a win. In fact, because of it, I did end up driving the Snickers car for Savolas the rest of the year. They called me and hired me to drive for them that year. So getting fifth in that race got me a ride for the rest of that year, not Winston car, but with another owner.

I've raced against and had fans from three or four genera-tions . . . grandpa, dad, son, son, you know? Usually a lot of times you'll see if grandpa and dad's got a Ford, the kid's got a Ford. Well, that's kind of how my fans went down through families.

KENNY WALLACE

■ *Like his older brother Rusty, Kenny Wallace started his career in the ASA series, winning Rookie of the Year in 1986 and then moving South to drive for his brother's Busch Grand National team. His Winston Cup career got off to a rocky start in the early 1990s, but Wallace redeemed himself from a difficult experience with Felix Sabates by winning at Bristol and capping off the victory with a Polish victory lap.*

Well, it was in 1994. I had won a night race at Bristol, and it was basically my comeback. I had been very successful in racing. I started in 1986 and won the ASA Rookie of the Year. And then I moved on to the Busch Grand National series in 1991 and won Rookie of the Year, and finished second in the points, and won races. And then in 1993 Felix Sabates fired me when I was driving the Dirt Devil car. He had me in an all-time slump, so in 1994 I went to drive for Philmar Racing. And when Ernie Irvan got hurt, Robert Yates asked me to drive the Texaco Havelin car.

Well, that very race in Bristol, Tennessee, the night race, in 1994— I won the Busch Grand National race that night, I'd just turned thirty-one years old. And the next night I went on to finish tenth in the Texaco car. So that was my greatest day in sports, because it was a major mark of achievement of my ability. And then I went on to win two more races that year, and of course that team—that Dirt Devil team—became defunct, and Bobby Hamilton missed a couple of races in that car.

I had won eight Busch races, eight poles, two-time most-popular driver, but that was probably the most satisfying day in my racing career.

That day, practice was in the daytime, and the car qualified very well. We qualified, I believe, in the top six. And I was going back and forth from the Texaco Havelin car to the number 8 Busch Grand National car. And the car was a little bit tight that day, it was pushing a little bit, and we started the race and we settled in third place behind Ricky Craven.

Harry Gant went out, and he was on Hoosier tires, and he was just killing the field. And before I know it, Harry Gant slowed up, the Hoosier tires gave up. We made a pit stop, I got the push out of my car, and went on to lap the whole field up to eighth spot. And Kenny Schrader finished second, and Ricky Craven was third.

I think the neatest part about it was, after I won the night race, I did the Alan Kulwicki, the backwards victory lap, the Polish victory lap. And then I was so happy that ESPN used the victory-lane clips in a lot of their promos, and it was a big night.

As a matter of fact, early in the race I was running right on the bottom of the racetrack. And I was pushing so bad that I was trying to get down on the left line to grab a little bit of stickier pavement. Well, after I made the pit stop I realized my car was turning a little bit better, and I moved to the middle of the track, and, as a matter of fact, a lot of people noticed it. And when I moved to the middle of the track, it was gone. The only thing I had to worry about was when I was lapping cars, that I didn't wreck myself.

Winning at night at Bristol, or any night race on the Cup circuit . . . Now, at that time, in 1994 . . . Bristol was the only night race on the circuit, and then along came the other ones. Bristol—if you win a race at Bristol, it gives you . . . It's a feather in your cap, because if you can win at Bristol, people think you're a good driver.

. . . The atmosphere was just great. You know, my motor home was parked outside. It just felt so good to have achieved something at a very famous racetrack with everybody watching.

I tell you, the next day was the Winston Cup race, we really didn't do nothing. Me and my wife were so relieved that I had come back after a bad year in 1993, we were so relieved that I came back and won, that I actually just slept so damn good it was unreal.

I think in professional sports it's hard to celebrate because people are always there to criticize every move you make. So if I would have celebrated and didn't do no good the next day, then they would have blamed it on me celebrating, so I just took my win and savored the moment with my wife, and went on to bed.

What that victory meant to me . . . it proved to never doubt your ability, because up until that point, after I got fired in 1993, after my Winston Cup stint, they had me doubting my own ability. I think, now that I look back at it, the lesson that victory taught me was to never, ever, no matter what people say, doubt your ability. Because people can ruin your faith if you let them, and if you don't have that constant positive mental attitude, you might as well just quit whatever you're trying to do.

The reason [the firing] played into the win was because Felix thought that I couldn't drive a Winston Cup race car, and he fired me. His reasoning was that he thought I couldn't drive a race car. Well, plus, he was easily influenced. Me and Felix are good friends to this day, but he was easily influenced, and he later . . . you can print this, too . . . I think one of my best victories was him being humbled after 1993, after the defunct departure of that team, and selling it out to Dick Brooks.

I think it meant a lot to me. . . . He recently, within the last couple of years—I believe it was in 1996—he personally came to my brother, Rusty Wallace, and me, and apologized. He said that he had made an error, that he listened to one person, that he should have never listened to that person, and realized that I was full of talent, that my rookie year was just a rough year. So anyway, that was it.

When you win you don't have to talk to anybody, it speaks for itself. As a matter of fact, he said to me . . . in Richmond . . . two weeks later in the drivers' meeting . . . after I won my second race in three weeks . . . he says, "Boy, them hiring you in that number 28 car sure has built your confidence."

So I knew he was just letting me know that Robert letting me drive the number 28 car—he thought it was building my confidence, that's why I was winning races. So it doesn't have to do with your confidence or your ability, it has to do with getting a chance, and good equipment, and making the most of it. That's what builds your confidence.

MICHAEL WALTRIP

■ *Marriage and motor sports? The combination was a match made in heaven for Michael Waltrip, who proposed in victory lane during a national television interview with ESPN's Benny Parsons after his Busch Grand National victory in Bristol, Tennessee, in 1993. Winning the Winston was Waltrip's biggest career victory, but it's hard to top this description of his personal greatest day.*

Well, probably the most important race of my career was definitely winning the Winston. That was a pretty big deal, and it remains to this day the biggest win that I've had. I think it's probably been talked about as much as any of the Winstons—passing Dale Earnhardt and Terry Labonte there in the last segment, and going on to win the race.

We started out the evening by being in the Winston Open. I never had won a Winston Cup race, so I was in the Winston Open and they transferred the top five finishers out of that race into the Winston. We finished fifth, and barely did that; I mean, my car just didn't handle real well in the Open, I just barely made it through into the Winston.

It started dead last in the Winston, but when I started the Winston, I knew my car was . . . We'd made the right changes, it was a lot better. And I remember the first thirty-lap segment, I was passing cars and moving up, and the crew was talking on the radio and they said,

"You know, every car you passed, you've gotta pass 'em again, because they invert the field [for the next segment]."

I was thinking, "Well, you're right, but I really need to see what I've got here, how good my car is." So I think I wound up finishing ninth, starting twentieth and finishing ninth in the first segment, and then when they inverted them I started eleventh, so I pretty much stayed where I was, and went from there to finish fourth in the second segment.

At the end of the second segment, I wasn't sitting there thinking to myself, "We're gonna win this race, or we're not," I was just . . . We were working on the car, trying to figure out what to do to it. And all the changes we discussed, we finally said, "Well, we were pretty good at the end of that deal, let's not screw it up, let's just leave it alone." Put four fresh tires on it, changed the air pressure a little bit, because it's not gonna go thirty laps, it's only gonna go ten, so we adjusted for that.

And when they threw the green flag, I got around those two—that was big when I passed 'em. But the best feeling I had that night was when I went down into turn three after passing them and having the lead. And the way my car stuck to the turns—I came off turn four, I looked at my mirror and said, "I don't care who's behind me, they ain't gonna catch me tonight." My car was just handling perfect, and we were able to run away and win, so that was probably the biggest night of my career.

The most important race I won in my career, the most memorable to me, was when I won the Busch race at Bristol. It was two days after Alan Kulwicki had unfortunately died, and I won the race, and just . . . didn't have it planned or anything, I just. . . . When I won I turned around and did that Polish victory lap for Alan.

It was the first one that was done. I don't know why I did it—that was his signature trademark, and I mean, everybody was just so distraught over what had happened to him. It was unbelievable. . . . He was the reigning champion and he had died, and everybody really respected Alan and the way he did things.

I did that for him, and got into victory lane and proposed to . . . my wife in victory lane. So I won a race, and then got engaged right after that, so that's probably the most memorable race for me personally. But the most important for my career, I'd say, was the Winston.

The Busch race, a lot of the practice had gotten rained out, the weather was a little iffy. It was real cold, very cold, and I went out on the racetrack for my first practice, and, this is the ironic thing about it, I pulled onto the racetrack for my first practice lap, and I come off turn four on the apron and spun out, just because the radial tires, you know, they didn't have any heat in 'em.

I just messed up, basically, and spun around. And when I did, a car went past me and hit the nose of my car. It didn't tear it all to pieces, he just brushed me, and it didn't hurt his car, and it just knocked the nose off of mine.

So we took duct tape and hammers and knocked it back around like it ought to be and taped it all up and went out and qualified ninth. And then on Saturday, started ninth, and just consistently had a good car, moved up, and made the right calls on the pit stops, pitted when I needed to, and got around a couple of really fast cars. Todd Bodine was running really good, he was probably a little faster than me, but I got around him during the pit-stop sequence, and then came out in front of . . . I guess Terry Labonte was running second.

I was leading with about a hundred to go, and I held him off forever, through some cautions and so forth. And I looked in my mirror and Todd Bodine had finally caught Terry, and I remember thinking, "Race him, Terry, because if you don't I'm gonna have to." Terry raced him for a while, and Todd finally got around him, but I had gotten out to a really pretty big lead by the end, and was able to win.

On Wednesday of that week, back in North Carolina, I decided . . . I made up my mind, I was gonna ask my wife, Buffy, to marry me. I went and bought the ring, I went to the jewelry store, got the ring, had the ring . . . hadn't thought about how I was gonna do that, either.

You know, it just so happened I won the race, and it felt appropriate to do it. And so I asked her to do that, with Benny Parsons, right there in victory lane, he was interviewing me, and I asked her to marry me right during the interview. He said, "Are you serious?"

And I said, "Yeah, I'm serious." And then she said, "Are you serious?" I said yes, and then she said, "Yes, I do," and we kissed. I sounded like a goofball . . . and I said, "Yeah, I got you a ring, it's in the truck."

I didn't have it with me, but as soon as we got out of victory lane I went over there and gave her her ring. I felt like I was in pretty good shape on that; [being on television] helped. We've been married five years now; that was 1993, we had been seeing each other for . . . maybe not quite a year and a half. . . . We were staying in Bristol, and we went back to the hotel, and there was all kinds of decorations on our room, congratulating us for winning the race and for getting [engaged] and everything. We just got room service and hung out.

Personally, the Busch victory is a tribute to Alan, and getting engaged—all that means more to me than winning the Winston did, personally. But winning the Winston gets talked about all the time now, whereas winning that Busch race doesn't. So careerwise, the Winston was more important. I wouldn't trade either one of them, they're both my best memories of a career that's fifteen or sixteen years old now. They're both very special to me, but that's kind of the way that I look at 'em.

The problem was in the Winston Open [the car] was just pushing terrible; the front end of the car would not turn in the corners. And I was racing Johnny Benson for fifth; we were running fifth and sixth, I was fifth and he was sixth, and he was just killing me. He was faster than I was, and was getting ready to pass me.

And I think prior to that, Lake Speed had had a flat or broke something, and he was running fifth, and I wasn't even in the top five. And I got around Lake when he had some sort of problem—I believe it was Lake, you might look at the finish, and if he's not one of the ones that finished ahead of me, it was definitely him.

But somebody in the top five fell out—it moved me into the top five, but I still didn't see how I was gonna be able to hold Johnny off, because he was just outrunning me. I just totally change my line, and totally adjusted what I was doing. I started letting off way early, I mean up on the back straightaway early, and rolling down into the corner and putting my wheels right on the white line and running the bottom off of four.

And the first time I did it in the three [turn], he about ran over, because I let off too early, but when we came off of four, I had a gap on him. And I said, "Man, that was cool, let's try that again." So we got back to come off [turn] two, and he caught back up because I was so tight down there, and then I got to three, and I did it again and I gained a little more, and I just was able to creep away from him doing that. That turned out to be key in the Winston, because when we got the car better, I continued to run the same line, and that was why I was able to pull away at the end, because I got my car working in that line.

It was just Charlotte, the whole deal where at the Winston you practice all day during the day, and you get your car how you think it ought to be and then you race it at night—and very seldom were you correct in what you guessed, you know?

Out in the sunshine, that track's really slippery and the cars slide around a lot, and in the night, they tighten up and they stick to the road better and they want to push. You know, while we thought we made the right decisions, we obviously hadn't, and the weather changing was a factor in us not being as good as we needed to be.

But then after the first 30-lapper, we changed the car a little bit, took spring rubbers out, moved the track bar, and took some wedge out. And then in the second 30-lapper, that's when I went from eleventh to fourth. And in doing that, I came in and we talked about rubber and we talked about wedge, and we couldn't make up our mind what to do, so finally we just all said, "Well, you know, heck with it, let's just leave it like it is."

And that obviously the right decision, because at the end of the race, it wasn't even close. . . . I was gone.

Victory lane was really neat, because the crew was just so excited. It was the Wood Brothers' first big win in a while, and it was only our eighth or tenth race together. And we kind of hit pay dirt there, and everybody was real excited. My brother Darrell, he came to victory lane and congratulated me, and I got a great poster of Winston, he and I hugging in victory lane.

And Dale Earnhardt came to victory lane to congratulate me, and it was jubilant. It was exciting, . . . fireworks that they shoot off after the Winston's over . . . I mean, I'll never forget all that, it was really special.

[Dale] kind of messed up a little bit; he got in the corner and underneath Terry and got a little bit loose, and when he corrected it turned right to save it and bumped into Terry and slowed them both up. I think Terry was a little perturbed, and Dale was doing what you expect him to do, he was going for it. It didn't work out for him, but I know he was happy that I won, so he gave it his best and it didn't work. I'm sure that after that, after the fact that he wasn't gonna get there, he was happy to see me win.

The significance is . . . that's one of our major races. Winning that event is something I'm very proud of, and obviously something no one can ever take away from me. They can say I haven't done this or haven't done that, but they can't say I haven't won the Winston. So it's important to me.

And what I learned from it that night was what Jim Valvano made so famous: Don't ever, ever give up. It would have been easy to say, "Our car's not right tonight," but that's just not my nature and it's not the nature of NASCAR racers. I mean, not just me—all of 'em are that way. We just didn't give up—they give you time to work on it, let's work on it and try to make it better.

Those are all the positive things about it. The negative thing about it is . . . I have to hear every day, "You've never won a points race." I'm like, Yeah, well . . . so what. I always tell people that when Mark Martin won the Winston this year and he jumped out in victory lane, they should have said, "Mark Martin, how do you feel?—you know, this isn't a points race." And he would have said, "I don't give a damn."

That's the ironic part about it—that it is one of our biggest races, and one of the ones you're most proud of winning, but . . . every time

I hear about it, I hear about it prefaced with [the fact] they didn't give me any points.

Time goes along, and you improve it, and you get closer and closer. You probably are more enthusiastic and maybe more charged-up about trying to win the race than someone that's led it all day, because the person that's led it all day has kind of gotten into that groove—"We've got the best car, we're leading the race"—and while that breeds confidence, you get a guy that gains on it all night long, and then all of a sudden puts himself in a position to win the race, he's jazzed up.

So that probably had a little bit to do with it, too. I'd rather be the pursuer than the pursuee in these races, more often than not.

H. A. "HUMPY" WHEELER

■ *One of NASCAR's most colorful figures, Humpy Wheeler has become famous for the outrageous stunt promotions that have been part and parcel of a day at the races at Charlotte. But the track president and general manager turned a bit more serious in describing his greatest day and the sequence of events that led to the first night race at Charlotte—a pivotal event in helping NASCAR go prime-time in televising night races at the superspeedways.*

   The greatest day was March, 16, 1992, at Charlotte Speedway, and it was the Winston, which is the all-star race. But more than that, it was the culmination of a year of anguish, risk-taking, et cetera, to become the first lighted superspeedway in history to run the first race under the lights.

   ... The Winston is an annual race, Winston can move at its discretion. So it'd been moved to Atlanta after the second one in 1986, and it came back to Charlotte. So we went up to make our annual presentation to R. J. Reynolds in 1991, and asked them ... we wanted to bring it back to Charlotte, obviously. Well, they had had a couple of strong proposals by other speedways to bring it to other tracks, so we knew we had to come up with something unique and different.

   So I said, "We will run it Saturday night, under the lights—the re-

turn to the Saturday-night short-track race—and do it that way."
Well, they really came alive when we said that, and I had three other
management people from the speedway with me, and they all looked
at me like I was flipped-out.

They said, "Well, that's a great idea," and in essence we knew we
had it. What they didn't know, that I knew, is that we didn't have the
slightest idea how we were gonna do it. We were coming back in the
car, after we got out of there, driving back to Charlotte, our guys just
jumped all over me—"This hasn't been done," "NASCAR's not
gonna let you do it," "Yackety yack . . ."

But Bruton Smith, the chairman of the company, and I have basically started off life the same way, and that was promoting dirt races
on Friday and Saturday night. And we would never run a race in the
daytime unless we had to. So my thinking was, Well, if you can light
a half-mile track, you can light a mile-and-a-half track.

And so the quest began when we got back, and, of course, like
everything, I figured I could engineer this myself. So I said, "Let's
light the fourth turn, because if we can light the fourth turn we can
light anything—that's the toughest part of the track."

So I rigged up my version of the lights, and we brought some
people out . . . I was the guinea pig, I took the pace car at several
drives through the lights at about 110 miles an hour. . . . I did, and
when I hit my engineer's lights, it blinded me for just a second, and till
I got the car stopped, I probably came as close to death as I ever have
in my life.

I was totally convinced that I had to get the experts in. So we
brought four or five lighting companies in, including two from Europe—they had done big stadiums, primarily, because no one had
ever done anything like this before. They had done horse tracks,
which are a mile, but a horse is running a lot slower than a car.

Well, besides the terrible expense that we were up against, one
thing I did not want to do was to create a picket-fence effect in the infield by having a bunch of poles standing up. So that was one of the
criteria, is that, "You light this track, you don't have poles in the infield." . . . Well, nobody could do that.

And now it's literally November, and the race is in May, and we haven't figured out how to do this yet. . . . Meanwhile, we had announced this—we'd announced it not knowing how we were gonna do it. NASCAR, and even RJR, was even skeptical of it, and said that if [we] didn't get NASCAR's approval, that we would have to run the race on Saturday afternoon.

Well, you know, here the cold winds of November are blowing, and I'm thinking this probably . . . has a good chance of not happening, and we're gonna get a lot of egg on our face. And NASCAR was extremely, extremely nervous about this timing, as they should have been.

The drivers were not terribly happy about it, because they had already heard about my escapade in the fourth turn. [Laughs.] Oh, everybody knew about it—you can't keep something like that a secret—and we'd brought a lot of people out, we thought we had cured the problem. But the problem that we were fighting was from the inside of the track, of the driver glancing to the left and a bright light hitting him—we could not have a bright light hit the race driver.

So I decided then . . . there was a company in Iowa called Musco, in a little town called Muscoteen, and they were the people that had portable lighting for a lot of the football games. They literally made Monday-night football possible in a lot of stadiums that did not have adequate lighting, or any lighting at all, and they enabled Notre Dame to go prime-time on Saturday night on NBC with the lights.

I decided to call them, and they were more than eager to jump into this. So they came down, and a guy named Joe Crookham—not a very good name for a businessman—and the chairman's name was Myron Gordon. Now, neither one of them looked like presidents or chairmen of anything, they're just a couple of guys that'll roll their sleeves up and go physically to work on something.

So Myron is an absolute genius, but he doesn't say much, and after I told him what we needed, and I said, "You've got to be able to do the fourth turn—if you can light the fourth turn you can light anything, because it's the most dangerous part of the track and it's narrow," and all that kind of stuff.

When I got through, Myron said, "Well, the first thing I want to do is go to the drivers' school, the Petty drivers' school." And I said, "We don't have time to do that . . . we've gotta get to work." He said, "That's why I want to go to the school. I want to find out what a race driver goes through."

Well, I didn't like that idea a whole lot, but I got with Teddy, and I got him in the school for three days. And at the end of the three days of driving, he said, "I think we can do this." So that was pretty good.

Well, at any rate . . . they go to work on this thing, and I didn't hear anything for a couple weeks. So I'm callin' 'em and buggin' 'em, and they're saying, "Well, they're working on it." One cold January day, they said, "Why don't you come up here and take a look at something?"

So I did. I went up to Muscoteen, and it was after six, it was dark, we were at the Muscoteen airport, which is . . . not exactly Dulles. They had a hangar in there, they'd taken all the planes out . . . and had built a quarter-scale model of the fourth turn, and had the lights up, which were regular outdoor lighting on the outside and reflective mirror lights low down on the inside, [which] reflected at an angle, so that when the driver looked left, to the inside, he wouldn't see anything.

Well, when I saw that, I thought, My God, this is unreal. . . . This might even work. So we just made the decision at that point to go with it, and we were really, really in a terrible rush at this point, to get it done and in by the middle of May.

In the meantime we had started a massive campaign before, literally called "One Hot Night." And we had spent a lot of advertising dollars, and a lot of promotion dollars getting this thing going.

So we had a test scheduled for the middle of April, for NASCAR to come up and . . . One of the critical things was that we have an emergency backup in case the lights went out, that we would have at least 10 percent lighting left so the cars could get off the track. Because nobody wanted forty race cars going 190 mph to get lost out there when the lights went out. And thunderstorms are prevalent in the area, so that was a concern.

So April 15 came, we had the lights in, we had turned the lights on, and they looked pretty good. But until we got race cars on it, we didn't know what would happen. The first test night was April 12, and we had probably top Winston Cup drivers in here, and NASCAR came up to look at the thing.

Les Richter was Vice President of Competition for NASCAR at the time, and Dick Beatty was the competition director, and they were going to approve or disapprove the lighting system. So they saw it, and it looked pretty good, but the cars got out there, and the drivers were a little bit . . . you know, the first couple of laps, a little queasy, and then they just got going and came back, and raved about it considerably.

Meanwhile I'm extremely nervous, because we've got something that's never been done before, and do we know if it's gonna last for three hours or four hours or whatever, and what if, what if, what if? So we did have to get to a point during the test that we had to turn the lights out and go to backup power to prove to NASCAR that we would have at least a couple laps where we could get the cars off the track.

. . . We told the drivers we were gonna do that, and nobody wanted to go out. And finally Kenny Schrader says, "I'll go out," and Kenny Schrader's probably run more night races than any Winston Cup driver, running from his many, many years of short tracks, maybe other than Dick Trickle. So at any rate, Kenny became the guinea pig, and we clicked the lights out and went down to 10 percent lighting, and he's supposed to come in that lap, but he stayed out and ran ten laps and came in. He said, "They're not only good, but they're better than most of the short tracks that I've run with full lighting."

So we felt pretty good about that. . . . But we move forward to the actual night of the Winston, under the lights, because this is the first time that we've got competition. And I can remember standing up on the roof, and looking down after qualifying was over, and everything was going real well. And . . . I'm looking down at these lights, and I'm thinking, If everybody in America could see this, it would give everybody new hope for the country, because we've been castigated so badly, because people were accusing us of losing our inventive motivation, [and] here's a bunch of farm-raised, corn-fed guys from a little town in Iowa, had done something nobody else could do And they used all American parts to do it with.

. . . At any rate, the night progressed, and you could tell . . . I've been in this business so long, you can always tell when the tension is, you have that same tension that you see before a major world-heavy-weight-championship fight—cut it with a knife. You had a sense that history was being made, you had a sense that every driver cared less about how much money was up for grabs; they wanted to win the first night race in history.

And so we ran the preliminary events, and they were exciting, because guys were just doing things that they just wouldn't normally do—you knew it was gonna be wild. And not only were we doing this under lights, but there was a full moon. . . . It was just gorgeous.

Of course, everybody in racing knows that, under a full moon, drivers just do things differently. And so . . . the Winston ends in a ten-lap showdown for almost a million dollars, and starts twenty cars. We drop the flag, and I thought that these guys, it looked like you had taken twenty people out of the French Revolution, and . . . told 'em . . . they were going to the guillotine if they didn't win the race, is how these guys were driving.

On the last lap, it was probably the most exciting last lap in the history of NASCAR. With one lap to go, with the white flag, Dale Earnhardt had the lead, Kyle Petty was second, and Davey Allison was third. Everybody knew that a big move was gonna be made coming off the second turn going down the backstretch.

Kyle Petty moved to second, and challenged Earnhardt for the lead, going into three. All of a sudden, he hits Earnhardt, he and Earnhardt tangle, Earnhardt goes into the wall—out of the race—this is right on the fourth turn.

And Davey Allison dove down, on the inside of Kyle Petty, and went from third to even with him as they came down the front stretch. They got down the front stretch and hit the finish line, and Davey Allison had about a six-inch lead, and they crashed right before the finish line. Kyle Petty went over and hit the wall, and Davey

Allison hit the wall extremely hard, at full tilt, on the driver's side, and the car ended up about twelve hundred feet away, down on the inside, severely torn up, and Davey was unconscious.

We had a great crowd that night, we had about 95,000 people, and usually when a race is over there's just a tremendous roar for the winner, and a lot of noise. But no one made a sound, because the crowd sensed that something was wrong in the car, the number 28 car, Davey Allison's, 'cause he wasn't moving.

And what made this even more dramatic was the fact that his father Bobby had had a near-fatal accident at Pocono in 1988, and had just really gotten himself back together after that accident. His brother, Clifford—Clifford had been killed before or after that—I can't remember.

At any rate, the feeling that I had of feeling good about accomplishing what had never been done before was certainly thwarted by this, because I've always been close to the Allisons, I've known 'em all my life. I knew Davey since he was little baby really.

So I left the control tower and went down to the emergency medical center at the speedway, and the whole Allison clan was down there, and they were in quite a tizzy, and kind of out of control. Bobby came in, I knew Bobby was back mentally when he went in and said, "I want everybody to shut up, and calm down, and let's find out first what happened before we go berserk."

And everybody did, it was just what they needed. Everybody calmed down, they brought Davey in, he slowly woke up . . . and he had to spend the night in the hospital, but he was okay, he had a mild concussion, he raced the 600 the next week. So we knew . . . after that he was in good shape.

But it was a great day for all of us, because not only was it the first night under the lights, and we had an absolutely fantastic race—but one other thing, my daughter Patty produced the race for the national network. It was probably the best telecast that had ever been on of racing; obviously the drama helped all that. So we just had a really good feeling about the whole thing.

I'm never one to get people to eat crow, I understand when people don't agree with me, or maybe publicly say what I'm doing is wrong. . . . I mean, you're in the public eye, you've gotta have a lot of thick skin and you get over that stuff, I just slough it off. But there was an awful lot of that, an awful lot of people, a number of people saying that this was not something that would ever work, and shouldn't be done, and was very risky, and all that kind of stuff.

I guess the thing that bothered me more about the whole thing was the risky part, because . . . in racing there's sort of an unwritten rule: You don't want to do anything riskier than what you're already doing; what you're already doing is risky enough.

But after the race, most everybody that had bad-mouthed it turned around and said, "Hey, you know, this really worked, and you guys were right, and this is really gonna put NASCAR racing eventually into prime time on superspeedways"—of course, short tracks had been done before.

And the drivers were extremely complimentary, I had some of 'em say, "I could see better tonight, at night, than I could in the daytime, because everything was focused so strong and the light was so focused." So, you know, all those things, and NASCAR . . . had done a complete about-face, and they were very pleased that everything turned out like it did. And a lot of people got to see the race that maybe wouldn't have gotten to see it if it was in the afternoon, because a lot of people do work on the weekends in the daytime.

So it was neat, and the next week, we were getting ready to run the 600, and we were starting that at one o'clock, Memorial Day Sunday, and it was about 90 degrees, hotter than the dickens. And Bruton Smith and I had been down to the pre-race stage, he had done "Gentlemen, start your engines," and we were running up the mid-aisle to go back up top, and every one of those fans were hollering at us, they were sitting there just drenched in sweat in that heat—"Hey, run this thing at night."

We're going up the stairs, and we got into the concourse, and I said to Bruton, "I think they just voted" . . . and that's when we decided to move the 600, the next year. We didn't move it completely to night, but we started it off in twilight, really, and it ended in the dark. And that changed that race completely.

I think that we all sit around and dream of . . . try to think of new ways to present a pretty exciting sport, and just keep pounding on the back of our brain, that, hey, there's something else here that's better . . . what is it? We've tried a lot of things that really didn't work, but at least we tried.

And this one was one that we felt could work, but there was some doubt there, too. And even though the argument, that, well, you can do a half-mile, you can do a mile-and-a-half . . . There is a completely different set of circumstances. You're dealing with twice the speed, and everything else. So the complexity of it, and the challenge, was probably so great that you felt a lot better at the end of it than you did before.

It's enabled us to do something . . . although we haven't done it yet—we were gonna find out last July—the first time a major network was gonna put NASCAR racing on prime time, and we got smoked out at Daytona. [*Editor's note:* The second race at Daytona in 1998 was canceled because of wildfires burning out of control in Florida.] But to enable us to go to prime time, to be up there with the NBA, Major League Baseball, the NFL, to actually have an event during prime time when the sports people at the networks weren't deciding whether they could do it or not . . . The entertainment people, who traditionally don't like sports, would say, "Hey, this is big enough, we'll take a gamble, we won't have the sitcoms or whatever that night, because we think you can drive ratings well enough to do it." In other words, you're there.

■ *Like his brother, Glen Wood chose the 1963 Daytona 500 won by Tiny Lund as one of his greatest days, offering a slightly different account of a race in which a driver who wasn't even supposed to run, took the checkered flag. But Wood, who along with his brothers Glen and Eddie, has been part of one of NASCAR's most innovative and successful ownership teams for almost a half-century, also chose a more recent race, one that had interesting repercussions given the events of the remarkable 1999 season.*

One would be when Dale Jarrett won the Michigan 400 over Davey Allison . . . by a foot, you might say—and it was Dale's first Winston Cup win. Ned was up there in the box watching it all; they sort of at first criticized us at the end for not changing all four tires.

We were gradually getting better all day. As we started, we were a little bit off, and we kept adjusting on it through the day, and finally got it to the best we'd had it at that particular time. And like I said, sometimes you try to do something to make it better, and all of a sudden you made it worse—it's not the first time that's happened. And so that was the lead-up to not changing the tires. We just adjusted the air pressure and the wedge a little bit during the race, various things, mostly tire things.

And we had run the best we'd run the whole day, so we chose to just put a little gas in it and go, and the rest of 'em changed tires. In this case, Davey's car pushed so bad, earlier maybe it would have gone all right and he'd have been ahead of us, but I guess there wasn't but ten laps to go and we chose to do that, and they knew they'd have to pass us rather than us having to pass them . . . so it worked out.

After the restart Dale was in front, 'cause everybody else stopped, and when we took off, the question arose in the booth up there as to whether we should have changed tires or not, and then we ran a lap or two, and he was staying out there. And then we ran about five laps, and he was still out there, had a little bit of lead, and they said, well, maybe they did the right thing.

The question was about the tire change, and normally that's true [that we should have], but sometimes the crews that are on top of everything know more than the announcers; they don't know that we were running better then than we had on some new tires earlier. So that was our decision, of course, along with Dale's—they both agreed on it, to go for it. The question was, "Shall we do it or not?" and [his input was], "Whatever you say."

Well, a lot of times it's just this combination of the set of tires you have on, the stagger that's in 'em, and how they work. You know, a lot of times you hear somebody say they've got a bad set of tires, and it's not exactly that, it's a badly matched set.

And possibly that same thing—if you had another, different one that you had in the stack to go with another one or something, you can't get a set matched closely that are measured the same or will act the same. And when you get a good set matched, you hear that a lot of times, "That last set of tires just pushed all day," or whatever, and the ones you had on was loose. That happens a lot, and there's not a whole lot you can do about it. But sometimes the stagger's . . . well, they don't have it quite as much with the radial tires, but just one set to another can just change whether you're a little bit loose or tight.

And it just kept on like that, [Allison and Jarrett] going back and forth; I'm not sure whether Davey was in front as they went by the white flag or not. It was real close then, and I just knew that he was bound to pass him; he had four tires, and they were fixing to come in and do better. And they went on around to the backstretch, so we couldn't see, and we didn't have a television in the pits at that time, and the crowd was sort of roaring is what happened. . . .

Afterwards we saw the replay on it after the race. Dale got a little bit sideways coming off [turn] two, but he managed to hold it, and they went through three and four side by side. Most of the time, you would think Yates's engine would have outdone us as they come off of turn four side by side, but they didn't. And they came across almost side by side, with us a little bit in front.

[Dale Jarrett] was determined to do everything he could to win the race there at the end. He drove a heck of a race; it's very tough to hold off David, so that'll go down as his first big win, and it was a great win for us, too.

Well . . . you know, we'd been there in that situation before—you just had to accept what happens, one way or the other. As it turned out, it was quite an emotional race for the whole bunch, especially Ned and I guess Dale, and Leonard and Eddie . . . and, of course, myself, too. It was just a nail-biting race.

Naturally, it was a first for Dale. He'd won quite a few times in the Busch series, but it seemed like he always missed 'em when he came to the Winston Cup. It's one we won't ever forget, I'm sure of that.

We knew he was good, and we'd been a little bit behind in the engine department and the chassis, too, and gradually, as we got to know each other better, and just about that particular time of the season, we had just got some better engines, and we knew we were gonna do better.

The ironic thing was that when he won that race, he had already signed with Joe Gibbs, and we didn't know it. We might not have been so jubilant about it if we had. Everybody went along, and Dale did what he had to do.

That other one [the 500], was . . . Marvin had qualified the car, and they were running a sports-car race during that speed week, and it was a Maserati, I think. And it had little tires [made with a] hard compound, and it was really hard to drive and really didn't have any downforce to it much, either, the way the car was designed. And he went into turn three, I guess it was, and it got away from him, and it turned over a few times and landed on its top.

Well, the doors to it were—what do you call that—a split: they go into the middle of the car and wrap over the top, a gull-wing sort of a thing. The weight was on that, and so it made it so he couldn't . . . he tried every way to make the door open, and he couldn't. And it had caught fire.

When the wreck happened, several of us went up there, just as fast as we could, got in a station wagon, and Tiny was one of 'em, and there was two more, Jerry Rayburn and somebody else from the Holman-Moody crew was up there, and one of the guys from Firestone. . . . Just half a dozen or so of us got ahold of the car when we got there and turned it back on its wheels.

As we did, Marvin kicked the door open and rolled out. It burnt him pretty bad, so come time to replace him with somebody for that race, we knew we'd be thinking about who, and all of a sudden we just said Tiny. He's as good as we could find, and he didn't have a ride, he was just down there. He may have had a ride in the sportsman class at that time, I'm not sure, but he didn't have a Winston Cup ride.

So we put him in it, and right away he was going real good. And then during the race . . . I think it started in the rain, maybe, I'm not sure about that. But anyhow, there was a caution at lap 36. Well, he wasn't leading the race at that time, it was Lorenzen, and Ned Jarrett, and two or three more—maybe him, all three of them—but he was just more or less just drafting with them and saving a little fuel by doing that. . . . As you well know these days, a lot of 'em wasn't paying attention to it back then, but we were.

And when we stopped at lap 36, we had put gas only in it, and so then the next stop came up, we had figured from that lap 36 stop we could easily go forty laps. So we went forty laps the next time, all this is green-flag, and all of a sudden that stop, looked like we could go another two—this is still green, all of it—there wasn't another caution all day.

And we had these next two stops, we ran forty-two laps, that made up for the thirty-six to forty. So then we only had forty to go at the end. By the time we were running and sort of saving fuel a little . . . he got a little bit behind at times, but always caught back up, he was in back of Lorenzen and Ned.

So then it came to about ten laps to go, Lorenzen came down pit road and gassed up, and so that left Ned leading, and us second. With about three to five laps to go, Ned came down pit road, all right? Then the announcers began wondering when Tiny was gonna stop. Well, we told 'em we weren't, and if we hadn't misfigured something, we felt like we could go all the way. So it just kept building and building: "Can he go, can he go?" And naturally, the people in the grandstands didn't know what we'd done, and none of the rest of the drivers had done that.

We won it, and Tiny thought it ran out of gas, but it made it a lap back around, and we loaded it onto the truck without adding any gas to it. And we did not change any tires, it was just gas and go every time. We never lost out of the pack; they wanted to lead worse than Tiny did, so he let 'em go and we'd save the fuel.

To put in a complete twenty-two gallons or whatever it took—twenty to twenty-two it had to take—you could easily change two tires before you could get all that in, but maybe not four. And pit stops then weren't a four-tire change in 16 seconds, they were more like in the low 20s.

The setup for the two drivers [Marvin Panch and Tiny Lund] was pretty close, I don't think we had to do anything different. Back then there weren't any spoilers, front or rear, no air dams, no nothing. The car was basically a street version. I don't think there was any templates or anything, you just got a '63 Ford that you bought off the showroom. It was just as near to that, like it was the same thing.

Marvin, I think, would have drove practically the same way, because of the way we were doing it to save the gas and try to make it on one less stop. I think he would have driven the car the same way. I'm not sure whether they had a television in the hospital where he could watch; I'm sure he listened to it on the radio.

We had agreed that if Tiny did drive it, whatever he won, we'd give Marvin a percentage of the winnings. Everybody in the pits was just really happy about it—his wife was in the pits, it was just real special.

Those two stand out because of the way they started out, at Daytona, the way that all came together, and, of course, this one, because we hadn't won a race in a little while when Jarrett won that one, and it was a big win and it stands out.

■ *As an ownership team, Dan Gurney compared the dominance of the Wood Brothers in the 1960s to that of the old New York Yankees, and the roster of drivers who drove for the team would form a sort of miniature Racing Hall of Fame in its own right. But Glen and Leonard Wood were best known for revolutionizing the pit stop in 1965, cutting the average time of almost a minute to a little under twenty seconds. In this interview, Leonard Wood talked about that experience, as well as a couple of his most memorable wins at Daytona.*

===

Well, one of 'em would be the time that Marvin Panch was scheduled to drive our car at Daytona. At that time he was down there for three weeks, and in the middle week you had sports-car racing, and this guy wanted Marvin to drive his sports car, and he'd already qualified the car, our car. Then he was involved in a wreck, the sports car got upside-down, caught fire, and Tiny Lund and Ernie Gahan and Steve Petrassic and another guy—there was four of 'em— came through the tunnel at the time, and saw the car burning, and ran up there and picked the car up and pulled Marvin out from under the car.

And then Tiny got in the car, in the 500, and won the 500. Tiny was able to practice in the car, and we set the car up for him. Then, during the race, they had a caution early, 36 laps, which is 4 laps shy of a hundred miles, so we stretched it 2 laps, ran 142 laps for the next three times. . . . I had it calculated out—at the end of the race we only had 40 to go. We'd been 42 laps the earlier times to make up the 4 laps that we were shy of a hundred miles.

And then we only had 40 to go at the end. . . . Well, the other guys hadn't made up their 4 laps, so at the end of the race we knew, we were setting back there maybe in third or fourth place, knowing that those other two guys were gonna have to stop.

Then [Tiny] began dicing it around a little, challenging them a little. Pretty soon you had to come down pit road, so we were kind of home free. He was running against Fred Lorenzen and Ned Jarrett— that was in 1963. His competition was fast, and he managed to draft, and then he was almost losing the draft at times. He came in, and we were getting such good tire wear that we didn't even have to change tires the whole race. So we kept it back up in the draft all day and it was just sort of a Cinderella story.

All I can tell you is that one of the reasons we picked him was because we had raced against Tiny earlier in races years before, and he was just a very aggressive competitive driver. You just didn't mess around with him. He was very good at it. I saw him drive in modifieds and stuff, over at Charlotte, over at the fairgrounds, and he was really just a strong competitor. The Pontiacs were very fast, I can remember he drafted onto Fireball a lot. The draft and effects were a little new to him, I think, and he hadn't had as much experience drafting as some of the other drivers—maybe Marvin. But he caught on, and there at the end he was challenging Lorenzen and Jarrett.

And then the other time would have been David Pearson, when Pearson and Petty wrecked on the last lap, in 1976, at Daytona. Pearson was spinning around in the grass, and kept his motor running, and it looked like Richard was gonna slide all the way across the finish line while he was wrecking, but he stopped short, and he couldn't get his motor started, and David won the race.

And then, when we went into Indianapolis in 1965, and pitted Jimmy Clark and won the Indy 500. Ford Motor Company wanted us to come up and pit Clark, because they'd had some problems in the pits in the past, and it had a Ford Motor in it, so Ford was very interested in it doing well. So we went up a week early, went into the shop—it was a foreign shop, we didn't know any of 'em. And we felt that if there had been any resentment it wouldn't have worked; but they seemed to welcome us with open arms to do it. So we just took the car over as if it had been our own. As far as pit strategy and preparation for the pit stops, we just took it and prepared it for the pit stop, and then [Clark] had a crew that was gonna go over it if it had had other problems. But we didn't have any other problems.

It was very interesting, we probably got the most publicity and did the least in the least amount of time we've ever done, because we got publicity all over the world, all over Europe, on account of it.

You had a big tank—at that time that was the first time that they went with gravity-flow fuel, so it was very important that you streamlined the fuel system so it flowed good. They were expecting us to be in there for about a minute, and we tested it beforehand, and went over and checked the fuel flow, and it put 58 gallons in in 15 seconds.

And then we practiced connecting and disconnecting the hoses without fuel in it, so nobody knew how quick our full stop was gonna be. And then the first one, I believe, was about 17 or 18 seconds.

I remember we ran so that Clark would give a signal when he switched his fuel tanks. You had one on each side, and he would give a signal. At one point they had some caution laps in there, Chapman came over and said he noticed one stop he didn't have cautions, and one he did, and then he gave the signal a little early.

And I said, "Well, if you recall, you had some caution laps in there that made up the difference when he switched." And I can remember the commentators—when we made the first stop, we weren't in there long—they said, "Well, you can bet they'll be back in in plenty of time to pit, because a new crew and all, you can bet that they'll need a full stop."

And I remember that when it came time to stop, it was when [the commentators said] we'd have to stop and we hadn't stopped yet. . . . Well, they didn't understand it. It must be running a mixture—that would mean if you were running half gasoline and half alcohol, you wouldn't have to put in as much because it would burn twice as much alcohol as it did gasoline. So they thought we were running a mixture, where we wouldn't have to put in as much. They sent a guy down there to ask Chapman what he was running, and he told 'em, "Pure alcohol" . . . that was funny.

A. J. and Parnelli and all of 'em were in there—but I can remember, I told 'em, "Now, it's very important you stop where you're supposed to, on the spot. Because the hoses are only a certain length, stop short and they won't reach; if you overshoot it, it'll buckle the hoses." And he said, "You just tell me where you want [me] to stop," and he put that thing right on the money every time. Then, when I disconnected it, my hose, I was on the far side, and I leaped back just as fast as I could, and as I'm leaping back the car just shaved me as it went out. I mean, he judged it to where he just hit it perfect for me to be out of the way and him leaving.

I remember he said he wasn't gonna run hard before the race. I believe one lap passed, and then the second lap—he just took over the lead and went off. Nobody challenged after that.

I can remember Chapman took us to dinner, and we had a victory celebration. We weren't that much into the media attention, we never were one to . . . I mean, sure, it's gratifying to know that you got all that publicity, but we weren't looking for that. It was just a great experience, and a nice bunch of guys to work with.

[At Daytona] I can remember David [Pearson] called on the radio and said he was running wide open, and that was all he could do. That was always his policy, he would always tell you he couldn't, and he usually would. He said he wasn't doing all he could do, and yet he passed [Petty going] into [turn] three. And then of course Richard tried to get it back, and got into him or got under him or something, I think.

But the crowd really roared, and I knew something was happening. There was a pause before they came, and they should have been there, and then I look up and see Richard up against the wall backwards, and I didn't see David. And then I looked down low, and he was down on the grass spinning around, and then Richard just slid—

I mean, it looked like he was running 150 sideways. Just grass flying, through the grass, and it was just gonna slide right across the finish line, on the grass. But it didn't.

I don't remember exactly what happened during the race all day, but I do know they were running close all day. There at the end, they were right there together, just them two—they did a lot of that.

Anytime you win in that respect, it's a lot more exciting when it happens like that, really, than it is if you've got a two-lap lead or something—you don't know who's gonna win until the last second. That makes it a lot more exciting.

I don't remember what the pit stops were, but I don't remember that it would have mattered, the way they were together at the end. Of course, pit stops were always important, you could lose out on a pit stop.

There's other races we had cars that I thought were superior to either one of those races. In 1970 at Daytona, when Cale was driving one of the Cyclones [that] was very superior. Something happened to the motor after twenty-one laps, but he already had a straightaway lead. The 1976 car was a great car, and then the 1963 car was a great car. But they didn't . . . It's kind of like David said, he was running wide open, so it wasn't anything that superior, as much as the car, in 1970.

You think you could top them? I don't know where you'd go to top [those experiences]. For sure, every race David won, we were excited about it, or Cale, or A. J. Foyt. A.J. won the Daytona 500 in 1972, but it wasn't the last lap-bible . . . The closeness, the Cinderella story of the way it all happened, you can't beat that.

■ *Although he was born in Timmonsville, North Carolina, it was the lure of Darlington that found Cale Yarborough following an unsuccessful venture into turkey farming, as well as a stint as a substitute running back for the semiprofessional Sumter Generals. One of NASCAR's most competitive and determined drivers, Yarborough conquered the track in 1968 and went on to win a total of five Southern 500s there, but it was his first victory at Darlington that stood out most among his eighty-three career wins.*

My biggest win, or the one that was most precious to me, was the 1968 Southern 500 in Darlington. I was born and raised only about fifteen miles from the Darlington racetrack. It was really the racetrack, really, that made up my mind that racing was gonna be my profession. I just got hooked on it.

Now, of course, like I said, I ran there when I was seventeen years old in the Southern 500, and I kept going back every year, trying to get a good ride and trying to be successful. If you could win Darlington, you could probably win anywhere.

Then I had some tough moments there. I went out of the racetrack in 1965, over the guardrail—that was when I was driving for Banjo Matthews. In 1968, I was in the Wood Brothers car, and was lucky enough to win the Southern 500 there, and went on to win five, to be the only driver in history to win five Southern 500s. That record'll be broken sooner or later, but that 1968 Southern 500, I wouldn't trade that one for any other.

I was a pretty hot young chew in the short tracks in South Carolina in my teenage years, and when I finally went to Darlington I thought I was ready. Then when I got out there and [there were] people like Fireball Roberts and Junior Johnson and all the greats of the time—you know . . . it didn't take me long to realize that I still had some learning to do to run with those boys.

And I did. I didn't back off. I wasn't ready when I got there, but all in all it worked out.

I was probably charging too hard, doing that all the time, and naturally I didn't have the equipment that those people had, either. I had to work my way up, and then . . . learning how to drive superspeedways, and also being able to get into the right equipment.

Well, of course you don't get equipment until you prove yourself, so I still had some proving to do, and the superspeedway was a lot more difficult than the short dirt tracks that I'd been accustomed to running. When you go from . . . I was just running dirt, I've always run on asphalt—but when you go from running quarter- and half-mile dirts to running a mile-and-three-eighths superspeedway, there's a *big* jump there. It's tough.

Now, for somebody that's never run any short track, or a dirt track especially, it would be difficult to come from superspeedways, or even asphalt tracks, to dirt. But going from dirt to a superspeedway is a pretty big jump.

Of course, it's been a long time ago, you gotta understand that. I can't remember all the details of it. But as I said, I was doin' real good on the short tracks around my part of the country, and a lot of my friends and people in this part of the country thought I was ready, so . . . it was more of a community-type effort than anything else. They donated money toward the car, and it was a 1957 Pontiac (1967 maybe?)—it had a Pontiac dealer that helped us some, and we got it ready, and of course, they were pretty much stock back then.

I felt good, I felt like I was ready. It didn't take me long to find out that I had to learn some more to learn how to drive on a superspeedway and go from 70 mph to 170 mph.

I don't even know where I started, I felt sure I was pretty far up, I'd have to look in the book to see where I qualified. [*Editor's note:* The qualifying speeds of Cale Yarborough and Charlie Glotzbach were identical. Glotzbach won the pole because he qualified ahead of Yarborough, but each was credited with being the fastest qualifier.]

It was a tough race all day long. I think Davey Pearson and I fought all day long, and when the race was [over] both our cars looked like they'd been in demolition derbies. And when it was over—I've got some pictures around—when I got out of that car, you can look at the pictures and they tell the whole story.

It was a hard fight, a hot day. . . . I remember after the race we were going up to the press stand, I got sick to my stomach, and I hardly even remember victory lane, really, that's how exhausted I was.

I don't know that I ever broke away. I think Pearson and I got together. . . . I think maybe Pearson spun late in that race. We were battling tooth and nail; it was one of the most exhausting races I've ever been through, if not the most. I wouldn't give up—I wanted to win that first Southern 500, that was a great victory for me. I don't hardly remember victory circle, much less what I said to anybody else, I was too exhausted.

I think being in good equipment . . . I was with the Wood Brothers; I was hungry; I wanted to establish myself; and I just worked hard and it just started coming together for us.

That's always gonna be the case, it always has been in the past—there are a few drivers that're gonna dominate for a few years, and then another group'll come along, and the same ones won't stay there all the time.

I think it's a great record. Nobody else has ever won five Southern 500s, it's gotta be up there pretty high. Gordon's got a good chance at it, because I think he's won, what, three in a row there now. If things go well for him, he'll be one that's got a shot at it. That's what records are for—they'll all be broken sooner or later—and who does or doesn't, it doesn't make any difference. I just wish that . . . some of these guys would have to go back and drive the equipment that we drove.

It was my home racetrack. I dreamed of winning there since I was a kid.

■ *The legendary Smokey Yunick was one of NASCAR's best and most creative mechanics, and "The Best Damn Garage in Town" has been a Daytona landmark for five decades. His greatest day in the sport was the 1960 Indianapolis 500, an epic battle between Jim Rathmann and Rodger Ward that Rathmann finally won when he waited a bit longer than Ward to slow down and conserved a badly worn tire. A. J. Watson built the engine for Rathmann's Ken-Paul Special, and Smokey Yunick worked on the car along with Takeo ("Chick") Hirashima. In this interview, Yunick more than lived up to his colorful reputation as he described the events that led up to that memorable race.*

I thought about it a little bit, and . . . my greatest day in racing would have been the 1960 Indianapolis 500. I guess you'll have to decide for yourself whether you believe the story, but I'm gonna tell it the way it was—I don't really give a shit how you interpret it.

[It was] in April. I was broke and retired—very broke, living in a machine shop, only had cold water. And I had an Indy car that was old, it was about five years old, I had qualified it in 1958, and I had it running fast enough in 1959 to qualify it, but I decided to qualify [with that one] . . . I had built another car, reverse rotation deal. A guy named Art Lincoln paid for it, so it wasn't my money, but the other car belonged to me, the 1958 car.

So I was going back to Indy with it, because if you qualified it probably [paid] forty-five grand. And I would have got, in them days the driver got about half, and the owner got half. So I figured that worst case—it didn't cost me more than a couple hundred to get the car ready. And I was pretty sure we could get it qualified. So I could have come home with eighteen, nineteen grand.

So I'm going up there with that, and about two weeks before I left—it would be about the fifteenth of April, 1960—I get a phone call from Jim Rathmann, and he says, "Smokey, I'd like you to help me at Indy this year." And I said, "I can't do it, Jim, I've already entered a car, a thousand-dollar entry fee."

He said, "Ah, I've run twice up there, three times, I think I've got the car to do it this year, it's brand-new. Got some rich kid backing it, and I need a crew chief." And I said, "Well, how do you get this far without a crew chief?"

And he said, "Well, we've got this Japanese guy, Chicky Hirashima, who's a pretty good man, but he's so nervous and everything, he tells us now, he can't even get in the pits on race day, he gets all shook up so bad he gets sick. . . . We need you to run the car on race day," he said. "We probably need you to help us keep the thing going a little faster."

So I said, "I can't handle the thing, I'm broke." And he said, "Okay, we'll pay you ten grand to be crew chief, and 10 percent of the prize money." So I'm thinking, "That's twenty-six grand if they win it. It's ten sure grand. 'Course I might run my own car and not be able to qualify and then come home with a pile of junk. I was so bad off I decided to take the sure thing, but I said, "What's the story on Hirashima?"

And he said, "Well, he wants to be involved in getting ready for the race and everything, and I don't like the sound of this thing." I said, "I'll get up there, he'll be all pissed off, and then we'll have a lot of dissension in the pit crew. I really can't work for somebody. . . . No thank you.

He called back after two or three days. Now we've got a three-way conference going: we've got Hirashima, Chicky's on the phone; the two owners . . . Four way—Miami, Daytona, Dallas, Los

Angeles. And I got right to it, I said, "Chicky, I think you were geared to be the chief on this thing, and I don't want no part of a deal where there's any hard feelings."

I said, "If I get involved in this thing, I'm not gonna listen to you, I'm not gonna ask you for any advice, I'm gonna do the goddamn thing the way I see fit. And if you're not willing to accept that . . . And [he says], "Oh, well, yeah, I can't get near that racetrack, I'll just go all to pieces, I get so worked up . . . I'll probably just stand there and puke."

And I knew about guys that had that problem, so I understood that. So we made the deal on the phone, that he would more or less just be the helper, and put his two cents in, but I would be the crew chief and run the whole deal and run the pits.

I got up there the first day of May, that was in the contract he sent me, and I showed up and I went in, and I signed and we agreed. And I thought, Oh, what the hell. I said, "Chicky, how about if we be co-chiefs on the thing?" Okay, okay, if you want to, if you want to, but he said, I wouldn't have to be the co-chief. Okay.

So I got up there, and I sign in as a co-chief. And Parky Baines was the registrar, and he said, "Smokey"—I run out the door—and he said, "Wait a minute, you signed on as co-chief and Chicky signed on as chief this morning." He said, "You can't do that." I said, "Yeah, you can't do that." So I said, "I'll go get it straightened out."

I walked around again, into the garage, and there was Rathmann and Lacey and Kenny Griggs, and Chicky. We do the handshaking contest, and I said, "Jim, Chicky, you and I agreed on the telephone who's gonna crew-chief this thing. I see that you signed in as the chief, Franky just told me." He said, "Hold it," and Rathmann said, "I'll go take care of it right now."

And I never, ever thought about it again. I built the engine for the son of a bitch, and I was crew chief during the race. Chicky Hirashima was in street clothes. And he finally showed up in the pits at 400 miles. It was a real good race, might have been the best race they ever had at Indy, between Rathmann and [Rodger] Ward swapping the lead, shit, maybe twenty, thirty times, and sometimes two or three times a lap.

Before the race started, I put air jacks on the car, and was running air jacks in practice. In 1959, a good pit stop was 50, 52 seconds, and I was practicing with air jacks, we got it down to 20 seconds. Well, Watson put air jacks on Ward's car that year, and we both stopped five times, there was only a 2-second difference in the pit times.

But Ward's tires wore out two laps from the end, and Rathmann . . . Back in them days, you had a breaker strip and you knew [if] you hit that you knew you had one or two laps at the most and it was gonna blow. So Rathmann got on the breaker strip, coming off of four, taking the checkered flag, and we ended up winning the race.

They got watches for all the pit crew, but when it came to Smokey's watch, he didn't get a watch, because Rathmann said, "Shit, I gave some of them to friends of mine, but we'll get another made next week and we'll give it to you."

We go to the victory banquet, and they introduced the chief mechanic, and they introduced Chicky. They never, ever even told me about it. I got my hands on my chair to get up—co-chief . . . it never happened. So in the record, I was never even there.

And yet, at the racetrack, back then they had a tradition that they watched the race, and the front page would change, you know, "Rathmann Wins Indy," or "Ward Wins Indy," and they would put 'em in with a helicopter, and maybe two or three times the race changed, and they'd change the front page, you know what I mean?

And finally, the Indy paper says "Rathmann and Smokey Win the '60 Indy 500"—I didn't know anything about it until the victory dinner. And to this day, it never got straightened out. Then about five years ago, six years ago, the speedway said, "Smokey, we want to straighten this thing out. We know about you and Chicky and the whole deal."

So [the question was], Who all was in the pit crew? In other words, about seven out of ten, and the driver was still alive, and they polled every one of them—Who actually was the crew chief?—and every one said Smokey except one guy . . . Jim Rathmann.

Now, the nice thing about him was . . . I told you how broke I was. Well, about the fifteenth of April, I got a check from General

Motors for $15,000, two weeks before I was supposed to go up there. And Jim Rathmann wanted to buy a Chevy dealership, and I had a friend in Elkman name of John Fordyce who had a Cadillac/Chevrolet dealership, and he had had a bellyful of it.

He said, "I've gotta sell this son of a bitch before I go crazy." And I said, "How much you want for it?" He said, "If somebody'll hand me 120 grand, I'm gone. They can have the goddamn inventory, the parts, the building, the grounds, the whole thing. One hundred twenty thousand dollars." He said, "I warn you, I ain't made any money in five years."

So, I knew his place, I knew the deal, I said, "That sounds like a reasonable deal to me." So I told Rathmann about it, and, "They gotta close it today at noon." I got the check for fifteen grand for General Motors out of the blue. I was so shocked I took it north of the river and put it in the bank.

And what it was, was I invented the variable-ratio power steering, and the power brakes, and the assisted-residual power steering, the hydraulic suspension that sat on top of the springs and then you pushed the button and it went up and down. I started to apply, I filed for the patents, I couldn't afford it, so I tried to sell the car; I talked to GM—they didn't want it.

So finally Saginaw Derringer, the president of GM, said, "You know, we're kind of interested in your variable-ratio power steering." And I said, "What would you give me for it?" He said, "Well, I can't give you much." So we ended up, I got $10K for the power steering, $4K for power brakes, $10K radiators, and one [K] for the suspension. That was all we got.

I signed the piece of paper and said it was theirs. I told 'em, "I applied for the patents, I couldn't afford it." They said, "Okay, we'll take care of it." . . . I invented this shit back in 1959—as a matter of fact, the Busch race in Atlanta; we used all that stuff on the 1959 Pontiac and won the race.

In 1960, about April 15, when I got that check, I was shocked. They gave me a letter that said, "We don't feel like we adequately compensated for your inventions, we're using the variable-ratio power steering now," and there was a check for $150,000 . . . and I said, "What a wonderful bunch of guys, they didn't have to do that."

So, two days later, there's a knock on the door from Thompson GM—"Uh, did you get your check?" "Oh yeah, thank you very much." "About that power steering . . ." And I said, "What's the problem?" And he said, "Well, Bendix has filed suit against us for royalties on power steering, because they filed and they got patents granted for a variable-ratio power steering."

And I said, "How the hell did that happen?" . . . It seemed like nobody watched what was going on with that deal with you and GM and they never paid the patents. And the patents that you applied for are worthless, and Bendix has got 'em, and they want a pretty healthy royalty on their material. As a matter of fact we sold some to Nash and sold some to Ford, and they're using quite a few.

They said, "What can you tell us to help us?" I said, "There's a sportswriter, a pretty good one in Atlanta, named Furman Bisher, a stick-and-ball man, he didn't know a fuck about race cars. He interviewed me after we won that race in Atlanta, and I gave him the story where I identified those four specific things—variable-ratio power steering was one of 'em, with a simple description of what a variable-ratio power steering was."

And I said, "So, you should have patented the fucking thing when you first had it." So he asked a couple more questions, and I said, "Your two minutes is up, get the fuck out of here" . . . I'm really getting hot now.

So . . . that's fifteen grand in the bank. And the next day, eight in the morning, I get a call from Jim Rathmann. Now, I got Jim Rathmann and this guy together, and Jim Rathmann had $60,000, and the other $60,000 was to be furnished by a guy from California by the name of Denny Weinberg.

Denny Weinberg was a Jew, and General Motors at that time wouldn't touch a Jew or a colored person with a twenty-foot pole. And when Denny and Jim decided to become partners, I asked Rathmann, I said, "I know Denny's got plenty of money, but GM ain't much on Jews."

So, about that time I get a call from Ed Cole—he's president of GM—and he said, "Smokey, do you know Denny Weinberg very well?" I said, "He's the best fucker in California, bar none, and he's got a lot of money, and he's one son of a bitch, and he's about as Jew as you can get. He works, he's not just some rich kid."

He said, "Well, I'm gonna have to go to bat to get him to be a partner for Rathmann. Do you think I should give him any trouble?" And I said, "No, I don't think so. Shit, for sixty grand, if Jim's gonna be in it with Denny, I would say that Rathmann could buy him out in a year or two, if it came to that. I'm sure that the only reason that Rathmann has got him in here is to try to figure out how to fuck him out of his interest, because Rathmann was kind of a chickenshit son of a bitch, always was—he was with Granatelli and the Chicago mafia.

So they got the deal. The morning the thing was supposed to close, Weinberg ain't there, and his sixty ain't there. It's supposed to close at noon today. . . . I get a phone call from Rathmann, he's in tears. "John's got my sixty—Denny, I just found out from my brother, ain't gonna put up his sixty, he ain't coming, he ain't here. And I'm gonna lose all my money."

So I says, "Is John there?" He says, "Yeah." I said, "Put him on the phone." Before I open my mouth, John says, "Goddamn it, Smokey, this deal was on the level, and you know the price was right, and he had two months to get the money up." And he said, "I have made arrangements to go on a world tour starting tomorrow morning. Now I gotta sit here through this goddamn mess, and I won't be able to get my money back, I don't owe him a goddamn thing."

And I said, "I don't think you do, John. All I want to do is ask you a question—will you give him twenty-four hours and fifteen thousand dollars?" And he says, "Smokey, I don't want to screw him out of his money," and I said, "John, goddamn it, just answer the question. Will you give him twenty-four hours for fifteen thousand in cash, if you get the cash in two hours?"

He said, "Well, if that's what it's gonna take to get you to believe that you're doing the right thing, yes." So I said, "Okay, I'll be there

308

in two hours." I had a car, driver working for me named William Harris. . . . I went over to the bank to get the money, and they said, "We can't cash that check, although you deposited it, for probably another two or three days."

I said, "Hey, the fucking check was on General Motors." I knew the president of the bank, I said, "Hey, I ain't got a lot of time. I need that fifteen grand I put in here, I need it now, I gotta have it down in Melbourne in an hour and fifty minutes to do this deal." He says, "Well, there ain't much I can do about it."

I said, "I told you I didn't have much time." His first name was Gil. I said, "Gil, I got about six pictures of you [with my girl-friend] . . . Now, would you like your wife to have them tomorrow, or are you gonna get me that fuckin' fifteen grand right now?

And I had the fifteen grand in about thirty seconds. And the last I heard from him is, "What do I gotta do to get them pictures back?"

They got the money down there. . . . I'm still sleeping on the army cot over there, with cold water only, and I gave him that fifteen grand to save the deal.

The next day, Rathmann found . . . Oh, he had a friend, and I had a friend that owned about half of Coca-Cola, his name was Lindsey Hopkins. And Lindsey's family owned the right to the syrup in Coca-Cola from day one, and Lindsey owned the Pan-American bank in Miami. And I figured, as soon as Jim could find Lindsey, Lindsey would loan him the money, which he did.

But Jim only borrowed forty-five thousand from him, and left my fifteen, and then the next day when the deal was saved, said, "I'm gonna make you a ten-percent partner." And I said, "I don't wanna be your fucking partner. If I gave you fifteen grand, and you paid $120K for the whole, I don't know if ten percent would be right on fifteen thousand, you know."

I said, "I know you didn't ever graduate from school, but you made it past sixth grade." So I said, "When you get the money, I want it back, I don't want to be your partner."

Now, this is another part of it. . . . I said, "I was not the mechanic in your pit crew." So if that ain't the greatest day I ever . . . Of course, to me, winning Indianapolis was everything. Ever since I was a little kid, I always wanted to go to Indianapolis—not as a mechanic, but as a driver.

But finally, to get there and actually win the son of a bitch, and then find out three or four days later you weren't even there . . . all the good feelings became bad feelings. And I could tell the son of a bitch—the next two years I worked for those rich guys in Texas, and we won two more years there—and every time I saw him, he said, "I gotta get hold of Frankie Baines and straighten that deal out." Then after the dinner was over, I didn't talk to him. Then . . . I got so pissed I just left. So I didn't see him.

So that was 1960, this is 1999—it ain't been fixed yet. Chicky's dead now, and he got voted into the Hall of Fame at Indy . . . and he belongs in there. It all happened in the conference call—he was willing to let me be the chief again, and me, like a dumb son of a bitch, I don't think it bothered him. But some of this stuff ain't exactly the way it looks like.

Other than that I ain't got no stories.